ISLAM

DENOUNCES

TERRORISM

As for those who believe and do right

actions, the All-Merciful will bestow

His love on them.

(Qur'an, 19:96)

HARUN YAHYA
(ADNAN OKTAR)

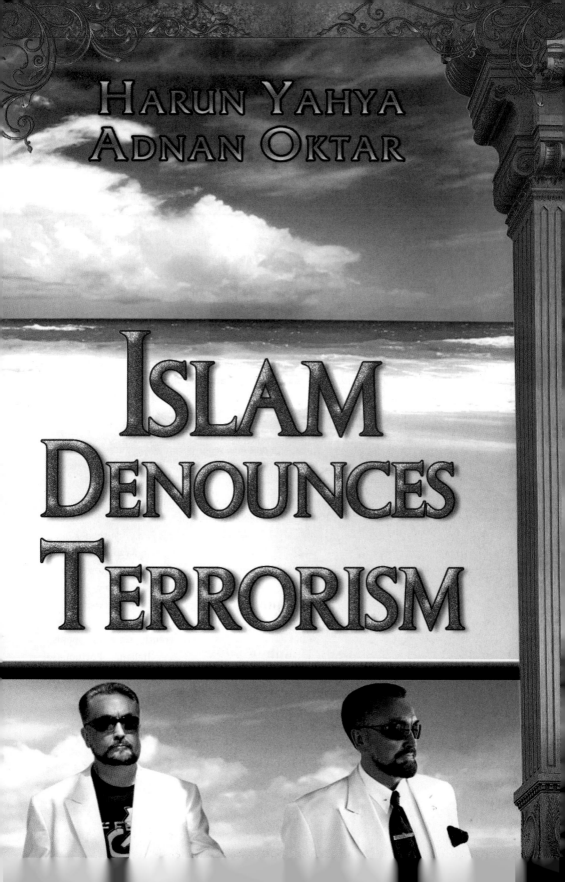

Harun Yahya
Adnan Oktar

Islam Denounces Terrorism

About the Author

Now writing under the pen-name of HARUN YAHYA, Adnan Oktar was born in Ankara in 1956. Having completed his primary and secondary education in Ankara, he studied fine arts at Istanbul's Mimar Sinan University and philosophy at Istanbul University. Since the 1980s, he has published many books on political, scientific, and faith-related issues. Harun Yahya is well-known as the author of important works disclosing the imposture of evolutionists, their invalid claims, and the dark liaisons between Darwinism and such bloody ideologies as fascism and communism.

Harun Yahya's works, translated into 76 different languages, constitute a collection for a total of more than 55,000 pages with 40,000 illustrations.

His pen-name is a composite of the names Harun (Aaron) and Yahya (John), in memory of the two esteemed Prophets who fought against their peoples' lack of faith. The Prophet's seal on his books' covers is symbolic and is linked to their contents. It represents the Qur'an (the Final Scripture) and the Prophet Muhammad (pbuh), last of the prophets. Under the guidance of the Qur'an and the Sunnah (teachings of the Prophet [pbuh]), the author makes it his purpose to disprove each fundamental tenet of irreligious ideologies and to have the "last word," so as to completely silence the objections raised against religion. He uses the seal of the final Prophet (pbuh), who attained ultimate wisdom and moral perfection, as a sign of his intention to offer the last word.

All of Harun Yahya's works share one single goal: to convey the Qur'an's message, encourage readers to consider basic faith-related issues such as God's existence and unity and the Hereafter; and to expose irreligious systems' feeble foundations and perverted ideologies.

Harun Yahya enjoys a wide readership in many countries, from India to America, England to Indonesia, Poland to Bosnia, Spain to Brazil, Malaysia to Italy, France to Bulgaria and Russia. Some of his books are available in English, French, German, Spanish, Italian, Portuguese,

Urdu, Arabic, Albanian, Chinese, Swahili, Hausa, Dhivehi (spoken in Maldives), Russian, Serbo-Croat (Bosnian), Polish, Malay, Uygur Turkish, Indonesian, Bengali, Danish and Swedish.

Greatly appreciated all around the world, these works have been instrumental in many people recovering faith in God and gaining deeper insights into their faith. His books' wisdom and sincerity, together with a distinct style that's easy to understand, directly affect anyone who reads them. Those who seriously consider these books, can no longer advocate atheism or any other perverted ideology or materialistic philosophy, since these books are characterized by rapid effectiveness, definite results, and irrefutability. Even if they continue to do so, it will be only a sentimental insistence, since these books refute such ideologies from their very foundations. All contemporary movements of denial are now ideologically defeated, thanks to the books written by Harun Yahya.

This is no doubt a result of the Qur'an's wisdom and lucidity. The author modestly intends to serve as a means in humanity's search for God's right path. No material gain is sought in the publication of these works.

Those who encourage others to read these books, to open their minds and hearts and guide them to become more devoted servants of God, render an invaluable service.

Meanwhile, it would only be a waste of time and energy to propagate other books that create confusion in people's minds, lead them into ideological confusion, and that clearly have no strong and precise effects in removing the doubts in people's hearts, as also verified from previous experience. It is impossible for books devised to emphasize the author's literary power rather than the noble goal of saving people from loss of faith, to have such a great effect. Those who doubt this can readily see that the sole aim of Harun Yahya's books is to overcome disbelief and to disseminate the Qur'an's moral values. The success and impact of this service are manifested in the readers' conviction.

One point should be kept in mind: The main reason for the continuing cruelty, conflict, and other ordeals endured by the vast majority of people is the ideological prevalence of disbelief. This can be ended only with the ideological defeat of disbelief and by conveying the wonders of creation and Qur'anic morality so that people can live by it. Considering the state of the world today, leading into a downward spiral of violence, corruption and conflict, clearly this service must be provided speedily and effectively, or it may be too late.

In this effort, the books of Harun Yahya assume a leading role. By the will of God, these books will be a means through which people in the twenty-first century will attain the peace, justice, and happiness promised in the Qur'an.

To the Reader

- A special chapter is assigned to the collapse of the theory of evolution because this theory constitutes the basis of all anti-spiritual philosophies. Since Darwinism rejects the fact of creation—and therefore, God's existence—over the last 150 years it has caused many people to abandon their faith or fall into doubt. It is therefore an imperative service, a very important duty to show everyone that this theory is a deception. Since some readers may find the opportunity to read only one of our books, we think it appropriate to devote a chapter to summarize this subject.

- All the author's books explain faith-related issues in light of Qur'anic verses, and invite readers to learn God's words and to live by them. All the subjects concerning God's verses are explained so as to leave no doubt or room for questions in the reader's mind. The books' sincere, plain, and fluent style ensures that everyone of every age and from every social group can easily understand them. Thanks to their effective, lucid narrative, they can be read at one sitting. Even those who rigorously reject spirituality are influenced by the facts these books document and cannot refute the truthfulness of their contents.

- This and all the other books by the author can be read individually, or discussed in a group. Readers eager to profit from the books will find discussion very useful, letting them relate their reflections and experiences to one another.

- In addition, it will be a great service to Islam to contribute to the publication and reading of these books, written solely for the pleasure of God. The author's books are all extremely convincing. For this reason, to communicate true religion to others, one of the most effective methods is encouraging them to read these books.

- We hope the reader will look through the reviews of his other books at the back of this book. His rich source material on faith-related issues is very useful, and a pleasure to read.

- In these books, unlike some other books, you will not find the author's personal views, explanations based on dubious sources, styles that are unobservant of the respect and reverence due to sacred subjects, nor hopeless, pessimistic arguments that create doubts in the mind and deviations in the heart.

Contents

Foreword to New Edition

*T*his book was written right after the 9/11 attacks that were staged in the two big cities of the United States of America in 2001 and it was explained with verses from the Qur'an, the practices of the Prophet Mohammed (pbuh) and examples from Islamic history that Islam denounces terrorism. However, terrorist attacks continued after 9/11, and spread to other countries including Great Britain, Spain, Turkey and France. This prompted politicians, academicians, religious leaders and writers, in other words, all conscientious people all around the world, to look for solutions to terrorism, to understand its causes and to work out the steps that should be taken.

When this book was first written in 2002, we explained with evidence that terrorists, and most importantly their leaders, are selfish,

cruel and merciless people who, as a result of Darwinist and material- ist education they received, see life as a constant struggle where only the fittest survive. Such people came to believe that violence and wars were justified means to their ends. Al Qaeda was very active at that time. Especially in recent years, many new terrorist organizations have emerged and they have used similar Islamic symbolism in their attacks against civilians.

These groups are getting stronger with new recruits joining them from all around the world. This forces political, academic, and reli-

If one is looking for the cause of an act of terrorism, one must look for its source in antireligious ideologies. Religion enjoins love, compassion, forgiveness, peace and living according to high moral standards. Terrorism, on the other hand, is on the side of cruelty and violence, causing pain, bloodshed and committing murder.

gious leaders to try to understand real Islam and determine ways to end terrorism with solutions from within the Islamic world. The ideological struggle against terror, particularly after the Charlie Hebdo attack that took place in the capital city of France, has shown once again that radical interpretations, which consist of superstitions that were added to Islam later and justify terrorist actions, were behind many terrorist attacks.

This deeply flawed understanding, which is diametrically opposed to Islam, a religion that favours peace over war, life over death, forgiveness over punishment, reconciliation over conflict, legitimizes violence against non-Muslims, and even against Muslims if they have different views or if they don't practice Islam or if they follow a different sect. Surely, this radical mentality is the biggest problem of the world today.

In this expanded edition of the book, we have included the sources of terrorism that result from this bigoted view of religion and how it needs to be countered intellectually. We hope that it will help those who seek solutions by force come to realize that twisted philosophical and religious interpretations cannot be ended with military means. And hopefully the money currently being squandered on weapons will be spent on education instead and they will join forces with illuminated, modern, loving and sensible Muslims.

INTRODUCTION

God commands justice and doing good
and giving to relatives. And He forbids
indecency and doing wrong and
tyranny. He warns you so that
hopefully you will pay heed.
(Qur'an, 16:90)

As Muslims, we strongly condemn all the terrorist attacks around the world, including those on two major cities of the United States of America on September 11, 2001, which caused the death and injury of thousands of innocent people.

The 9/11 attacks propelled the important issue of the true source of terrorism to the forefront of the world agenda. Thus, it has been announced to the entire world that Islam is a religion of peace and love that summons individuals to compassion and justice. Many world leaders, leading media organizations, television and radio stations said that the Islam defined in the Qur'an by no means permits any terrorist attacks on innocent people, and commands peace between people and between nations. The Western circles that have come to a full grasp of the morality of Islam and are well-informed about Islam as commanded by God in the Qur'an noted clearly that the words "Islam" and "terror" cannot stand side by side, and that no Divine religion permits terrorist attacks.

This book maintains that the source of the terror that we condemn is definitely not from a Divine religion, and that there is no room for terrorism in Islam. This is made clear in the Qur'an, the sole source of Islam, and in the practices of the Prophet Muhammad (pbuh) and many other Muslim rulers. However, surely there have been groups throughout history that interpreted the religion of Islam according to fabricated hadiths and superstitions that were produced after the Qur'an. As a result of following such superstitions that justify violence, these groups have carried out many terrorist atrocities that our beautiful religion strictly forbids.

This book reveals, in the light of the verses of the Qur'an and the practices of our Prophet Muhammad (pbuh) with examples from history, that terrorism is forbidden and bringing peace and security to the world is aimed in Islam.

As is known, for centuries, various acts of terrorism have been carried out in different parts of the world by different groups for a variety of purposes. Sometimes a communist organisation, sometimes a fascist group, and sometimes radical and separatist factions assume responsibility for these acts. While some countries like America have recently often become the target of attacks by racist and marginal terrorist groups, the European countries have been centre stage for violent acts carried out by terrorist groups. 17 November in Greece, the RAF (Red Army Faction) and Neo-Nazis in Germany, ETA in Spain, the Red Brigades in Italy and many other organisations killed innocent and defenceless people through terror and violence. The PKK, a Marxist and Stalinist terrorist organization, has been carrying out terrorist attacks for the past 30 years in the south-eastern part of Turkey resulting in the martyrdom of tens of thousands of people. The nature of terrorism changes with changing world conditions and increases its impact and power with the new means made possible by high technology. In particular, mass communication tools such as the Internet extend the scope and influence of the terrorist activities considerably.

Besides the Western organizations, there are also other terror organizations of Middle East origin. Terrorist attacks are carried out by these groups in all corners of the world. The fact that the perpetrators of various

For centuries, various acts of terrorism have been carried out in different parts of the world by different groups for a variety of purposes. Sometimes a communist organisation, sometimes a fascist group, and sometimes radical and separatist factions assume responsibility for these acts. 17 November in Greece, the RAF and Neo-Nazis in Germany, ETA in Spain, the Red Brigades in Italy and many other organisations killed innocent and defenceless people through terror and violence. The PKK has been carrying out terrorist attacks for the past 30 years in Turkey resulting in the martyrdom of tens of thousands of people.

terrorist acts carry Christian, Muslim or Jewish identities cause some people to put forward claims which do not concur with Divine religions. The truth is that even if terrorists have Muslim identities, the terror they perpetrate cannot be labelled "Islamic terror", just as it could not be called "Jewish terror" if the perpetrators were Jews or "Christian terror" if they were Christians. That is because, as will be examined in the following pages, **murdering innocent people in the name of a Divine religion is unacceptable.** These people grossly misinterpret the holy Scriptures that God sent to people for peace and brotherhood, and through their self-invented superstitions, work to

Murdering nnocent people in the name of a Divine religion is unacceptable. No one who is religious, and loves and fears God would do such a thing.

legitimize violence against people from different beliefs and thereby completely violate their faith in the process. We need to keep in mind that, among those who were killed, for example in New York and Washington on 9/11, there were people who loved the Prophet Jesus (pbuh) (Christians), the Prophet Moses (pbuh) (Jews) and the Prophet Muhammad (pbuh) (Muslims). Unless forgiven by God, murdering innocent people is a great sin that leads to torment in hell. No one who is religious, and loves and fears God would do such a thing.

The aggressors, regardless of which faith they claim to be a member of, may commit such violence either out of ignorance or with the intention of misusing religion for their own ends, or out of their enmity against religion. This violence divorces people from religion and generates hatred towards those who are religiously inclined. Consequently, every attack on innocent people having a so-called religious facade is actually an attack made against religion.

Religion commands love, mercy and peace. Terror, on the other hand, is the opposite of religion; it is cruel, merciless and demands bloodshed and misery. This being the case, the origins of a terrorist act should be sought in disbelief or in radical views that misinterpret the commands of religion rather than in religion itself. People with a fascist, communist, racist, materialist or radical outlook on life should be suspected as potential perpetrators. The name or the identity of the triggerman is not important: If he can kill innocent people without so much as batting an eye, then he cannot possibly represent a Divine religion. For this reason, "Islamic terror" is an erroneous concept which contradicts the message of Islam. The religion of Islam can by no means countenance terrorism. On the contrary, **terror (i.e. murder of innocent people) in Islam is a great sin, and Muslims are responsible for preventing these acts and bringing peace and justice to the world.**

Eat and drink of God's provision and do not go about the Earth corrupting it.
(Qur'an, 2:60)

ISLAMIC MORALITY: THE SOURCE OF PEACE AND SECURITY

Some of those who say that they are members of a particular religion and something is done in the name of that religion may, in fact, misunderstand that religion and as a result, practice it wrongly. For that reason, it would be very wrong to form ideas about a religion or make judgments based on people's actions. The best way of understanding a religion is to study its Divine source.

Islam's Divine source is the Qur'an, which is based on concepts of morality, love, compassion, humility, sacrifice, understanding and peace. A Muslim who lives by those precepts in its true sense will be most polite, careful of thought, modest, decent, noble, just, trustworthy and easy to get on with. He/she will spread love, respect, harmony and the joy of living all around him. Despite this fact, the Qur'an and Islam have been associated with the word "fear" in recent years thus causing Islamophobia to spread even more. However, the real source of the fear in people's hearts isn't Islam; it is the religion of bigotry. The radicals that act in the name of Islam and the Islamophobes who fear those radicals, are making the same mistake. Both parties fail to grasp that Islam has nothing to do with the religion of bigotry, which is a horrid and hateful system devoid of love. For this reason, it is crucial to understand the real meaning of Islam according to the Qur'an and to show the grave mistake of those who are trying to associate terrorism with it.

Is it sufficient to say that "Islam is the religion of peace"?

While saying that Islam is a religion of love, the existence of some references that order the killing of those who do not fulfil their prayers, or those who do not fast or even trim their beards is both a serious contradiction and a grave danger. Those who make lengthy speeches about the importance Islam attaches to women constitute an exceedingly important problem when they do not admit to the invalidity of some so-called hadiths suggesting things such as, "Women are imperfect", "Do the opposite of whatever a woman does" or "A great part of hell is full of women." It will not be sufficient to say that "Muslims are loving people" or "Islam is the religion of peace" without putting an end to the hateful and violent rhetoric that have been added to Islam over the centuries and that directly contradicts the Qur'an.

Surely, according to the Qur'an, Muslims are supposed to be loving, compassionate and friendly, and no one has any right whatsoever to impose anything on other people; however the problem is most Muslims today follow not the Qur'an, but their tribal, local or regional traditions and superstitions. Therefore, unless all those superstitions are completely eliminated, unless Muslims completely turn to the Qur'an, it is simply impossible to prevent those violent people that act in the name of Islam or to stop Islamophobia.

It is not sufficient to say that "Muslims are loving people" or "Islam is the religion of peace" without putting an end to the hateful and violent rhetoric and practice.

The only way to remove the impact of those extremists who portray as "Islam" the bigoted mindset that forbids science, technology and the arts to Muslims, and thus condemns them to oppression and ignorance, is through education.

Modern Western education is definitely obligatory; however, the number of people educated in the West but then going to the East - and Africa - to participate in acts of terror is far from insignificant. Therefore the question that demands an answer is this:

How is it possible to convince those who are well-educated in all fields to become involved in terrorism?

When observed carefully, we understand that the crux of the problem is those teachings which legitimize violence and are widely seen in both West and the Islamic world. Everyone knows about the negative aspect of the Darwinian worldview, which is the basis of Western-style education, and we will be talking about this in detail in the coming chapters. However, what must be explained before is the fact that praises of violence that exist in some Shia and Sunni references are mostly ignored, and that during their primary Islamic education, many young people are first taught about these sources. A generation totally unaware of the content and context of the Qur'an and whose minds are moulded by radical views are readily directed to violence. For this reason the cause of terrorism is not a Divine religion, but it is a blend of Darwinist education and a bigoted state of mind. Spreading the true Islam based on the Qur'an, cleansed of bigotry, is the definitive solution to terrorism.

Islam Is the Religion of Peace

Terrorism, in its broadest sense, is violence committed against non-military targets for political purposes. To put it another way, targets of terror are civilians whose only crime, in the eyes of terrorists, is to represent "the other side."

For this reason, terrorism means subjecting innocent people to violence, which is an act bereft of any moral justification. Each and every terrorist act, as in the case of the atrocities committed by Hitler or Stalin, is a crime committed against humanity. For a believer, this is clear act of defiance of the orders of God. Those who are trying to associate Islam with terrorism need to remember this important fact.

The Qur'an is a true Book revealed to people as a guide to the true path and in this Book, God commands men to adopt good morals. This morality is based upon love, compassion, understanding and mercy. The word "Islam" is derived from the word meaning "peace" in Arabic. Islam is a religion revealed to mankind with the intention of presenting a peaceful life through which the infinite compassion and mercy of

God manifest on earth. God calls all people to Islamic morals through which compassion, mercy, peace and love can be experienced all over the world. In the Qur'an, God addresses believers as follows:

> **O you who believe! Enter absolutely into peace (Islam). Do not follow in the footsteps of satan. He is an outright enemy to you. (Qur'an, 2:208)**

As it is made clear in the verse, security can only be ensured by "entering into Islam", that is, living by the values of the Qur'an. The values of the Qur'an hold a Muslim responsible for treating all people, whether Muslim or non-Muslim, kindly and justly, protecting the needy and the innocent and **"preventing the dissemination of mischief"**. Mischief comprises all forms of anarchy and terror that remove security, comfort and peace. As God says in a verse, **"God does not love corruption"**. (Qur'an, 2:205)

A society in which Islamic moral values are truly honored is a society characterised by peace, forgiveness, love, compassion and mutual support and joy.

Murdering a person for no reason is one of the most obvious examples of mischief. God repeats in the Qur'an a command He formerly revealed to Jews in the Torah thus:

> **... if someone kills another person – unless it is in retaliation for someone else or for causing corruption in the earth – it is as if he had murdered all mankind. And if anyone gives life to another person, it is as if he had given life to all mankind... (Qur'an, 5:32)**

As the verse states, a person who kills even a single man, "unless it is in retaliation for someone else or for causing corruption in the earth", commits a crime as if he had murdered all mankind.

This being the case, it is obvious what great sins are the murders, massacres and attacks, popularly known as "suicide attacks", committed by terrorists. God informs us how this cruel face of terrorism will be punished in the hereafter in the following verse:

Terrorists aim to create a world of violence, conflict, disorder, and fear.

There are only grounds against those who wrong people and act as tyrants in the earth without any right to do so. Such people will have a painful punishment. (Qur'an, 42:42)

Organizing acts of terror against innocent people is entirely against Islam and it is unlikely that any sincerely believing Muslim could ever commit such crimes. On the contrary, Muslims are responsible for stopping these people, removing "mischief on earth" and bringing peace and security to all people all over the world. Islam cannot be reconciled with terror. Just the contrary, it should be the solution to and the path to the prevention of terror. This is the basis of Islam; peace is the spirit of Islam. However, the bigoted worldview, which practices Islam according to superstitions rather than the Qur'an, believes the opposite is true.

The fanatics' problem is that they regard what they've learned from specious superstition as their faith. However, those who criticize those fanatics are sometimes just as radical as them and believe in the accuracy of that same superstition. The more one produces evidence from the Qur'an, the more they try to produce their own from the superstitions the fanatics subscribe to. That is where they make their gravest mistake: If they want to know the true Islam and find a solution to fanaticism, they must heed the true faith described in the Qur'an.

Until the clear difference between bigotry and Islam is demonstrated, radicalism and Islamophobia is going to continue to plague the world.

For this reason, it is very important to explain the beautiful morals of the Qur'an, in other words Islam all around the world with serious education campaign intended to display the clear difference between bigotry and Islam. Various facts need to be made clear, such as that God prohibits corruption and encourages virtue, and that freedom of thought and the finest democracy are enshrined in the Qur'an:

God Has Condemned Wickedness

God has commanded people to avoid committing evil: oppression, cruelty, murder and bloodshed are all forbidden. A few of the many verses on this matter in the Qur'an read:

> **Eat and drink of God's provision and do not go about the earth corrupting it. (Qur'an, 2:60)**

> **Do not corrupt the earth after it has been put right. Call on Him fearfully and eagerly. God's mercy is close to the good-doers. (Qur'an, 7:56)**

Those who think that they will be successful by causing wickedness, upheaval and oppression, and by killing innocent people are committing a great error. God has forbidden all acts of wickedness involving terrorism and violence and condemned those who engage in such acts.

In Surat al-Ma'ida, verse 32, God says that if anyone kills someone unjustly, it is as if he had murdered all mankind. To murder even one person is totally opposed to the moral teaching of the Qur'an.

In the present era, however, acts of terrorism, genocide and various massacres occur all over the world. Innocent people are being savagely killed, and countries where communities are being brought to hate each other for artificial reasons are drowning in blood. These horrors in countries with different histories, cultures and social structures may have causes and sources peculiar to each. However, it is evident that the fundamental cause is a moving away from the Qur'an. As a result of lack of religion, communities emerge that have no love for or fear of God and that are deceived by the lie that they will not be called to account in the hereafter. Since they falsely believe that "I will not have to account for my actions to anyone," they can easily act with no compassion, morality or conscience.

The existence of hypocrites who emerge in the name of God and religion, but actually organise themselves to commit wickedness condemned by God, is indicated in the Qur'an. The fact that some people

These people are not representatives of Christians and Muslims.

do things "in the name of God" or even swear in His name, in other words that they use the kind of language designed to show themselves as very religious, does not mean that what they do is in conformity with religion. On the contrary, what they do can be quite against the will of God and the morality of religion. The truth of the matter lies in their actions. If their actions are "causing corruption and not putting things right", as the verse reveals, then you can be sure that these people cannot be truly religious, and that their aim is not to serve religion.

It is quite impossible for someone who fears God and has grasped the morality of Islam to to take part in such actions as violence or wickedness. That is why Islam is the true solution to terrorism. When the sublime morality of the Qur'an is explained in a way purified of superstition, it will be impossible for people to connect true Islam with those who support or join groups that aim at hatred, war and disorder. That is because God has forbidden wickedness:

Whenever he holds the upperhand, he goes about the earth corrupting it, destroying (people's) crops and breeding stock. God does not love corruption. (Qur'an, 2:205)

It is out of the question for someone who fears God to turn a blind eye to even the smallest action that might harm mankind. Someone who does not believe in God and the hereafter, however, can easily do all kinds of evil, since he thinks he will not have to account to anyone.

The first thing that needs to be done to rid the world of the present-day scourge of terrorism is to explain the errors of bigotry that stirs up radicalism, to use education to do away with irreligiousness as well as with deviant beliefs that are put forward in the name of religion, and to teach people true Qur'anic morality and to love and fear God.

Islam Encourages Justice, Kindness and Everything that is Beautiful for Everyone

One of the reasons behind terrorism is the failure to see differences as a source of beauty. Today, all around the world, some people are being treated unfairly and ruthlessly only because of the colour of their skin or owing to their ethnicity. However, God orders mankind in the Qur'an to treat everyone equally regardless of language, faith, race or ethnic background.

God informs us in the Qur'an that the purpose in the creation of different tribes and peoples is "that they should come to know each other". Different nations or peoples, all of whom are the servants of God, should get to know one another, that is, learn about their different cultures, languages, traditions and abilities. In brief, one of the purposes of the creation of different races and nations is not conflict and war but richness. Such variation is a bounty of God's creation.

The fact that someone is taller than someone else or that his skin is yellow or white neither makes him superior to others nor is it something to feel ashamed of. Every trait a person has is a result of God's purposeful creation, but in the Sight of God, these variations have no ultimate importance. A believer knows that someone attains superiority only by having fear of God and in the strength of his faith in God. This fact is related in the following verse:

> **O mankind! We created you from a male and female, and made you into peoples and tribes so that you might come to know each other. The noblest among you in God's Sight is that one of you who best performs his duty. ... (Qur'an, 49:13)**

The understanding of justice recommended by God in the Qur'an calls for equal, compassionate and peaceable treatment of everyone, with no discrimination between them. For example, hatred and anger are the major sources of evil, and are likely to prevent people from making just decisions, thinking soundly and conducting themselves rationally.

People in societies where hatred and anger prevail worry that they can fall victim to someone else at any time. Having lost their sense of mutual trust, they also lose their human feelings such as compassion, brotherhood and co-operation and start hating one another.

However, the feelings someone holds in his heart towards a person or community should never influence a believer's decisions. No matter how evil or hostile the person he is considering may be, the believer sets all these feelings aside and acts and makes his decisions justly. His feelings towards that person cast no shadow over his wisdom and conscience. His conscience always inspires him to comply with God's commands and advice, and never to abandon good manners, because this is a command God gives in the Qur'an. In Surat al-Ma'ida, it is related as follows:

> **O you who believe! Show integrity for the sake of God, bearing witness with justice. Do not let hatred for a people incite you into not being just. Be just. That is closer to faith. Heed God (alone). God is aware of what you do. (Qur'an, 5:8)**

As is related in the verse, displaying a just attitude is what most complies with having fear of and love for God. A person of faith knows

Islamic morality commands Muslims to protect the rights of orphans and those in poverty and need, to mutually support one another, and to be well-disposed towards one another.

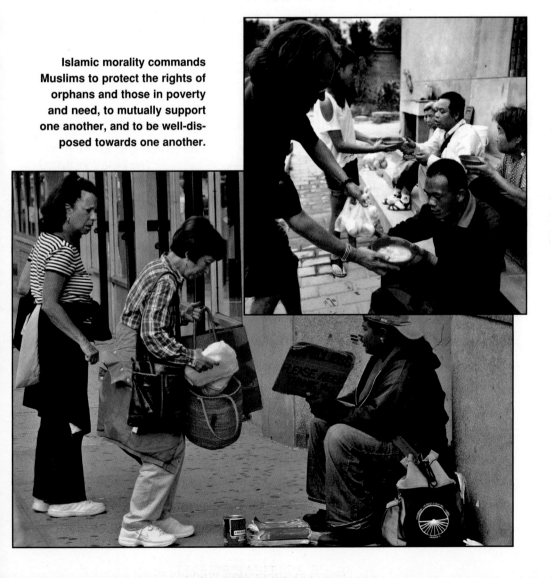

that he will attain the pleasure of God only when he acts justly. Every person who witnesses his or her good manners will trust this person, feel comfortable in their presence and trust them with any responsibility or task.

It is obvious that those who fear and heed God hold spiritual values in high regard and are filled with eagerness to serve people. In general, such people are there to serve humanity and bring with them great benefits to mankind. For this reason, it is very important for people to learn about the true religion and live by the morals explained in the Qur'an – the final Revelation from God.

God Has Commanded Forgiveness and Compassion

In the verses of the Qur'an, God has always described forgiveness as a superior quality, and in one verse, He has given the good news that such behaviour will be rewarded: **"The repayment of a bad action is one equivalent to it. But if someone pardons and puts things right, his reward is with God. Certainly He does not love wrongdoers."** (Qur'an, 42:40)

God has revealed in the Qur'an that it is virtuous behaviour to forgive someone even if one has been wronged, and to respond to bad with something better. Verses on the subject read:

... You will never cease to come upon some act of treachery on their part, except for a few of them. Yet pardon them, and overlook. God loves good-doers. (Qur'an, 5:13)

A good action and a bad action are not the same. Repel the bad with something better and, if there is enmity between you and someone else, he will be like a bosom friend. (Qur'an, 41:34)

Islamic Morality Envisions
a Life Filled With Peace,
Well-being, Love and Joy
For All People...

Islam Defends Freedom of Thought

Islam is a religion which provides and guarantees freedom of ideas, thought and life. It prevents tension, disputes, slander and even negative thinking among people. In the same way that terrorism and all acts of violence are determinedly prohibited in Islam, even the slightest ideological pressure to be put on them is also forbidden:

> **There is no compulsion in religion. True guidance has become clearly distinct from error. (Qur'an, 2:256)**

> **So remind them! You are only a reminder. You are not in control of them. (Qur'an, 88:21-22)**

Forcing people to believe in a religion or to adopt its forms of belief is completely contrary to the essence and spirit of Islamic morality. According to Islam, true faith is only possible with free will and freedom of conscience. Of course, Muslims can advise and encourage each other about the features of Qur'anic morality. All believers are charged with explaining Qur'anic morality to people in the nicest manner possible. They will explain the beauties of religion in the light of the verse, **"Call to the way of your Lord with wisdom and fair admonition..."** (Qur'an, 16:125), however, they must also bear in mind the verse, **"You are not responsible for their guidance, but God guides whoever He wills."** (Qur'an, 2:272)

They will never resort to compulsion to force others to embrace faith, nor any kind of physical or psychological pressure. Neither will they use any worldly privilege to turn someone towards religion. When they receive a negative response to what they say, Muslims will reply along the lines of: **"To you your religion, and to me, mine,"** as revealed in the verse (Qur'an, 109:6). Muslims must respect and be compassionate towards all beliefs they encounter, no matter what they may be, and behave forgivingly, justly and humanely towards everyone, even if they don't believe in any faith at all. This responsibility placed on believers is to live by the beauty of the religion of God by means of peace and compassion. The decision whether or not to implement these truths, whether or not to believe, lies with each individual himself. Forcing that person to believe, or trying to impose anything on him, is a violation of Qur'anic morality. In fact, God issues a reminder to believers in the Qur'an:

If your Lord had willed, all the people on the Earth would have believed. Do you think you can force people to be believers? (Qur'an, 10:99)

A model of society in which people are forced to worship is completely contradictory to Islamic morality. **Belief and worship should be directed to God by the free will of the individual**. If a system imposes belief and worship on people, then they will act as if they are religious out of fear of that system. This will mean the encouragement of hypocrisy and no Muslim would approve that. From the point of view of Islamic morality, what really counts is that religion should be lived with the love of God, for God's good pleasure, mercy and paradise in an environment where peoples' consciences are totally free.

The history of Islam is full of the compassionate and understanding practices of Muslim rulers who have respected all religions and built religious freedom with their own hands. For example, Thomas Arnold, a British missionary employed in the service of the Indian government, describes that Islamic morality favours freedom in these words:

But of any organised attempt to force the acceptance of Islam on the non-Muslim population, or of any systematic persecution intended to stamp out the Christian religion, we hear nothing. Had the caliphs chosen to adopt either course of action, they might have swept away Christianity as easily as Ferdinand and Isabella drove Islam out of Spain, or Louis XIV made Protestantism penal in France, or the Jews were kept out of England for 350 years. The Eastern Churches in Asia were entirely cut

In 1492, the Jews who refused to convert were exiled from Spain by King Ferdinand and Queen Isabella (above). The Jews were accepted by the Ottoman Empire, a haven of Islamic justice and compassion.

off from communion with the rest of Christendom, throughout which no one would have been found to lift a finger on their behalf, as heretical communions. So that the very survival of these Churches to the present day is a strong proof of the generally tolerant attitude of the Muhammadan governments towards them.[1]

Killing A Person Is One of the Greatest Sins Related in the Qur'an

Killing a person for no reason is one of the greatest sins related in the Qur'an:

> ... if someone kills another person – unless it is in retaliation for someone else or for causing corruption in the earth – it is as if he had murdered all mankind. And if anyone gives life to another person, it is as if he had given life to all mankind. ... (Qur'an, 5:32)

> ... those who do not call on any other deity together with God and <u>do not kill anyone God has made inviolate</u>, except with the right to do so,

and do not fornicate; anyone who does that will receive <u>an evil pun-</u>
<u>**ishment.**</u> **(Qur'an, 25:68)**

As the verses suggest, a person who kills innocent people for no
reason is threatened with a great torment. God informs us that killing
even a single person is as evil as murdering all mankind on earth. A
person who observes God's limits can do no harm to a single human,
let alone massacre thousands of innocent people.

All of this shows that the morality that Islam recommends to
mankind brings to the world the virtues of peace, harmony and justice.
The horror known as terrorism, that is so preoccupying the world at
present, is the work of ignorant and fanatical people, completely
estranged from Qur'anic morality, and who have absolutely nothing to
do with religion. The solution to these people and groups who try to
carry out their savagery under the mask of religion is the teaching of
true Qur'anic morality. In other words, demonstrating to them the
errors of their bigotry, causing them to completely abandon it; explaining Islam based on the Qur'an will fundamentally destroy the ideology
of terrorism and terrorists and therefore is the only solution to save the
world from the nightmare of terrorism.

True Democracy Is Only Possible When People Live by Islamic Moral Values

God wishes ease, comfort, happiness and joy to people. God does not wrong people. The religion, which is the commandment of God, also shows people the way to the most peaceful, blissful, safest, highest quality, comfortable, and delightful life. There is no compulsion where religion is concerned. A person believes in God and lives by religion, by seeing God's existence and oneness by using his conscience. Religion is an acceptance by the heart.

God describes in the Qur'an freedom, love, compassion, forgiveness, justice and an environment where everyone can live freely, can speak up their minds freely and live in peace. This is a summary, a description of democracy; therefore, the true source of democracy is in the Qur'an. Anyone seeking social justice and equality will find the best manifestation of these in the Qur'an:

1- SOCIAL JUSTICE: Almighty God commands social justice and sharing

Social justice is one of the basic principles of democracy. People learned social justice from the Prophet Noah (pbuh) and the Prophet Abraham (pbuh). According to religious sources, when the Ark came to dry land after the flood, the Prophet Noah boiled together the small quantities of remaining chickpeas, lentils, raisins, figs, wheat and the like to make a kind of sweet broth. Everyone on the Ark then ate it together. That is one of the best examples of social justice, because by this example the Prophet Noah teaches everyone equality, solidarity and generosity and the importance of distributing food to all.

As revealed in the Qur'an, in verse 69 of Surah Hud, **"Our messengers brought the good news to Abraham. They said,**

'Peace!' and he too said, 'Peace!' and brought in a roasted calf
without delay" the Prophet Abraham immediately killed a calf
when guests arrived and had it prepared for them to eat.
Almighty God notes that by offering food to people whom he
had never met, the Prophet Abraham was behaving in the best
way, and wisely stresses the importance of feeding the poor
and of social justice.

2- EQUALITY: Almighty God reveals in the Qur'an that no race is superior to any other

As Almighty God reveals in one verse of the Qur'an, superiority lies in piety alone. In this verse God tells us:

Mankind! We created you from a male and female, and made you into
peoples and tribes so that you might come to know each other. The
noblest among you in God's Sight is the one with the most piety. God
is All-Knowing, All-Aware. (Qur'an, 49:13)

Our Prophet (pbuh) expresses this truth commanded by God as
follows:

"You are sons of Adam, and Adam came from dust. Let the
people cease to boast about their ancestors." *(Sunan Abu
Dawud, Book 41, Number 5097)*

During his final sermon, the Prophet (pbuh) called on Muslims
in these terms:

"There is no superiority for an Arab over a non-Arab and for
a non-Arab over an Arab; nor for white over the black nor for
the black over the white except in piety. Verily the noblest
among you is he who is the most pious." *(The Prophet Muhammad's Last Sermon; http://www.stanford.edu/ ~jamila/Sermon.html)*

3- JUSTICE: Almighty God commands justice

God issues this commandment to believers in the Qur'an: **"...You who believe! Be upholders of justice, bearing witness for God alone, even against yourselves or your parents and relatives. Whether they are rich or poor, God is well able to look after them. Do not follow your own desires and deviate from the truth. If you twist or turn away, God is aware of what you do."** (Qur'an, 4:135)

The commands that our Prophet (pbuh) issued among Muslims and his just and affectionate attitude toward people of different religions, languages, races and tribes, as well as the way he treated everyone equally, making no distinction between rich and poor as God revealed in the Qur'an, represents an excellent example of the conception of democracy.

Democracy Will Come About When People Are Living by the Moral Values Commanded by God

As we have seen, in the essence of Islam, there is intellectual freedom, freedom of faith and expression. Some people assume that democracy entered the history of humanity with the ancient Greeks. However, it is God Who teaches democracy to people. From the time of the Prophet Adam (pbuh), all prophets have been the genuine representatives of intellectual freedom and respect to views. The essence of all the primary concepts – freedom of justice, not putting any pressure upon anyone, treating everyone as a first class citizen, respecting and trusting people, not judging anyone due to his views - which are associated with democracy, are present in the morality of religion.

Throughout history, people have learned these concepts from the righteous religions revealed by God and witnessed its most beautiful examples during the times when people lived by the righteous religions.

When we look at the times when people were oppressed due to their opinions and their different ideologies, members of various religions were humiliated, while the arts, science and architecture died out; times when people lost their joy in living and almost turned into robots, or when book burnings, murders, massacres, genocides became widespread, we see the influence of irreligious, atheist ideologies or those who misinterpreted religious morality with a radical mindset by distancing it from its essence.

Once God's righteous religion is lived in the form it is commanded by God, the true justice, democracy, respect and love, that people have been longing for, can be experienced. Very soon, democracy, brotherhood, love, friendship and peace will, by God's leave, dominate the world and people will experience the joy, bliss and abundance of faith as much as they can. As one can clearly see from the signs of the verses, hadiths of our Prophet (pbuh) and words of great Islamic scholars, the time in which we live is the End Times.

The difficult and troublesome days of the End Times will, in this century, come to end, and the world will enter a brand new, bright era. Communicating the Oneness and Unity of God in the most beautiful and wise manner, and introducing people to Islam as described in the Qur'an and lived in the Age of Felicity lays a very important foundation for the bright days that we will attain in the near future.

Do they then seek the judgement of the Time of Ignorance?

Who could be better at giving judgement than God for people with certainty? (Qur'an, 5:50)

...God is All-Gentle,

Most Merciful to mankind.

(Qur'an, 2:143)

THE QUR'ANIC VIEW OF SHARIA, JIHAD AND WAR

*T*here are two concepts widely exploited by radicals who perform terrorist acts supposedly in the name of the religion of Islam in their bid to show Islam as a religion of violence: Sharia and jihad.

As God explicitly states in Qur'an, 12:111, the Qur'an is **"a clarification of everything,"** although the radical mindset that takes fabricated hadiths as its guide has never seen the Qur'an as entirely sufficient. For that reason, throughout the course of history they have maintained that some of the commandments of the Qur'an are "not sufficient" (surely the Qur'an is beyond that) and need to be interpreted. From that, they developed the idea that we can only understand the Qur'an through the hadiths.

The hadiths have come down to the present day as the words of our Prophet (pbuh). While some are entirely trustworthy and accurate quotations and practices, others have gradually been distorted and the meanings of some have been changed entirely. There are two ways of determining whether a hadith is really the words or the practice of our Prophet (pbuh) and that is if it is in agreement with the Qur'an or if it has already occurred. It is without doubt a grave slander to maintain that words or practices that conflict with the Qur'an actually belong to the Prophet (pbuh) because our Prophet abided by the Qur'an alone.

The idea that we can only understand the Qur'an through the hadiths has wrought enormous harm on the Islamic world because some Muslims thinking along those lines began to abide by fabricated hadiths. They even eventually abandoned the Qur'an altogether, taking those hadiths alone as the source of their religion. When fabricated hadiths conflicted with the Qur'an, some even had the effrontery to say, "This hadith overrules the commandment of the Qur'an." Hundreds of fabricated hadiths gave rise to different faiths, and the result was four schools that disagreed with one another on many areas within Islam. The scholars all called

"Interior of a Mosque, Afternoon Prayer", by John Frederick Lewis, 1847. Oil painting on wood panel, private collection.

themselves Muslims, but they all espoused something very different. They even said that the others had abandoned the faith entirely.

Our Prophet (pbuh) complains to Almighty God of the state into which the Islamic world has fallen as follows in the Qur'an:

The Messenger says, "My Lord, my people treat this Qur'an as something to be ignored." (Qur'an, 25:30)

Indeed, the problem of a large part of the Islamic world today is that people regard the Qur'an as a book that has been abandoned.

Once the Qur'an had been abandoned, it was time for "ijma." (Ijma means eminent religious figures living at any time producing commandments regarding Sharia law on the basis of deductive analogy.) Since the Qur'an was not their guide they were smothered by thousands of fabricated hadiths and they finally decided that "neither the Qur'an nor the hadiths could properly explain the commandments." After a while these "religious leaders" began producing laws in the name of Islam.

The schools began clashing with one another, and the agreements of the Muslim communities came into conflict with those of other schools. Every "religious leader's" own interpretation was regarded as law, each community based itself on a different set of practices and the whole community of Islam began splitting up into sects, classes and finally tiny groups. The Qur'an, however, was left as little more than a decorative item hung up on the wall, still inside its case. As a result, a large part of the Islamic world "abandoned and ignored the Qur'an."

Looking at some of the opponents of Islam, we see that their problem is quite ironically the same as that of the peddlers of superstition: They do not learn about Islam from the Qur'an. Just like the peddlers of superstition, they concentrate on fabricated hadiths, tra-

The Ka'aba, to which almost two million Muslims come every year from the four corners of the world, is a symbol of the peace and compassion that are an integral part of Islamic teaching.

ditions and interpretations of Islam by religious leaders that are generally incompatible with the Qur'an. In their eyes, "Islam" is the lifestyle and practices of the peddlers of superstition. In their view, "Islam" is the imaginative power of historians, not the faith as revealed in the Qur'an. They call the practices of this fabricated religion "Sharia," not the laws of the Qur'an. They are unaware of the values and concepts imparted in the Qur'an, but have a great knowledge of all the rules of the false religion of the peddlers of superstition. In criticizing the rules of that false religion, they imagine they are criticizing Islam. So attached are they to the religion of the peddlers of superstition that they do not believe it when they are told, "This is not Islam." And this is an exceedingly serious error.

These people must believe this if they are not opposed to Islam owing to any philosophical or religious opposition and if they genuinely seek a solution to the darkness of the fanatic mindset. Their religion is not Islam. The Qur'an by itself is sufficient for a Muslim. Hadiths are true and reliable so long as they are compatible with the Qur'an. A hadith that is incompatible with the Qur'an has no place in Islam. If a Muslim cannot find Islam in the Qur'an, it means he is looking for another religion and the Sharia of that faith is not Islam.

The True Sharia in the Qur'an

The word Sharia means "path." A Muslim can easily tell what "path" to follow by looking at the Qur'an. Few things are unlawful in the Qur'an, and these are made clear with explicit prohibitions. They are not open to discussion or interpretation. For example, killing, adultery, earning interest, eating pork or drinking blood are all unlawful actions revealed in verses of the Qur'an in the most definitive terms. This is one important characteristic of the Qur'an. People who aim to come up with prohibitions by interpreting verses in the light of their own desires always produce their own deductions from them. Yet God prohibits what is unlawful with definitive pronouncements, as in this verse:

> **He has only <u>forbidden</u> you carrion, blood and pork and what has been consecrated to other than God. (Qur'an, 2:173)**

God reveals in the Qur'an that there will be people who fabricate what is lawful or prohibited in the name of Islam:

> **Do not say about what your lying tongues describe: "<u>This is lawful and this is unlawful</u>," inventing lies against God. Those who invent lies against God are not successful. (Qur'an, 16: 116)**

Following the time of our Prophet (pbuh), numerous communities emerged who invented lies against God. Since these communities did not take the Qur'an as their guide, they could call whatever they wished to be lawful or unlawful.

However, there are some communities whose characteristics God particularly emphasizes: "They make unlawful the good things made lawful." Our Lord says in the Qur'an:

> **You who believe! <u>Do not make unlawful the good things God has made lawful for you</u>, and do not overstep the limits. God does not love people who overstep the limits. (Qur'an, 5:87)**

The system of savagery applied under the name of Sharia, yet which is completely incompatible with Islam, is a result of being distanced from the Qur'an. The true Sharia set out in verses, the true path of the Qur'an in other words, can be defined as follows:

The Sharia of the Qur'an means love, respect, and affection and protection toward people of all faiths and opinions. The Sharia of the Qur'an insists on democracy, and freedom of ideas prevails. Under the Sharia of the Qur'an, people are knowledgeable, educated, open-minded, respectful of other ideas, happy, outward-looking, modern, high quality, optimistic, value art and science and value love and friendship. There is no hatred, intolerance, conflict, fighting, despotism, imposition, threatening, unhappiness, anger or war in the Sharia of the Qur'an.

Is there an Islamic country in the world today that meets these definitions of the Sharia of the Qur'an? Certainly not; this Sharia has not been applied since the time of our Prophet (pbuh). The countries that say they are governed under Sharia law apply the Sharia of a fanatical faith that various violent groups impose in the name of Islam. They adopt various untrue hadiths as their guides, but abandon the Qur'an.

The failure to apply the true system of the Sharia in the Qur'an, which would bring with it the delights cited above, and savagery being misrepresented as the Sharia of the Qur'an is of course a very terrible thing: Blaming Islam is not the answer, however. Those who blame Islam do grave harm by trying to eliminate it as the sole answer to radicalism, violence and savagery. They are actually smoothing the radicals' path by striving to weaken Islam. It is not their accusations or the weapons they manufacture that will eliminate radicalism and the false beliefs propagated under the name of Islam. The only way to accomplish that is with the conception of the true Islam. There is a problem of a false belief and false beliefs can only be done away with by replacing them with true ones.

The Sharia of the Qur'an requires that a Muslim be modern, well-groomed, noble, wise, cultured, democratic, open-minded, respectful of all ideas and full of love. The Sharia of the Qur'an is based on brotherhood, peace and love. War, cruelty, hatred, anger and conflict are all forbidden to Muslims in the Qur'an. Those who wish to know the true Sharia must look to the Qur'an alone.

The True Jihad in the Qur'an

There is no killing in the jihad in the Qur'an. There is no raining bombs down in the jihad in the Qur'an. There are no suicide bombers or cowardly attacks on the civilians. There is no hatred or cursing people in the jihad in the Qur'an. The children of the Prophet Abraham (pbuh), of the Prophet Jacob (pbuh) and the Prophet Moses (pbuh) are not accursed in the jihad in the Qur'an. There are no threats and intimidation in the jihad in the Qur'an. Islam is not that kind of faith.

There is no slaughter, death, hatred and rage in Islam, nor in Christianity or in Judaism. Therefore, if someone says, "I learned from the Qur'an that I must kill, bomb and curse people" then he is lying, or has been mistaught.

"Waging jihad" in Islam means to educate the other side, to teach moral virtue and to strive to turn people away from evil. Those who murder in the name of jihad are not acting in the light of the Qur'an.

KILL THOSE INSU[...]

No Democracy We want Just Islam

A radical who says he is a Muslim follows a faith invented solely for the purpose of killing, bombing and cursing. That invented faith does not stem from the Qur'an.

The Holy Book they kiss and touch to their foreheads and hang on the wall may never actually have been read. That is the kind of faith in which everything is dark. It offers hatred instead of love, anger instead of affection, enmity instead of brotherhood, afflictions instead of beauty and ignorance instead of art, beauty, science and culture. It is easy to put a gun in the hand of someone who believes in such a faith. It is easy to say, "That community are your enemies." It is easy to stir such a person up. It is easy to produce communities of rage. **This terrible scourge, which exists not only in Islam but also in all the true faiths and even in Marxism, satanism and materialism, in short in all religions, ideologies and ways of thinking, is the scourge of radicalism and bigotry.**

Why does radicalism or bigotry exist? The answer is evident: Because that is what many people are taught. They know no other faith. That is all the radicals who appear in the name of Islam know as Islam. They have been left in ignorance, in a ghetto. They have been turned away from society, art and science. They have always been misinformed about the concept of "jihad" and have applied it wrongly because that is what they were taught. They have always imagined that by acting on what they were taught they were doing a good thing. They never even imagined they were actually harming themselves, their faith, their own families, their own peoples and, of course, others. However, the "jihad" described in the Qur'an is very much different than the picture of jihad painted by the radicals.

So what does the word *"jihad"* mean?

The word *jihad* comes from the Arabic word *"jahd."* Its meanings are 1) To work, to strive, to exhibit determination and persistence or self-sacrifice and 2) To control one's lower self. On the basis of these definitions, waging jihad in Islam means to inform the other side, to teach people proper moral values and to turn them away from evil. In doing this, a Muslim must train his own lower self in the direction of moral virtue and train himself to be someone far removed from rage and hatred. In other words, what a Muslim engaged in jihad must do is to train himself on the one hand, and strive to teach people truth and goodness on the other. He must be a role model with his own moral values in order to spread love, peace and affection and to turn people away from evil.

The word "jahd" is never employed in any other sense in the Qur'an. Those who perpetrate slaughter under the name of *"jihad"* saying "Our point of reference is the Qur'an" are either lying or misinformed.

In the eyes of the Qur'an, those who are now slaughtering people in the name of jihad, suicide bombers taking their own lives as well as lives of defenceless civilians or those who are inciting war are committing a grave sin. The verses of the Qur'an these people misinterpret in the name of war will be set out in detail in the following pages. There is one important point that needs to be remembered here; the great majority of radicals spread violence out of ignorance. They do not

know the true faith. Most of them have likely never even read the Qur'an. That is why it is no use to condemn, curse, threaten, imprison or exile someone who kills under the misapprehension he is waging jihad. His problem is that he has not been educated with the Qur'an and has not understood the law of God. Since that is the problem, we have to accept the fact that so long as false education persists, there will also be radicals who are ignorant of what they do. If one properly understands what the problem is, one can also grasp the fact that the only thing that those who spread violence and terror under the name of jihad need is true education.

Killing Oneself (Committing Suicide) Is not "Jihad", It Is Forbidden in the Qur'an

The main act of terrorism carried out in the world in the past 20 to 30 years, especially those by terrorist groups originating in the Middle East, usually took up the form of suicide bombing. Killing oneself, or suicide, is a sin in the eyes of the Qur'an. But how can a person strap bombs to his chest and walk into a crowd before blowing himself up, or drive a bomb-laden car right into the middle of a crowd of civilians?

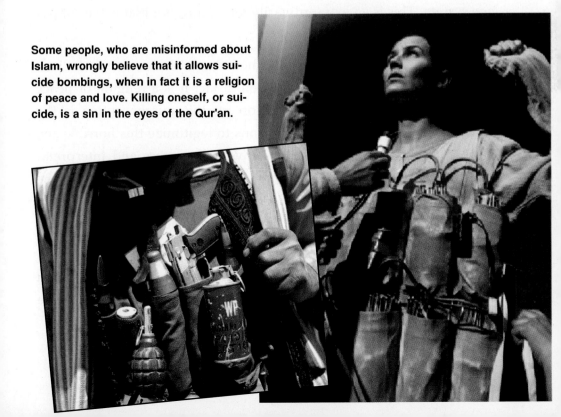

Some people, who are misinformed about Islam, wrongly believe that it allows suicide bombings, when in fact it is a religion of peace and love. Killing oneself, or suicide, is a sin in the eyes of the Qur'an.

The majority of Arab countries were to some extent touched by post-World War II communism. The Ba'ath Party that became strong in Egypt, Syria and Iraq, the Shanghai block that was established under Chinese auspices and quietly placed Arab countries and Iran under its protection, and al-Fatah, which grew under Yasser Arafat's leadership, never concealed their communist/socialist leanings. It is no secret that much blood was shed by Arab socialism mixed with extreme nationalism in Arab countries. Those who are unaware of that history should have a look at the situation in those countries now or how Hafez Assad's legacy is preserved in Syria.

Such savagery is inevitable in the socialist or communist mindset. In that false worldview, putting an end to one's own life is regarded as much a contribution to world progress and to the "cause" as putting an end to someone else's life. Therefore, putting an end to one's own life, regarded as valueless, in order to put an end to other lives also regarded as worthless, is an even greater contribution in the eyes of this savage system. This is an extraordinarily false logic, but that is the subject of separate criticism.

Some people, who are misinformed about Islam, wrongly believe that it allows suicide bombings, when in fact it is a religion of peace and love. The most important reason for this misconception is the effort of the said terrorist organizations to legitimize this horrible act, banned by Islam, through various invented sources and interpretations. If a suicide bomber claims to be perpetrating his action in the name of Islam, then that is a disgrace, and a slander against Islam. There are the most profound and terrible errors here.

A Muslim can never kill. This is a sin. God reveals in the Qur'an that **"... if someone kills another person – unless it is in retaliation for someone else or for causing corruption in the earth – it is as if he had murdered all mankind."** (Qur'an, 5:32)

The verse is explicit. Just like it is a sin and murder to kill some-one else, it is also a sin and murder to kill oneself. It is not "jihad," but a sin to blow oneself up in a restaurant. Those who honour and glorify such things and imagine that the person has become a "martyr" are applauding murder, not jihad. Killing defenceless civilians together with himself is not jihad, but murder. As we will explain in detail later on, Islam bans waging a war against a community that is not offensive.

Jihad means to strive through knowledge and science to bring someone to the truth and to establish communication with love and respect; not to kill him.

Martyrdom means losing one's life while striving on the path of God, while seeking to spread the love, friendship and brotherhood demanded by Islam. Killing is a murder and a sin. It is not a virtue to be honoured.

But suicide bombers and their supporters spread the propaganda of a religion that commands others' deaths. And their religion is not the religion of God, either. Very few of those who follow that faith may realize that. There are many people who imagine this false religion to be true and who seek to adhere to it.

The real problem is this: People who do not know their own reli-gion are being diverted toward nonsense. And unless they learn their own religion and the true love in the Qur'an, there will continue to be suicide bombers and those who encourage and even honour them. Bombs are not the way to teach them the truth. The only way is correct education. And in order to provide a true education, people of love from among Muslims, Christians and Jews must all come together. Once the power of unity has been established, then those people on the wrong path will begin to listen to us.

What are the reasons for the rise in suicide attacks?

Politically-inspired suicide attacks in the Middle East initially emerged in the 1980s, during the Lebanese Civil War, when Hezbollah began to use suicide attacks against its targets. From then on until the early 21st Century, some 200 suicide attacks were carried out in different parts of the world. Yet, it was only in the 2000s when these attacks began to grab the headlines with an ever-increasing frequency as the number of total attacks over the past three decades reached 3,500. Only in 2013, 291 suicide attacks were carried out in eighteen countries, claiming the lives of 3,100 people, marking a dramatic increase of 25% compared to previous year (with 230 attacks).

Most of these attacks were staged in Muslim countries. The Middle East, with Iraq coming in at the top of the list, saw too many suicide attacks to count over the last ten years. Afghanistan, Pakistan, Syria, Lebanon, Tunisia, Libya, Somalia, Mali and Nigeria are among the Muslim countries that are frequently hit by suicide attacks.

What drove the increase in the attacks? The political instability in these countries is an important factor. Despite the common assumption that suicide bombings target occupying powers, only 32% of the attacks were actually carried out in countries where a foreign army was present. 68% of the bombings target the own citizens of the country; in other words, innocent civilians are overwhelmingly the victims in these attacks.

In countries like Iraq and Syria, the attacks are usually prompted by sectarian and ethnic differences, while in Egypt they are usu-

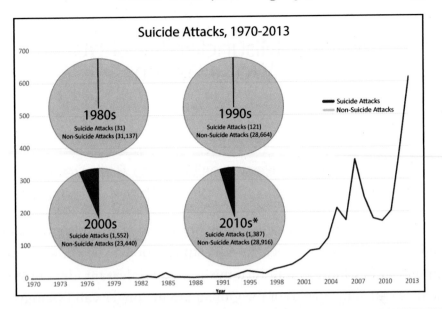

ally carried out due to conflicts between nationalist secular forces and Islamic groups. The suicide attacks usually target the most crowded areas like restaurants, markets, mosques and public transportation; places where civilians can easily be found and where women, children and the elderly, are specific targets in these attacks. Indeed, attacks can even be perpetrated as Muslims are worshiping during the Friday prayers, as we've seen in Iraq, or while religious celebrations are going on, as in Yemen. This is very thought-provoking.

Many Muslim groups condemned Israel for sending its troops into a mosque in Jerusalem, and even denounced it as a foe needing to be destroyed; interestingly, however, those same groups have remained utterly silent in the face of a suicide attack against a mosque where Muslims were praying, and some have even encouraged such attacks.

When the perpetrators are asked to explain the reasoning behind their actions, because of their deficient educational background and unawareness of true Qur'anic moral values, which in truth embody for-giveness, peace and love, they claim to be doing these atrocities in the name of Islam. For this reason, explaining the morals of Islam based on the Qur'an is a priority. It is essential to start a world-wide campaign to this end.

What Is Misunderstood about War In Islam

A Muslim Has A Responsibility to Believe in Every Verse of the Qur'an, Without Exception

The reason for this section is to show the false nature of claims made by fanatics who seek to add superstition to Islam and some opponents of Islam, who in turn misuse the unpleasant ideas of those fanatics that some verses of the Qur'an are no longer valid (Surely the Qur'an is beyond that). They cite this verse as supposed evidence for their claims:

Whenever We abrogate an ayat or cause it to be forgotten, We bring one better than it or equal to it. Do you not know that God has power over all things? (Qur'an, 2:106)

Those who twist their tongues against the Qur'an have misinterpreted this verse as evidence to allow them to impose their own superstition. They have foolishly imagined that they can invalidate some verses and even replace them with fabricated hadiths. Some opponents of Islam, on the other hand, maintain that there are verses about the use of intoxicants or war that no longer apply and seek to divide Muslims into those who abide by that and those who do not.

The true interpretation of this verse is as follows;

The Arabic word "ayat" in "Whenever We abrogate an ayat" is singular. The word means sign or miracle when used in this form. When the word "ayat" appears in the singular in the Qur'an, it always means evidence or sign, and that is how it is translated in all other verses. The word "ayat" used to refer to the verses of the Qur'an never appears in singular form in the Qur'an.

The meaning here is therefore not "verses of the Qur'an" but "signs, rules and Sharia" that went before it. According to this verse, some practices and commandments applied by previous communities to whom Divine books were sent down, that is, the Jews and the Christians, but which were forgotten in time, have either been recalled or else abrogated by the Qur'an. A similar or better version has thus been brought forth with the Qur'an.

We also need to concentrate on the words "cause it to be forgotten" in the verse. In order for one commandment to abrogate another, the earlier one has to have been "forgotten." Since the Qur'an has remained unchanged for 1,400 years there can be no question of one verse replacing another. The commandments that fanatics allege have been abrogated have not been forgotten; they are still in the Qur'an. This clearly shows that the abrogation being referred to here is not of one verse by another, but of commandments belonging to earlier communities that have since been forgotten. Commands that have been sent down to earlier societies but "forgotten" have been restored with the Qur'an, with more auspicious or similar versions being sent down to those communities.

The Qur'an Is a "Preserved" Book

As our Lord explicitly states in a verse, the Qur'an is a "preserved" Book.

It is We Who have sent down the Reminder [the Qur'an] and We Who will preserve it. (Qur'an, 15: 9)

It is impossible for some verses in a book which is "preserved" and whose commandments apply to all Muslims to be regarded as valid, while others are not. The perfection in the entirety of the Qur'an, its mathematical and scientific miracles, the fact that it is a guide and the verses regarding how it has been preserved all rebut these claims made by fanatics and some opponents of Islam.

Those who reject the Remembrance [the Qur'an] when it comes to them –truly it is a Mighty Book; falsehood cannot reach it from before it or behind it – **it is a revelation from One Who is All-Wise, Praiseworthy. (Qur'an, 41:41-42)**

Let us now look at where these people have gone wrong.

The Mistakes in Differentiating between the "Meccan Period Muslims" and "Medina Period Muslims"

Some opponents of Islam refer to moderate Muslims as "Meccan period Muslims." In their view, the time when our Prophet (pbuh) was in Mecca was a peaceful time of no wars, yet wars suddenly started following our Prophet's (pbuh) migration to Medina. Some people claim, on that basis, that the proponents of war in Islam recognize only the verses revealed in the Medina period, while peace-loving Muslims recognize only the verses from the Meccan period. That idea is as illogical as it is ignorant.

As we have already seen, the essential precondition for a Muslim to acquire the identity of a Muslim is to believe in all the verses of the Qur'an, without exception. If someone rejects a single verse, then he loses the attribute of being a Muslim as described in the Qur'an. There is therefore no possibility in the eyes of the Qur'an of someone who says, "I am a Muslim" to discriminate by saying, "I recognize this verse but not that one."

It is true that there was no fighting in the Meccan period in the life of our Prophet (pbuh), but that there was fighting in the Medinan period and that verses were sent down concerning those particular battles. In order to understand the reasons for this, we need to understand the difficult conditions in the time of our Prophet (pbuh).

The Harsh Testing of Muslims in the Meccan Period

The revelation to our Prophet (pbuh) took a full 23 years. During the first 13 years of this, Muslims lived as a minority in the pagan society of Mecca and were subjected to tremendous pressures. Many Muslims were subjected to physical torture, some were martyred, the homes and possessions of most were looted and they were constantly exposed to threats and insults. Yet Muslims continued living without resorting to violence, merely keeping their distance from the pagans and always calling them to the path of peace.

Yet the aggression of the pagan communities in question was unrelenting.

Muslims lived as a minority in the pagan society of Mecca and were exposed to much oppression. Many Muslims were physically tortured, some were martyred, most had their homes and possessions pillaged and they were subjected to constant insults and threats. Yet Muslims continued to live without resorting to violence, merely keeping their distance from the idolaters and calling on them to live in peace.

The Quraysh initially seemed to regard the prophethood of Muhammad (pbuh) as unimportant. While continuing not to believe, they made no protest against the Prophet's (pbuh) call so long as he said nothing against their idols. When they saw the Prophet (pbuh) however, they attacked him verbally. They unwisely mocked and belittled Muslims. The Quraysh's "verbal assault" period began in that way.

The Qur'an describes the position in these words:

Those who did evil used to laugh at those who had faith.

When they passed by them, they would wink at one another.

When they returned to their families, they would make a joke of them.

When they saw them, they would say, "Those people are misguided." (Qur'an, 83:29-32)

Mecca was the centre of idolatry. Mecca would fill to overflowing every day with people coming to visit the Ka'aba and the idols around it, thus earning the Quraysh a good deal of money and prestige. The Quraysh regarded the spread of Islam in Mecca as a threat, because they thought that this would act against their own interests and also attract the hostility of other tribes. They also knew that Islam regarded everyone as equal and made no discrimination on grounds of lineage or wealth. Leading members of the Quraysh therefore believed they needed to take precautions to stop the spread of Islam. These "precautions" frequently included the torture and even the killing of Muslims. *(Ibn Hisham, 1/287)*

The pagans of the time could not do much harm to members of strong and eminent families, such as Hazrat Abu Bakr and Hazrat Uthman but they viciously mistreated poor and unprotected Muslims. Worthy Muslims exposed to such severe mistreatment included Abu Fakih, Khabbab ibn al-Aratt, Bilal ibn Rabah, Suhaib ar-Rumi, Ammar ibn Yasir, Yasir ibn Amir and Sumayyah bint Khayyat.

This mistreatment of Muslims took place simply because they had faith and preached Islam to others. Despite all that oppression, torture and violence, Muslims never harmed those who were harming them, which is one of the requirements of Islam, and never tried to defend themselves, which is their most basic human right. Seeing that the Muslims were not fighting back, the Quraysh stepped up their aggression and tortures. The Quraysh in question were now martyring Muslims the moment they saw them.

As the persecution worsened, the Muslims, who did not respond to it in any way and did not even defend themselves since the Qur'an prohibits the shedding of blood, found themselves unable to remain in Mecca any longer. That meant they had to migrate to Medina.

The Medina Period and the Battles

As the idolaters' attacks grew in severity in Mecca, the Muslims migrated to the city of Yathrib (later known as Medina), where the climate was a great deal freer and friendlier, and set up their own administration there. Yet even after they established their own political structures, the attacks by the pagans of Mecca did not come to an end. The Quraysh followed the Muslims and persisted in violent attacks against them. But our Prophet (pbuh) and the Muslims around him never embarked on a battle against the idolaters.

No person, community or country in the world will fail to respond if they are attacked. They will always respond to the aggressor in "self defence" and at the very least, take defensive action. People who engage in self defence are invariably exonerated by the courts, and countries that act in self defence are exonerated under international law because they have been subjected to an unjust attack, and people's lives, families and loved ones, or countries' peoples, lands and honour, are endangered.

Our Prophet (pbuh) was given permission to engage in self defence for himself and his community in the following verses which were revealed after the migration to Medina:

Permission to fight is given to those who are fought against because they have been wronged – truly God has the power to come to their support – those who were expelled from their homes without any right, merely for saying, "Our Lord is God"... (Qur'an, 22:39-40)

With these verses, the Muslim community that had been unjustly forced into exile merely for saying "Our Lord is God" started to make preparations to defend themselves. As explicitly stated in the verse, a

Muslim community "who are fought against because they have been wronged" are permitted to defend themselves; but they are not told to attack. Following this verse, Muslims began to defend themselves and fought back against the ferocious community that was attacking them. Verses concerning war and defence revealed after that contain descriptions regarding measures during the fighting taking place then. To put it another way, a special description is provided specific to the situation in that particular war. Therefore, all the verses about war in the Qur'an were specially revealed as referring to the particular attacks taking place at that time to enable us to see the difficult conditions of the time and the justice of our Prophet (pbuh).

The pagans of the time barbarically mistreated and tortured Muslims, in a way never seen before. Our Prophet (pbuh) was given permission in the verses to engage in self defence for himself and his community in the face of these attacks and wrongdoing.

Who Were Battles Fought Against in the Time of the Prophet (pbuh)?

One important point that needs to be remembered regarding the battles described in the Qur'an is "the other side" in the fighting. Some religious and historical sources say that the battles fought in the time of our Prophet (pbuh) were against the Jews. Some people who read those sources then go on to look for anti-Semitism in the Qur'an, claiming that the verses revealed for specific battles in the Qur'an are generally directed against the Jews. That is a grave error, however.

It was the pagans who engaged in that persecution against our Prophet (pbuh) and Muslims. A great many of these were idol-worshipers. Their aim was to prevent any harm from coming to their idols and perverse beliefs. Some were hypocrites and polytheists who had come out of Jewish communities but it would be very wrong to refer to these as Jews. In the same way that it would be very wrong to regard a polytheist or hypocrite who emerged from a Muslim community as a "Muslim," it is equally wrong to regard polytheists and hypocrites who emerged from among Jews and began spreading violence as "Jews." It is impossible for a true Jew to start fighting and take the lives of believers.

The Qur'an curses anti-Semitism. For that reason, those who look for expressions of enmity toward the Jews in the Qur'an return empty-handed; people who interpret the verses in question as referring to fighting against the Jews need to understand this. Our Prophet (pbuh) always enjoyed good relations with Jews. He treated them with respect and affection, and true, devout Jews treated our Prophet (pbuh) with that same respect and affection. This topic is explained in detail later in the chapter about the People of the Book. (See chapter "The Outlook of Islam on the People of the Book")

The Description of War in the Qur'an

The Qur'an is quite explicit on when and how war is to be waged:

Fight in the Way of God against those who fight you, but do not go beyond the limits. God does not love those who go beyond the limits. (Qur'an, 2:190)

War can only be waged **against those who attack Muslims;** it must be a **defensive** war. It is absolutely prohibited in the Qur'an for Muslims to **attack** the other side for no reason.

What God commands Muslims in the Qur'an is that they must always keep justice at the fore, even if they are angry at a community because of its injustices and aggression. God reveals in one verse:

You who believe! Show integrity for the sake of God, bearing witness with justice. Do not let hatred for a people incite you into not being just. Be just. That is closer to devoutness. Have awe of God. God is aware of what you do. (Qur'an, 5:8)

For example, in one verse God prohibits Muslims from going beyond the limits regarding communities that try to stop Muslims from entering the Ka'aba, advising them to treat them and everyone else with kindness:

... Do not let hatred for a people who debar you from the Masjid al-Haram [the Sacred Mosque] incite you into going beyond the limits. Help each other to goodness and piety. Do not help each other to wrongdoing and enmity. Have awe of God. ... (Qur'an, 5:2)

Muslims are warned by Almighty God not to overstep the bounds, even though they have deliberately been prevented from performing their religious obligation of the Hajj (pilgrimage) and have been treated unjustly. God commands Muslims to behave justly even under those conditions, and commands them to behave well and not be angered. Muslims have an obligation to obey this commandment in the

Qur'an, no matter what the circumstances.

The verse that describes the only justification for fighting – self-defence – also contains another condition on the subject of war: not to go to excess. This means that in the event of an attack a Muslim must simply defend himself, must not overreact and must take no other action than defensive measures. In other words, aggression, violence, anger and extremism are banned in the Qur'an.

Other verses reveal the obligation to engage only in defence war against aggressors in these terms:

> **God does not forbid you from being good to those who have not fought you in the religion or driven you from your homes, or from being just towards them. God loves those who are just. God merely forbids you from taking as friends those who have fought you in the religion and driven you from your homes and who supported your expulsion. ... (Qur'an, 60:8-9)**

There is an important distinction here. It is unlawful for Muslims to attack people who have never attacked them, even though they are strongly opposed to Muslims on the level of ideas. A Muslim has a responsibility to treat such people with respect and justice. According to this verse, Muslims are only permitted to engage in defensive warfare against people who oppress them because of their beliefs and actually physically attack them; against people who initiate hostilities, in other words. Everyone will, of course, defend himself if he is attacked. This is the right of every person, nation and country, and is also the correct thing to do.

The fact that our Prophet (pbuh) engaged in no self-defence until the revelation of the verses permitting such activity represents enormous self-sacrifice and religious devotion. Until that time, our Prophet (pbuh) had merely resorted to methods of compromise and trying to convince the other side, as required by the verse **"... argue with them**

in the kindest way ..." (Qur'an, 16:125) even though the sole aim of the pagan Quraysh was slaughter.

Having made that important point, we shall now examine all the verses that the peddlers of superstition and opponents of Islam seek to offer as evidence for the violence perpetrated supposedly in the name of Islam, and will refute their errors on the subject one after the other.

Before looking at these verses, we need to know that all the battles described in the Qur'an were waged against a particular community in that region, and that these special conditions are expressed in the verses. That community was a polytheistic one, with which an agreement had been reached. Therefore, all these battles were determined by the behaviour and aggression of the community in question which had breached the peace and friendship agreements. The verses sent down therefore concern the state of affairs at that time and describe that specific climate.

In order to better understand this fact, let us look at the definition of "polytheist" at the time and the agreements reached with them:

Polytheists with Whom Agreements Were Made

Although, according to some commentaries of the time, the word polytheist simply means "those ascribing equals to God," the term really refers to pagans who worship idols, who explicitly ascribe equals to God and who believe in countless deities and who are not Muslim, Jewish, Sabaean, Christian or Magian.

While the Qur'an refers to the various religions that existed in Arabia during the time of the coming of Islam, the polytheists are always mentioned as a separate group. Looking at the time of our Prophet (pbuh), although it was made lawful to marry women from and eat food prepared by the People of the Book, Jews and Christians; it was forbidden to marry women from or eat food cooked by the Magians and Sabaeans, and also the polytheists.

After our Prophet (pbuh) migrated to Medina, he signed numerous agreements with polytheistic communities and people living in the region, and always invited them to be united in order to build peace, despite the extreme attitudes of the polytheists. This proved that people could live in peace with peoples of different beliefs, faiths and languages. One of the greatest proofs that he was a messenger of peace and love is that the first text he had written was a peace agreement. After capturing Mecca, the Prophet Muhammad (pbuh) even released all the polytheists who had previously tortured Muslims and treated them with great compassion. This superior moral virtue exhibited by the Prophet Muhammad (pbuh) was something that had never been seen before in Arab society, and was met with great approval.

The Prophet (pbuh) is a role model for all Muslims on the subject of the implementation of justice in conquered territories. Our Prophet (pbuh) applied the justice revealed in the Qur'an to the inhabitants of countries that were taken over and made agreements with them that would content both sides and under which nobody would suffer the slightest victimization. Our Prophet (pbuh) and the Companions with him represented a community that established justice between people, as expressed in the verse, **"Among those We have created there is a community who guide by the Truth and act justly according to it."** (Qur'an, 7:181)

The agreement that our Prophet (pbuh) made with the Christian Najran people in the south of the Arabian peninsula is one of the finest examples of his understanding and justice.

One of the articles in the treaty reads as follows:

"The lives of the people of Najran and its surrounding area, their religion, their land, property, cattle and those of them who are present or absent, their messengers and their places of worship are under the protection of God and guardianship of His Prophet." (The Pact of Najran, Article 6, http://www.islamicresources.com /Pact_of_Najran.htm)

Following the agreements with all the societies in that region, our Prophet (pbuh) founded the state of Medina by drawing up the first constitution in the history of Islam, the Constitution of Medina. This was the first and most perfect example of a democratic and multilateral constitution.

The First Multilateral and Most Democratic Constitution Ever: The Constitution of Medina

With the Constitution of Medina, the first constitution of the state of Medina, our Prophet (pbuh) brought a democratic and peaceful order never before seen on the Arabian Peninsula to an urban community composed of various races, religions and tribes.

Under this constitution, all the communities in Medina were to live together in peace, arrange their lives according to their own faith and beliefs, and have the power to operate and regulate their own institutions and laws. In doing this, they would live together in peace and unity with all the communities in Medina.

The Constitution of Medina was written in 622 AD, under the leadership of the Prophet Muhammad (pbuh) some 1,400 years ago, to respond to the demands of peoples of differing beliefs, and has come down to us as a written legal treaty. As a result, communities that were hostile to one another for 120 years and consisted of different religions and races were included under this constitution. By means of this agreement, the Prophet (pbuh) showed that conflict could come to an end between communities that used to attack one another at every opportunity, were hostile to one another and never compromised with one another, and that they could easily live together.

Under the Constitution of Medina, everyone was free to make his own religious, political or philosophical choices, free from any pressure from anyone else. They could establish a community with people holding the same views. Everyone was free to exercise his own justice system. However, nobody committing an offense was to be protected by anyone else. The parties to the agreement were to help and support one another, and would be under the protection of the Prophet Muhammad (pbuh). Disagreements between parties would be brought to the Messenger of God (pbuh). Indeed, even polytheists preferred the arbitration of our Prophet (pbuh), as he was the most just person of all.

This treaty drawn up by our Prophet (pbuh) was implemented gradually between 622 and 632 AD. Through that constitution, people moved beyond the tribal structure based on ties of blood and family, and people with very different geographic, cultural and ethnic roots came together to constitute one whole. The Constitution of Medina also established very wide-ranging freedom of belief and religion. One of the items expressing that freedom reads:

> *"The Jews of Banu 'Awf are a community along with the believers. To the Jews their religion and to the Muslims their religion." (The Constitution of Medina, http://www.islamic-study.org/jews-prophet-page-2.htm)*

The Constitution of Medina was the first pluralist and the most democratic constitution in history, showing the protective attitude of Muslims toward the rights and laws of members of all other faiths and even idolaters.

The Constitution of Medina consists of 47 items. Items 1 through 23 concern Muslims, while items 24 through 47 concern Jewish tribes settled in Medina. Reference being made to Christians, who were much fewer in number, is also important in terms of participation by members of different faiths.

An analysis of the Constitution of Medina in a report titled "A Reassessment of Medina Charter according to Professor Leonard Swidler's Pluralism Perspective" states that the Constitution is a significant document in displaying the Prophet's efforts in uniting the city and bringing the groups together around the law, which was explicitly announced to the people.

According to this report, in terms of law, each individual had equal rights, enjoyed the freedom to choose their own religion and participating in war together with Muslims while under all circumstances, they were prohibited from engaging in any separate agreements with the enemy, showing an effort to establish a strict solidarity of the Medina groups. The author of the report says that this political and religious text aimed at establishing a new society around the values of equality and freedom. As it was emphasized in the Constitution, the superiority of the law over the individual was the basic step in attaining the goal of securing an atmosphere of dialogue and co-existence. The items of the Constitution also signified the equal responsibility of each individual in defending the city. According to this report, given that the names of all the groups in the city are cited one by one, the Constitution - and thereby the Prophet - recognized all these groups in the city as legal entities and took them into account. *(Kenan Çetinkaya, Amerika'da Diyalog anlayışı ve Medine Vesikası [Understanding of Dialogue in America and Medina Charter])*

The text of the Constitution of Medina shows that Muslims adopted a protective attitude toward the rights and laws of the polytheists, and that these polytheists wished to act alongside Muslims in the defence of Medina. Such an attitude toward the polytheists is not at all surprising because in the Qur'an, Muslims have a responsibility to protect polytheists with whom they have signed agreements, even at the cost of their own lives. (This will be set out in greater detail in due course.)

In conclusion, the constitution in question is regarded as a highly important document containing the nucleus of unity and union, love and affection, friendship and peace, and represents an example of dialogue between Muslims and non-Muslims in general and between Muslims and Jews in particular. The conception of love and peace of our Prophet (pbuh) was based on the Qur'an but it is hard at present to identify a Muslim society capable of living by that same conception. This is highly important evidence that the first most democratic constitution in history was written and implemented by our Prophet (pbuh).

The subsequent sections of this book therefore need to be assessed in the light of this information. The practices of today's peddlers of superstition are radically different from the advice of the Holy Qur'an, which commands that polytheists be protected and says that the People of the Book (Jews and Christians) enjoy a special status for Muslims, and from the practices of the Prophet Muhammad (pbuh), who always aimed for peace and democracy. The peddlers of superstition are always looking for evidence for unceasing conflict in the Qur'an, yet the Qur'an itself always counsels peace. This important fact therefore needs to be borne in mind while interpreting the verses about war.

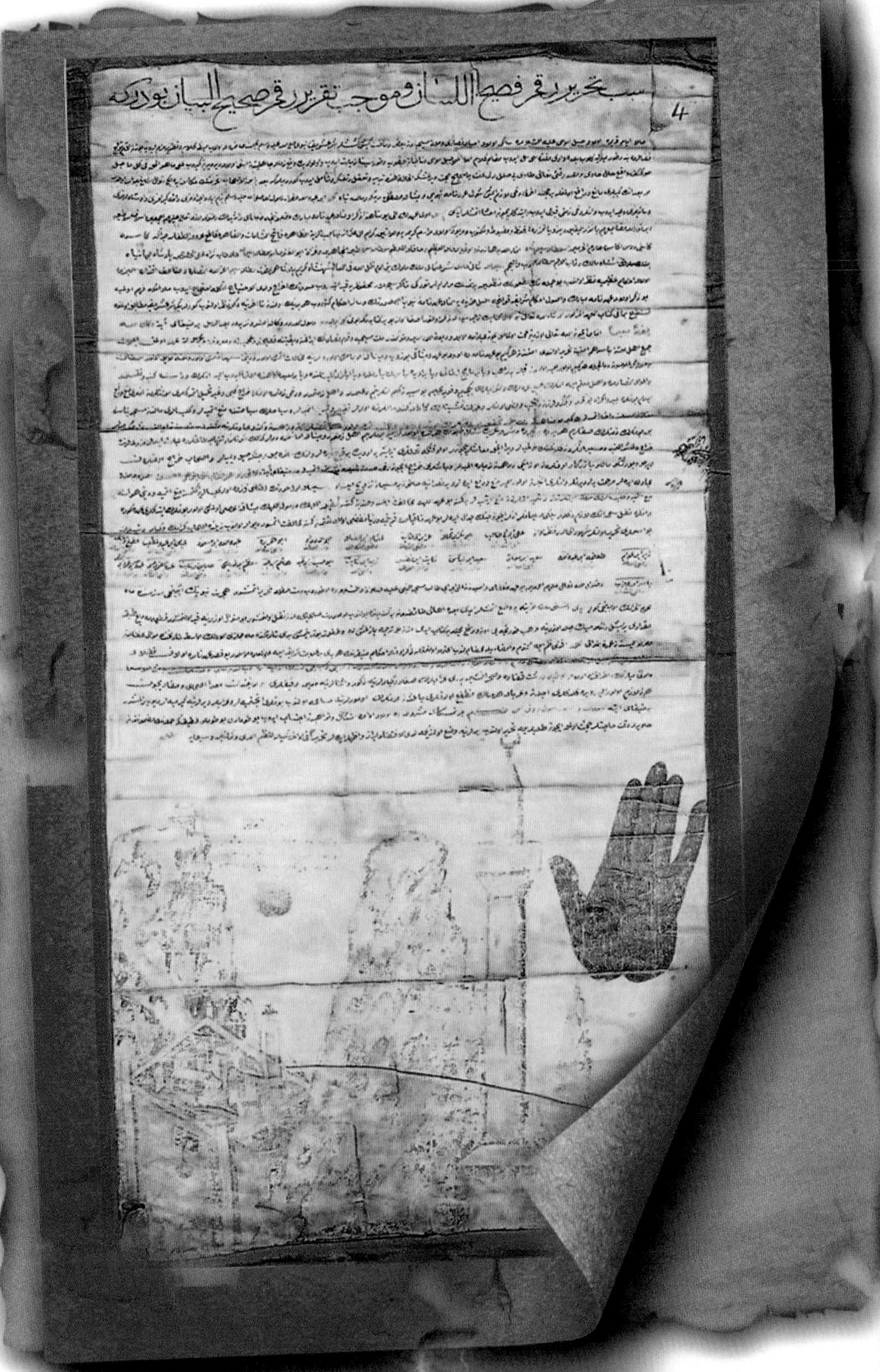

سبب تحریر رقم فصیح اللسان وموجب تقریر رقم صحیح البیان بودرکه

4

Prophet Muhammad's
Charter of Privileges to Christians
(Letter to the Monks of St. Catherin Monastry)

This is a message from Muhammad İbn Abdullah, as a convenant to those who adopt Christianity, near and far, we are with them.

Verily I, the the servants, the helpers, and my followers defend them because

Christians are my citizens; and by Allah I hold out against anything that displeases them.

No compulsion is to be on them.

Neither are their judges to be romoved from their jobs nor their monks from their monasteries.

No one it to destroy a house of their religion, to demage iy, or to carry anything from it to the Muslims' houses.

Should anyone take any of these, he would spoil God's covenant and disobet His Prophhet. Verily, they are my allies and have my secure charter against all that they hate.

No one is to force them to travel or to obligate them to fight.

The Muslims are to fight for them.

If a female Christian is married to a Muslim, it is not to take place without her approval, She is ot to be prevented from visiting her church to pray.

Their church are to be repected. They are neihter to be prevented from repairing them nor the sacredness of their covenants.

No one of the nation (Muslims) is to disobey the convenant till the Last Day (end of World).

This charter of priviliges has been honoured
and faithfully applied by Muslims throughout
the centuries in all lands they ruled.

Verses about War and the Interpretation Thereof

After seeing the definition of war in the Qur'an, let us now examine the verses about war that are misused by some radicals and used for criticism of Islam by some opponents of Islam:

Examination of Verse 191 of Surat al-Baqara:

> **Kill them wherever you come across them and expel them from where they expelled you. Fitna [sedition, strife] is worse than killing. Do not fight them in the Masjid al-Haram [the Sacred Mosque] until they fight you there. But if they do fight you, then you also fight them. That is how the unbelievers should be repaid. (Qur'an, 2:191)**

This verse is one that was sent down after Muslims were subjected to severe pressure and violence and were forced to migrate from Mecca to Medina. The conditions we discussed in detail above came about and Muslims received the command to defend themselves against direct attacks. They used the methods of that community, which never stopped oppressing them, that refused to heed pleasant words and that turned a deaf ear against all calls to peace or negotiation, against it.

However, the verse also contains a reminder of the rules of war: **"Do not fight them in the Masjid al-Haram until they fight you there. But if they do fight you, then you also fight them."** As we have seen, the only condition for fighting is for the other side to have attacked first. If they do not wage war, if they do not attack, then it is absolutely unlawful for Muslims to fight idolaters.

It is of course very suspicious how the radicals and opponents of Islam who distort this verse ignore this rather important provision. The verse explicitly grants Muslims only the right to self-defence: The verse is not therefore commanding warfare and aggression.

Another important element in the verses is revealed as follows: **"Fitna [sedition, strife] is worse than killing."** Inciting communities, encouraging hatred, spreading hatred, anarchy and terror by engaging in slander and outright falsehoods thereby producing hostile masses of people is fitna, and the verse tells us that fitna is worse than killing; thus, the communities that attack Muslims are the ones that engage in actual, psychological and covert fitna and the harm they do is very great. Muslims naturally defend themselves when their aggression rears its head.

The way that some fanatics are taken in by hearsay or superstition and declare individuals, societies or faiths to be spreading fitna and then seek supposed evidence for their perversions from verses of the Qur'an is exceedingly wrong. Fitna involves actions that will lead to corruption, such as spreading division among Muslims, leading them into loss and sin by inflicting all kinds of troubles on them, then establishing the infrastructure for mass rebellions and engaging in physical and verbal assaults on Muslims. Therefore, in order to be able to accuse someone of fitna, they have to have committed one or more of these actions. Those who seek to accuse Jews or Israel by branding them as engaging in fitna thus flies in the face of this verse.

According to the Qur'an, it is a sin to accuse all Jews or Israel of engaging in fitna. People who spread fitna may emerge from any religion or country. Yet in the same way that it is impossible to brand all Arabs, Turks or Muslims as spreaders of fitna simply because there are some Arabs,

Turks or Muslims who engage in fitna, there is also no question of branding all Jews or all Israelis as spreaders of fitna. According to the Qur'an, a Muslim can dine in the home of a Jew, can be his guest and friend, and can even marry a Jewish woman (this will be clarified in detail in chapter "The Outlook of Islam on the People of the Book"). That being the case, it is impossible for a Muslim to unconditionally brand a Jew as a spreader of fitna. People who make such sweeping claims know nothing of the Qur'an, as we said at the beginning, and are acting out of ignorance resulting from being raised under the influence of countless fabricated hadiths regarding fitna and the Jews. The position of the People of the Book according to the Qur'an will be examined in due course in later chapters.

Examination of Verses 89, 90 and 91 of Surat an-Nisa':

They would like you to be unbelievers as they are unbelievers so that you will all be the same. Do not take any of them as friends until they have emigrated in the Way of God. But if they run away then seize them and kill them wherever you find them. Do not take any of them as either a friend or helper – (Qur'an, 4:89)

Except for those who seek shelter with people with whom you have a treaty, or who come to you greatly perturbed at the prospect of fighting either you or their own people. If God had willed, He could have given them the upper hand over you and then they would have fought you. If they keep away from you and do not fight you and submit to you, God has not given you any way against such people. (Qur'an, 4:90)

You will find others who desire to be safe from you and safe from their own people. Each time they are returned to fitna they are overwhelmed by it. If they do not keep away from you or submit to you or refrain from fighting, seize them and kill them wherever you find them. Over such people We have given you clear authority. (Qur'an, 4:91)

These verses refer to hypocrites. They say they are Muslims, live among Muslims and appear to be one of them, but actually harbour a great hostility toward God and Islam, and seek to stab Muslims in the back. God reveals that those who die as hypocrites are cast into the lowest circle of hell. As can be seen, because of its two-faced and treacherous nature, hypocrisy is an especially dangerous and despicable human model, quite unlike the deniers or the polytheists.

It is forbidden in verse 89 of Surat an-Nisa' to adopt hypocrites as friends, those who abandon Muslims and who strive to make Muslims fall into the same perversions as themselves. What justifies fighting against them is the state in which the hypocrites in question engage in physical attacks on Muslims. We can see this from the verse that follows, verse 90. As is clear from the words **"If they keep away from you and do not fight you and submit to you,"** there is nothing to be held against a community that does not engage in attacks. The community the killing of which is permitted is quite clearly one that has declared war on Muslims first. Muslims are clearly given the right to defend themselves in the face of attacks here.

In addition, verse 90 of Surat an-Nisa' is another manifestation of the just, forgiving and affectionate language that always favours peace, of the Qur'an. Some hypocrites, who until then had always stabbed Muslims in the back and betrayed them but who later adopted a peaceful attitude toward Muslims are also immune, as we can see from the words; **"Except for those who seek shelter with people with whom you have a treaty, or who come to you greatly perturbed at the prospect of fighting either you or their own people."** In the same verse God says, **"If they keep away from you and do not fight you and submit to you, God has not given you any way against such people,"** again emphasizing their immunity. This is the very definition of justice.

Verse 91 contains a situation described on the basis of the same conditions. Hypocrites who repent and who say they do not want to fight later return to fitna and begin attacking Muslims again. In that event, the provision regarding war is recalled in the Qur'an, saying that these people are not to be touched as long as they do not attack, but that if they do, then self-defence is legitimate.

We need to remember that the situation described in the verse was a specific one that came about during the Battle of Uhud and concerns those hypocrites who engaged in treachery on the battlefield.

Examination of Verse 5 of Surat at-Tawba:

> **Then, when the sacred months are over, kill the polytheists wherever you find them, and seize them and besiege them and lie in wait for them on every road. If they repent and perform their prayers and pay alms, let them go on their way. God is Ever-Forgiving, Most Merciful. (Qur'an, 9:5)**

In order to understand the conditions in the above verse we need to start reading from verse 1 of Surat at-Tawba; in that way we see that the polytheists deserving to be counter-attacked are not "all polytheists" but those perpetrating savage attacks on Muslims and who **then come to agreements** in order not to fight during the sacred months. The polytheists here are the ones who have cunningly tried to hunt Muslims down and have continued to attack them during the sacred months and have taken Muslims' lives, **although they have made a fair agreement with Muslims and they very well knew that Muslims would not enter into a war during the sacred months.**

Under these conditions, Muslims are given the right in this verse to defend themselves against savage attacks. As shown in the verse, although the polytheists carried out their savage attacks in the sacred

months, Muslims did not respond during those months, as commanded by God. They exhibited patience during those months and only
began defending themselves once the sacred months were over. We
also see that the verse describes the method that needs to be adopted
in defence: seizure, siege and lying in wait on all roads. The primary
conditions in wars based on international law are siege and seizure.
The passages required for the siege are taken and held and the other
side is thus prevented from moving. This verse therefore described the
method adopted and now regarded as legitimate under international
law. The only difference is that it is not Muslims doing the attacking;
they are simply trying to put an end to the attacks against them.

There is also no question in this verse of engaging in any fight
against those who stop their attacks and repent. They must be released;
that is explicit.

When we look at the very next verse, we find a very important
statement that describes the loving and protective spirit of the Qur'an.
This verse eliminates all the claims made about Muslims by the opponents of Islam. The verse reads:

> **If any of the polytheists ask you for protection, give them protection
> until they have heard the words of God. Then convey them to a place
> where they are safe. That is because they are a people who do not
> know. (Qur'an, 9:6)**

Through this verse, Muslims are advised to help a polytheist who
has taken shelter with them and seeks their help, even if that endan-
gers their own lives. The verse even suggests that such a Muslim
should **use himself as a shield** to protect such polytheists. To put it
another way, he has a responsibility to risk his own life to protect
someone who denies God and to carry him to safety.

This is what the Qur'an commands. According to that command-ment, someone is not to be killed for not believing in God. On the con-trary, he must be protected, even at the cost of Muslims' lives. There-fore, the justification for war has nothing to do with whether the other side believes in God or not or belongs to another faith. The justification for war is that the other side engages in assaults and torture, and takes people's lives.

Another fact set out in the verse is that all people will be under the protection of Muslims so long as they do not attack or engage in extreme behaviour, irrespective of their religion, language, ethnicity or beliefs. A Muslim has a responsibility to protect the People of the Book, or an atheist or a communist, in the same way that he does other Mus-lims; this is a requirement of being a Muslim; this is the description of a Muslim in the Qur'an. If someone says, "I am a Muslim," he must be protective of others.

Examination of Verse 13 of Surat at-Tawba:

> **Will you not fight <u>a people who have broken their oaths and resolved to expel the Messenger, and who initiated hostilities against you in the first place?</u> Is it them you fear? God has more right to your fear if you are believers. (Qur'an, 9:13)**

This verse is another of those that show the commandments regarding fighting in the Qur'an. When a polytheistic community that had come to a truce with Muslims - in other words, that lived in peace with them as required under those agreements - broke that truce and started attacking, when they tried to force our Prophet (pbuh) to leave his own land and go into exile and when, as the verse explicitly states, they **initiated hostilities**, Muslims had the right to fight back against them.

Examination of Verse 33 of Surat al-Ma'ida:

> The reprisal against <u>those who wage war on God and His Messenger,</u> <u>and go about the earth corrupting it,</u> is that they should be killed or crucified, or have their alternate hands and feet cut off, or be banished from the land. That will be their degradation in the world and in the hereafter they will have a terrible punishment. **(Qur'an, 5:33)**

The subject we have particularly stressed in all the verses about warfare is also noticeable in this verse. The characteristics of the community to be fought against are set out in great detail here: They wage war on God and His Messenger and go about the world corrupting it. These people do not merely engage in physical attacks on Muslims; they also spread corruption across the world. The verse is speaking of a community that represents a problem for the whole world, that everyone regards as a perverse, corrupt and warlike society.

As in all wars, killing is possible in resisting a community that has actively declared war on Muslims, so long as it is a last resort, and one of the measures that can be imposed is to force those people from their lands. To put it another way, according to the verses of the Qur'an, Muslims are permitted to do things that would normally be forbidden – such as killing and forcing people into exile – only in the event of such a state of war.

Examination of Verse 57 of Surat al-Anfal:

> So if you come upon such people in war, make a harsh example of them to deter those coming after them so that hopefully they will pay heed. **(Qur'an, 8:57)**

We also need to assess this verse in the light of the perspective and evidence we have been looking at in detail. It must not be forgotten that the Medinan period when some verses were sent down was a time of intense fighting. This was purely the result of injustice perpetrated against Muslims **"who were expelled from their homes without any right, merely for saying, 'Our Lord is God'..."** (Qur'an, 22:40) as stated in one verse. Moreover, as the verse goes on to say, **"If they keep away from you and do not fight you and submit to you, God has not given you any way against such people."** Muslims have a responsibility to stop the fighting and not to insult the other side when it does come to an end.

Looking at a few verses before verse 57 of Surat al-Anfal, we see that communities with which Muslims had reached agreement are being referred to. As almost every verse that gives permission for legitimate self-defence states, these communities are ones which had broken their truce with Muslims and then immediately attacked them.

It is important to produce a deterrent force in the face of that community which engages in one attack after another, refuses to listen to

reason and creates corruption by constantly breaking peace agreements because once that is done, those communities that have become accustomed to spreading corruption will no longer have the strength to do so and other groups of polytheists preparing to follow their lead and create corruption and start attacking will thereby lack the courage to do so. This is a necessary and important precautionary measure against that community that breaks every peace treaty, and one that will prevent subsequent conflict.

Great importance is attached to sanctions being "deterrents" in the constitutions of just about all countries of the world and in international law. The aim is to prevent an offense being committed by the same or another person. These precautions in international law are extremely appropriate, and it is unjust, as well as a violation of both common sense and fairness, for people who regard them as necessary for states of law to oppose the same measures when it comes to Islam.

Examination of Verse 4 of Surah Muhammad:

> **Therefore when you meet in war those who are unbelievers strike their necks. Then when you have decimated them, tie their bonds tightly and <u>set them free or ransom them</u>, until the war is finally over. That is how it is to be. If God willed, He could avenge Himself on them. But it is so that He can test some of you by means of others. As for those who are killed in the Way of God, He will not let their actions go astray. (Qur'an, 47:4)**

As with other verses, what this verse is emphasizing is the presence of a climate of war. The treaty has been broken, the polytheists have gone on the offensive and there is now no alternative but to respond to that aggression. What this verse is describing is the international rules of warfare. In addition, it also describes something that is not applied under the international rules of warfare: the release of prisoners as soon as the fighting is over. Yet, prisoners of war are still being held in Guantanamo Bay in Cuba even though the war in Afghanistan is over, and organizations such as the U.N. and NATO regard this as legitimate. But the Qur'an does not regard that unlawfulness as legitimate: In the view of Islam, all prisoners must be released as soon as the fighting is over.

The verses concerning war are clearly describing defensive wars under the conditions of the time, being waged solely against polythe-

Under Islamic law, war is only permissible for defensive purposes, and prisoners must be released when it is over.
This is a practice not even found in the international law of war. Indeed, prisoners from past conflicts are still being kept under harsh conditions in prisons such as Guantanamo Bay.

ists and hypocrites who initiate hostilities and spread fitna and corruption. The main reason why these verses are misinterpreted and used for the policies of rage and hatred of the radicals is that hundreds of false hadiths have been added to Islam and the false perspectives of some analysts. Yet the Qur'an needs to be read with a pure and enlightened mind, purged of all false hadiths and other superstition. When considered in the light of the reality of war at that time, the meaning of these verses is crystal clear.

There Is No Justification for War in Islam

Those who allege that Islam has spread through war and is a militant religion (surely Islam is beyond that) must realize that such a perspective is in fact diametrically opposed to the teachings of Islam. All the misconceptions regarding Islam stem from fabricated hadiths and superstitions that emerged after the revelation of the Qur'an and the passing of the Prophet Mohammed (pbuh). Some radical groups, based on these fabricated hadiths, misinterpreted Islam and came up with explanations to justify war. That is how they found so-called justification for their attacks on non-Muslims, and even on those Muslims who had different views.

As we explained in detail previously, there is no justification for attacking the other side in the Qur'an. The Qur'an provides the very finest description of democracy and freedoms. In a climate of democracy and freedom there is no question of denouncing the other side as the enemy or seeking to silence it. That climate is one in which everyone is respected and everyone can speak freely and Islamic Sharia describes just that environment. Therefore, there is no justification for offensive warfare in the Qur'an. However, according to the sharia invented by the superstition-followers, there are countless reasons to fight, to attack and to kill. Let us examine this fact through the words of verses of the Qur'an:

War Cannot Be Waged to Enforce Conversion to Islam

Those who employ war, force or coercion to impose Islam on someone are betraying the Qur'an. One of the most explicit statements in the Qur'an is that "there is no compulsion in the religion":

There is no compulsion where the religion is concerned.... (Qur'an, 2:256)

This is an explicit commandment of the Qur'an. No Muslim can disobey that command and force anyone else to be devout. That is expressly forbidden in the Qur'an.

Our Prophet (pbuh) is only an adviser. He has a responsibility to preach and introduce communities to Islam, the last revealed religion. At that time, some of those who heard about Islam from the mouths of our Prophet (pbuh) and other Muslims came to believe, while others

did not. As explicitly required by the Qur'an, neither our Prophet (pbuh) nor the other Muslims with him ever resorted to compulsion. Our Prophet (pbuh) is reminded in the Qur'an; **"So remind them! You are only a reminder. <u>You cannot compel them [to believe].</u>"** (Qur'an, 88:21-22) Compulsion is therefore absolutely forbidden.

According to the Qur'an, all Muslims have a duty to tell people of the moral values of Islam, but nobody can use compulsion and say, "You must become a Muslim" or "You must perform the religious observances." The purpose of the Qur'an is to bring love and peace to the world. Such pressure is therefore incompatible with the Qur'an.

Other verses in which compulsion is prohibited read:

Say: "It is the truth from your Lord; so let whoever wishes have faith and whoever wishes be irreligious"... (Qur'an, 18:29)

If your Lord had willed, all the people on the earth would have had faith. Do you think you can force people to be believers? (Qur'an, 10:99)

We know best what they say. You are not a dictator over them. So remind, with the Qur'an, whoever fears My threat. (Qur'an, 50:45)
Say: "Unbelievers! I do not worship what you worship and you do not worship what I worship. Nor will I worship what you worship nor will you worship what I worship. You have your religion and I have my religion." (Qur'an, 109:1-6)

Since force and compulsion are prohibited in the Qur'an, there is no justification for war, aggression, enmity or anger. What things, apart from converting, would Muslims compel polytheistic communities to do? It is clear that it is unlawful for someone to be forced to convert. Therefore, **according to the Islam of the Qur'an, imposing Islam can never be a pretext for war.**

War Cannot Be Waged for Ideological or Ethnic Superiority

Islam respects all ideologies, all nations, all ethnic groups, all ideas and all faiths. Islam is a religion in which all ideas are listened to and that permits the maximum possible freedom of ideas. **War due to any clash of ideas or clash of ethnicities is of course impossible in a faith with such an excellent conception of democracy and freedom.**

War Cannot Be Waged for the Purpose of Spreading the Rules of Islam to be Introduced by A Muslim Leader

According to the Qur'an, a Muslim leader must be someone who also embraces Christians, Jews, atheists, communists, agnostics, Buddhists and people who adhere to other beliefs and ideological systems in the community he leads. He must implement complete freedom of ideas. He must allow people complete liberty.

Conflict, slander and hypocritical people appear where there are no freedoms. He must prevent that and do what the Qur'an requires. As stated in the verse **"You who believe! Be upholders of justice, bearing witness for God alone, even against yourselves or your parents and relatives."** (Qur'an', 4:135) every believer has a responsibility to maintain justice without regard for individuals, beliefs or origins, even if that works against himself.

War Cannot Be Waged to Eliminate Those Regarded as "Enemies"

How can there be enemies in Islam? Islam is a religion that requires all people to be equal and brothers. According to Islam, no matter what someone's colour, language, religion, race, citizenship or social standing, he is worthy of respect simply for the fact that he is an entity with soul. As all the revealed religions say, human beings are brothers as we are all the children of the Prophet Adam (pbuh). This principle of brotherhood is a requirement of religious belief.

Islam is opposed to all fascist-type ideologies and ideas and Darwinist/materialist philosophies that are based on racial superiority and divide people into false categories such as "advanced" and "primitive." It therefore engages in an intellectual and rational struggle against these conflicts that these ideologies bring with them, and has no room for them within itself.

The rule in Islam about all humans being worthy of respect represents the basis of all relations between people. In the view of Islam, even someone who acts wrongly always has the potential to be turned in the direction of goodness. It is therefore impossible for a true Muslim to have any enemies. Every Muslim has a responsibility to treat others with affection and to tell them about moral virtues, not to make enemies with others and plot to bring them down.

While there is no distinction among people on the subject of superiority when they are addressed in the Qur'an, the use of the term "the sons of Adam" shows that in that respect all people are created equal:

We have honoured the sons of Adam and conveyed them on land and sea and provided them with good things and favoured them greatly over many We have created. (Qur'an, 17:70)

The way that a religion is heralded by many as a religion of war, even though there are no pretexts as summarised above, stems entirely from the practices of the peddlers of superstition. Some people are generally mistaken about Islam because they are simply unaware of these clarifications regarding it and only witness the practices of the radicals. People with a radical mindset are unaware that they are applying commandments outside the Qur'an and have adopted another faith quite different to the true Islam. However, the religion of Islam and Islamic sharia are based on the Qur'anic verses. Other sources that are based on fabricated hadiths and superstitions have no validity for a true Muslim. So do Muslims desire war?

Who Desires War?

The armaments sector is always kept alive by certain groups. It is also the only sector not affected by economic crises. It is a vibrant sector in which supply and demand never end and in which novelties are always being offered to the market. The way of keeping this sector alive is no doubt "wars." To this end, an ignorant mass of people who regard their own faith as one of war and who are ready to kill and be killed, in other words the radical groups that appear in the name of Islam, are provoked.

Some Neocons and opponents of Islam in the West are entirely correct about violence being spread by the radicals. However, these people are wrong when it comes to some leaders, such as Osama bin Laden. Such so-called leaders are generally people with no interest in Islam and Muslims but who are kept ready under the supervision of various intelligence services. They are immediately involved whenever a climate of turmoil or war is desired. They spend their time in bars and cafes in Western countries, but when the command comes, they let their beards grow, change their clothing and language, assume a typically Middle Eastern appearance and set to work implementing the superstition they have learned over the years.

It is usually radical groups that are encouraged to wage war, but those who need war for their own evil ends manage them all. Ignorance is of vital importance to those "managers" in question. Ignorance gives them pawns to make use of.

This scenario has become reality many times; Osama bin Laden was just one of the actors of this scenario. The coming of Hazrat Mahdi (pbuh), the greatest event in the End Times foretold by our Prophet (pbuh), and Muslims' sincere expectations on the subject were used to give the impression by some circles that bin Laden himself was the Mahdi and efforts were made to convince many people of this. The journey that began with bin Laden struck not just Afghanistan but the whole Muslim world; the scenario was to end with images of bin Laden's dead body. This was perhaps the most striking part of the whole plan. Under that plan, the Muslim world would see that their Mahdi is dead and lose all hope and expectations. This was a system-

VIOLENCE, HATRED AND LOVELESSNESS ARE CHARACTERISTICS OF RADICALS. THEY HAVE NO PLACE IN ISLAM.

Some supposed religious leaders are pawns set in motion when needed to create war and turmoil. They are supervised by various intelligence units and play a role in bringing about the war with which they are charged.

atic scenario aimed at the weakening and further exploitation of the Islamic world.

People with radical mindsets are no doubt guilty on the subject, but we must not ignore the forces that feed them. War always serves some people's interests at a time when the armaments industry is so strong. It is usually radical groups who are incited to fight, but it is those who need war for their own wicked ends who pull their strings. These groups ready for war because of their ignorance are an ideal "cover" for these forces behind the scenes; they are merely pawns that can easily be sent to war.

Americans or Europeans who complain about the radicals must not forget these managers running them. This does not of course mitigate the crimes of those who have fallen into the clutches of radical groups and peddlers of superstition, split up into sects and declared one another to be the enemy, but neither should this important reality be ignored. Indeed, the various organizations that openly stage and manage protests and uprisings, particularly in Muslim countries, have no hesitation about openly expressing their aims.

Considering this, in order for there to be peace, the benefit of all mankind need to be pursued rather than personal advantage, the hunger for land and enmities need to come to an end, and the fanatical mindset has to be eliminated. The true faiths, religious moral values, the believers and the Qur'an are all essential to that end. Conflicts based on a desire for political or material advantage, territory or ideology always grow and assume the most terrible dimensions. What can do away with all this is proper education in the true understanding of faith using the Qur'an as its point of reference. This education can eliminate all these errors and absorb all enmities. Once people's mindset has changed, there will be no grounds for hostility or war and the only way to achieve that change in mindset is through education according to the morality of the Qur'an.

An important reason that fuels radicalism: Guantanamo

The comprehensively revised form of a CIA report was published in early 2015. The report attracted great attention across the world. While it is a known fact that the U.S. inflicted severe torture on prisoners detained on grounds of suspicion, particularly after September 11, this report documented torture.

The world already knew more or less how intelligence activities worked in the U.S. after September 11 through pictures from the notorious Abu

Ghraib Prison, the techniques of persecution emerging from Guantanamo and witness statements and accounts from released detainees. Torture is a practice that was used even before September 11 in the U.S., but the whole world saw in detail in this report what new methods of torture were invented and what funds were appropriated to pay the experts to implement these techniques. So what did the years of torture actually benefit the U.S. or the free world?

We can easily answer that question in the words "nothing at all." U.S. Senator Harry Reid admits that torture achieved nothing other than giving the U.S. a bad name. Contrary to what some Republicans maintain, researchers have confirmed – following an examination of a staggering six million pages of CIA documents – that the agency acquired no vital information at all.

It is a well-known fact that it is next to impossible to obtain real-time or accurate information about radical terror organizations from its leaders or members. Terrorists in possession of such infor-

mation will either shoot it out with the security forces, military or police or else have themselves killed or commit suicide if they are about to be captured. That has happened time and time again. However, examination of the profiles of people captured and imprisoned by the U.S. shows that the majority were put under arrest without resistance. These people are imprisoned without trying to harm themselves or the people around them, and the information acquired as a result is admitted to be outlandish and intended solely to put an end to the torture. Therefore, this historic lesson once again shows that terrorists in possession of information that might be elicited through torture cannot be captured alive.

Another point we need to concentrate on is the values which the U.S. fights to protect, and the place of torture among those values. The U.S. wants its own people to be free, not afraid of attack, and to build a country in which its own traditional values are preserved in peace and tranquillity, and it spends trillions of dollars to that end and knowingly loses thousands of young lives on the battlefield. The sole aim is to stand up for American values and defy any threats to them.

As we all know, although the U.S. is governed by a secular Constitution, it describes itself as a Christian society and it is much more conservative than Europe. Does not the Bible, the holy scripture of that conservative community, command love, compassion, forgiveness and unity? What Christian could support the idea that a person whose having committed any crime merits being savagely tortured to death? What Christian could be pleased by the innocent lives lost for that reason? If the U.S. wishes to stand up for its values, it has to remain true to those values when times get tough. Speaking in the Senate, Dianne Feinstein, Democratic Party Senator for California, also admitted that torture was a stain on American values.

Torture is not a means of combat, but a culture of cruelty. Information gathered through torture during 12 years of war has not helped eliminate or even weaken such terror groups as al-Qaeda or the Taliban. On the contrary, terror organizations have grown even stronger in the face of violence, savagery and cruelty, have spread across even more parts of the world and have become even more of a threat by setting up new groups. The U.S. attacks have led to the deaths of scores of civilians, and instead of fighting the causes that gave rise to al-Qaeda through an intellectual campaign, its seeking to eliminate by military means those people influenced by those causes has led to a widening of the terror organization's sphere of activity by encouraging other sub-groups to join it.

Responding to a destructive action with an even more destructive method cannot prevent a repetition of that action. Violence will always lead to more violence, and bloodshed to further bloodshed. Therefore, resorting to even more radical techniques in the fight against radical terror will simply result in a vicious circle that confirms the claims of those terror organizations and strengthens their base. That will mean opening the door to further unending conflicts. We need to return to a foundation of common affection and love if future generations are to live in a humane climate where human rights are respected.

Say: "Truth has come and falsehood has vanished. Falsehood is always bound to vanish."

(Qur'an, 17:81)

THE ERROR OF
RADICALISM AND
THE TRUTH

There is another idea that we must examine together with that of terror; that is, the phenomenon of radicalism.

Radicalism means supporting sudden revolutionary destructive changes in any sphere and applying a strict uncompromising policy in order to achieve them. Radicals are characterised by their desire for revolutionary change and the stern, sometimes aggressive attitude they adopt.

In this, as in every sphere of life, the guide for the Muslim is the verses of the Qur'an and the life of our Prophet Muhammad (pbuh). When we look at radicalism in the light of the Qur'an, we see that it has nothing to do with the way in which God commands the believers to behave. When God describes a believer in the Qur'an, He depicts him as a loving, soft-spoken person, shunning conflicts and arguments, approaching even the most hostile people with warmth and friendship.

An example to guide us in this matter is the command given by God to the Prophet Moses (pbuh) and Aaron (pbuh) to go to the Pharaoh and speak gently to him:

Go to Pharaoh; he has overstepped the bounds. But speak to him with gentle words so that hopefully he will pay heed or show some fear. (Qur'an, 20:43-44)

Pharaoh was one of the most cruel and rebellious unbelievers of his time. He was a despot who denied God and ignorantly worshipped idols; moreover, he subjected believers (the Israelites of the time) to terrible cruelties and murder. But God commanded His prophets to go to such a hostile man and speak to him gently.

You will notice that the way shown by God was the way of friendly dialogue, not the way of conflict with sharp words, angry slogans and agitated protests.

Some examples of speaking pleasant words in the Qur'an

There are a few other examples to show Muslims how to behave in the dialogue between the Prophet Jethro (pbuh) and the deniers. This dialogue is related in the Qur'an in this way:

And to Madyan their brother Jethro. He said, "My people, worship God! You have no deity apart from Him. Do not give short measure and short weight. I see you prospering and I fear for you the punishment of an all-encompassing Day.

My people! Give full measure and full weight with justice; do not diminish people's goods;

and do not go about the earth, corrupting it.

What endures with God is better for you if you are believers. I am not set over you as your keeper."

They said, "Jethro, do your prayers instruct you that we should abandon what our fathers worshipped or stop doing whatever we want to with our wealth? Yet you are such a lenient, normal person!"

He said, "My people! What do you think? If I do possess a Clear Sign from my Lord and He has given me His good provision, I do not want to oppose you in what way I am forbidding you. I only want to put things right as far as I can. My success is with God alone. I have put my trust in Him and I turn to Him." (Qur'an, 11:84-88)

When we examine what he says, we see that the Prophet Jethro (pbuh) invited the people to believe in God and to adopt high moral principals and he did this with friendliness and humility. We can explain some of the reasons behind the things said in these verses:

❒ When the Prophet Jethro says **"I am not set over you as your keeper"** to the people, he does not want to dominate them; his only intention is to inform them of the truth that God has revealed.

❒ **"You are clearly the forbearing, the rightly-guided"**: These words of the deniers to the Prophet Jethro show his warm, gentle and courteous character and that this was particularly appreciated by the deniers.

❒ **"My people! What do you think?"** This expression used by the Prophet Jethro shows that he calls on the deniers to use their intelligence and conscience. In other words, he does not use insistent pressure, but questions their ideas from an opposing stance and invites them to consider and come to a conclusion based on their own free conscience.

❒ **"I do not want to oppose you in what way I am forbidding you"**. The Prophet Jethro's prohibition here is not actually a prohibition. He explains that some acts are sinful and invites the people to abandon them. Moreover, when the Prophet Jethro says **"I do not want to oppose you"**, it is not his purpose to dispute with the people; he does not want to make them uncomfortable and incite a quarrel; he wants only to invite them to faith and the practice of high moral principles.

If you examine the Qur'an you will see that a warm, gentle and compassionate disposition characterised all the prophets. God reveals that the Prophet Abraham (pbuh) was **"tender-hearted and forbearing."** (Qur'an, 9:114) and in another verse, the Prophet Muhammad's (pbuh) moral principles are described in this way:

> **It is a mercy from God that you were gentle with them. If you had been rough or hard of heart, they would have scattered from around you. So pardon them and ask forgiveness for them, and consult with them about the matter. Then when you have reached a firm decision, put your trust in God. God loves those who put their trust in Him. (Qur'an, 3:159)**

God commands people to avoid angry words

An obvious characteristic of radicalism is its anger. This disposition can be clearly seen in the speeches, writings and demonstrations of radicals. However, anger is not an attribute of Muslims. When God describes believers in the Qur'an, He describes, **"those who give in times of both ease and hardship, those who control their rage and pardon other people – God loves the good-doers"** (Qur'an, 3:134).

There is no situation in which a Muslim displays anger. Every Muslim of course wants other people to believe in God and live according to moral principles, but this is possible only by the grace of God. No matter what we do, no matter how much we try to explain the truth to people, human hearts are in God's hands. God reminds Muslims of this very important fact in this verse, **"... Do those who believe not know that if God had wanted to He could have guided all mankind? ..."** (Qur'an, 13:31)

Therefore, it is the duty of a Muslim only to explain the facts and to invite people to accept them. Whether or not people accept the invitation is completely up to their own conscience. God reveals this truth in the Qur'an when He says that there is no compulsion in religion.

There is no compulsion in religion. True guidance has become clearly distinct from error. Anyone who rejects false deities and has belief in God has grasped the Firmest Handhold, which will never give way. God is All-Hearing, All-Knowing. (Qur'an, 2:256)

Therefore, there is no coercion to make people believe and become Muslims, or to make Muslims perform prayers and beware of sin. There is only advice. God reveals in a

few verses addressed to the
Messenger of God (pbuh)
that Muslims are not oppressors:

> **We know best what they say. You are not
> a dictator over them. So remind, with the
> Qur'an, whoever fears My Threat.
> (Qur'an, 50:45)**
> **Say: "Mankind! The truth has come to you
> from your Lord. Whoever is guided is
> only guided for his own good. Whoever is
> misguided is only misguided to his detri-
> ment. I have not been set over you as a
> guardian." (Qur'an, 10:108)**

Muslims are responsible only for
explaining the religious morality, they
apply no pressure or coercion on anyone
and are enjoined to speak gently to even the
most tyrannical deniers. Such persons cannot be radicals, because radicalism stands
for the opposite of those qualities we have
enumerated. Indeed, radicalism is an unIs-
lamic current of thought and a political
stance that came into the Islamic world from
outside. When we examine social phenomena described in terms of radicalism, it will
be seen that these are basically a collection
of methods and pronouncements used by
communists, or an expression of the "fanatical rage" that has no place in true Islam.
(Qur'an, 48:26)

How Can the Vicious Circle of Radicalism and Terror Be Broken?

As stated in earlier sections, one concrete fact stands after 13 years of military operations, from Afghanistan to Libya and from Nigeria to Iraq; radical terrorist groups have not ceased to exist through military force, violence and oppression, and to the contrary, they've grown even stronger.

What is more, all kinds of military operations, including air strikes and ground operations just **lead to more civilian deaths, damage cities and destroy infrastructure, resulting in mounting fury in the countries concerned and that fury mostly benefits radical organisations**. Spending billions of dollars on producing people opposing it, and thus providing human resources for terror organisations, is a most undesirable state of affairs.

Although killing off the leaders of terror organisations is presented as an effective technique by some military analysts, looked at from a wider perspective, no results are actually obtained from it at all. The killing of Osama bin Laden obviously did not spell the end of al-Qaeda.

Besides, **terror organisations are capable of skilfully turning even these armed attacks against them into propaganda**. They have the skills to portray the attacks against them as evidence of the righteous nature of their cause. For that reason, organisations either grow stronger or continue their activities underground and that makes the military struggle against them ineffective.

In order to break the spiral of terror, socioeconomic improvements need to be made and policies such as ensuring the implementation of democratic processes clearly need to be brought to the fore in regions where there are intense terrorist activities. In order for all these things to happen, however, it is essential to remove the ignorance that lie at

RADICALISM

TERROR

the roots of all the errors of a radical mindset. The way to do that is through educational and cultural activities. **Correct education with accurate ideas needs to be implemented**, this would be far more economical than spending trillions of dollars on weaponry and later spending billions more on humanitarian aid, and is a method that will produce infinitely better results.

It is possible to stop these militants before they turn into killers through precautions taken against the intellectual foundations of these organisations. Moreover, it would then be possible to prevent new recruitment to those organisations. No terror organisation could ever

**Military Budgets
$US Dollars**

500+ billion
100-500 billion
50-100 billion
20-50 billion
10-20 billion
5-10 billion
1-5 billion
0.5-1 billion
0.1-0.5 billion
-0.1 billion

The world states pour money into fighting extremism with armed force; yet this menace keeps growing. An educational mobilisation against terrorist organisations is what it will take to prevent the outrageous terror all over the world.

resist such an intellectual struggle via television and radio and the internet. **A movement that loses its intellectual basis cannot survive.** The states should either take over this task or support non-governmental organisations that make themselves available for this task.

An educational mobilisation against all terrorist organisations, no matter what their ideological roots are, is what it will take to prevent the outrageous terror we encounter all over the world.

NATO keeps pouring money into fighting extremism with armed force; yet why does this menace keep growing? The answer is in the direction the finances are being directed. Trying to fight an extremist ideology solely with physical force will do little but increase the number of the supporters of that ideology. As the military campaign in the

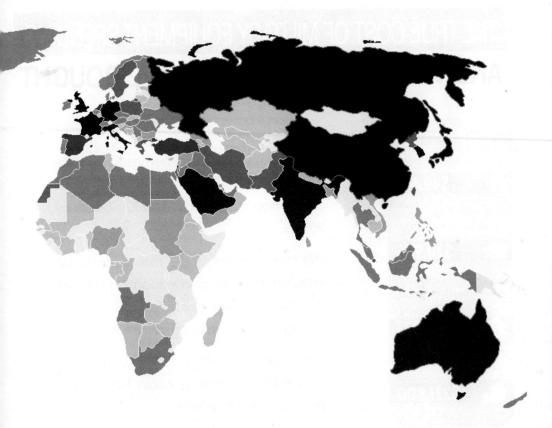

region costs more innocent human lives, the relatives and the close circle of those who died in those attacks will be motivated to join the extremists due to their resentments toward the West.

Such dangerous movements must be brought to an end and their ideological basis should be annihilated all over the world. As a matter of fact, this is something that can only be done by the Middle Eastern nations with the help of their Western allies. In that regard, in order to eradicate radicalism and its effects globally, and to uphold the positive ideals of humanity such as democracy, pluralism and human rights, education is the most important step. To prevent the proliferation of radicalism – a major threat against global security – world leaders should realize the urgent need for an intellectual campaign and seek ways to correct ignorance with intellectual efforts.

THE TRUE COST OF MILITARY EQUIPMENT SPENDING
AND WHAT ELSE IT COULD HAVE BOUGHT

[LEGEND]

REAL MEDIAN
HOUSEHOLD INCOME
$49,445

AVERAGE COST OF 4-YEAR
COLLEGE EDUCATION
$20,986

AVERAGE FAMILY
HEALTH INSURANCE PLAN
(Through Employer)
$15,073

MEDIAN SALE PRICE
OF NEW HOMES SOLD IN THE U.S.
$221,800

The U.S. military budget increased by 104% over 11 consecutive years. Expenditure of $354 billion in 2001 rose to $721 billion by 2011.

The money spent on the military could be invested in health and education instead, and employment opportunities could be employed for thousands of people.

These two pages show some examples of how military spending could have been employed in other fields.

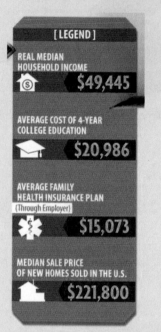

EQUIPPING ONE U.S. SOLDIER $17,500	CRUISE MISSILE $830,000	ABRAMS TANK $6,210,000
►WHICH AMOUNTS TO	►WHICH AMOUNTS TO	►WHICH AMOUNTS TO
0.35 AVERAGE HOUSEHOLD INCOMES	16.8 AVERAGE HOUSEHOLD INCOMES	125.6 AVERAGE HOUSEHOLD INCOMES
0.83 4-YEAR EDUCATIONS	39.6 4-YEAR EDUCATIONS	295.9 4-YEAR EDUCATIONS
1.16 FAMILIES' HEALTH INSURANCE	55 FAMILIES' HEALTH INSURANCE	412 FAMILIES' HEALTH INSURANCE
0.08 HOMES	3.7 HOMES	28 HOMES

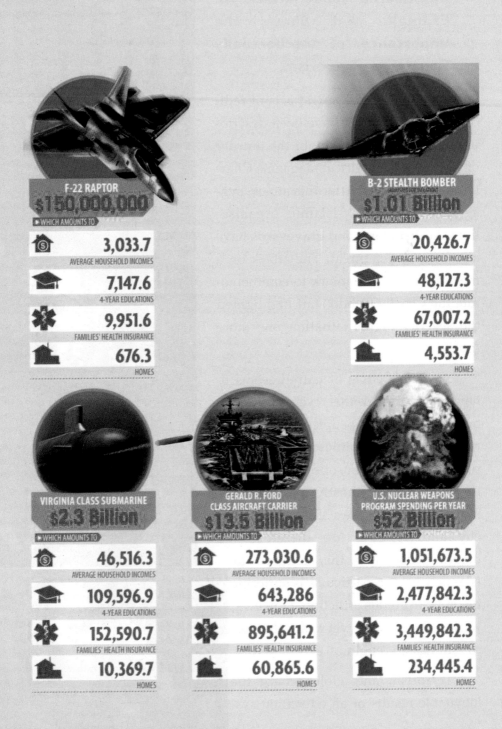

F-22 RAPTOR
$150,000,000
▶ WHICH AMOUNTS TO

3,033.7
AVERAGE HOUSEHOLD INCOMES

7,147.6
4-YEAR EDUCATIONS

9,951.6
FAMILIES' HEALTH INSURANCE

676.3
HOMES

B-2 STEALTH BOMBER
ADJUSTED FOR INFLATION
$1.01 Billion
▶ WHICH AMOUNTS TO

20,426.7
AVERAGE HOUSEHOLD INCOMES

48,127.3
4-YEAR EDUCATIONS

67,007.2
FAMILIES' HEALTH INSURANCE

4,553.7
HOMES

VIRGINIA CLASS SUBMARINE
$2.3 Billion
▶ WHICH AMOUNTS TO

46,516.3
AVERAGE HOUSEHOLD INCOMES

109,596.9
4-YEAR EDUCATIONS

152,590.7
FAMILIES' HEALTH INSURANCE

10,369.7
HOMES

**GERALD R. FORD
CLASS AIRCRAFT CARRIER**
$13.5 Billion
▶ WHICH AMOUNTS TO

273,030.6
AVERAGE HOUSEHOLD INCOMES

643,286
4-YEAR EDUCATIONS

895,641.2
FAMILIES' HEALTH INSURANCE

60,865.6
HOMES

**U.S. NUCLEAR WEAPONS
PROGRAM SPENDING PER YEAR**
$52 Billion
▶ WHICH AMOUNTS TO

1,051,673.5
AVERAGE HOUSEHOLD INCOMES

2,477,842.3
4-YEAR EDUCATIONS

3,449,842.3
FAMILIES' HEALTH INSURANCE

234,445.4
HOMES

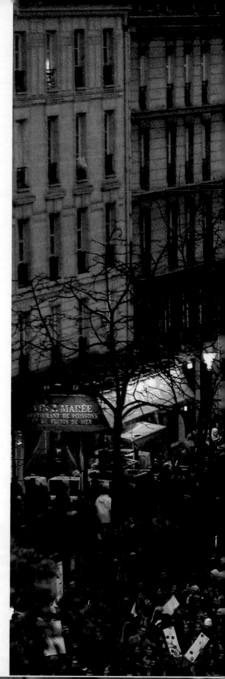

The Charlie Hebdo Attack: An Example that Shows the Importance of Intellectually Countering Terrorism

One of the most horrid acts of radical terrorism that we have been describing in this book is no doubt the murder of 12 staff of the satirical magazine Charlie Hebdo in Paris. After this attack, synagogues, mosques, Islamic organisations, kosher stores and graveyards have also been under threat. The attack on a meeting held in Denmark to commemorate the Charlie Hebdo staff highlighted the severity of the situation one more time.

A vicious circle of hatred seems to have formed and this cycle hurts the ordinary, innocent people the most. The radicals of every philosophy have the potential to make Europe uninhabitable for everyone and mostly for minorities like Muslims and Jews. Terrorism, anarchy and violence are therefore the biggest problems of this century. The Islamic world in particular is suffering the most from this affliction. However, we have to reiterate yet again that terrorism has no religion.

Terrorism and violence are the inevitable results of an education sys-

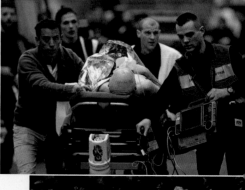

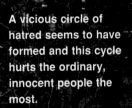

A vicious circle of hatred seems to have formed and this cycle hurts the ordinary, innocent people the most.

tem that believes human beings are mere animals fighting for their lives in a cruel setting; this system teaches people cruelty, selfishness and mercilessness. In this system, altruism, cooperation, compassion and love are not valuable. A human becomes strong only if he is cruel and selfish. When a spiritually weak person is educated like this and especially if he doesn't know how to use his conscience, he will be easily swayed by any ideology that sees "violence as a means to prove himself and to obtain his rights." To sum it up, a person who is trained with such education can be convinced to adopt the ways of terrorists, sometimes through communist principles and sometimes through radical influences which pose as Islamic. For this reason, the first measure the world needs to take against terrorism is fixing this wrong education system.

It is true that content of Charlie Hebdo and other similar publications offend Muslims. This magazine published content that offended not only Muslims, but also Christians, Jews, Buddhists and many other people. However, what a Muslim should do in the face of such a situation is resorting to legal recourses, to ask that his values are not offended. Better yet, he can approach the offenders (or those with similar ideas) in a friendly manner and explain to them - kindly - that their attitude is not nice, that humour can be made in a more elegant style, and encourage them to adopt a more loving and compassionate attitude instead. They can write and talk about the fact that such wrong ideas should be fixed and let the whole world know about these facts. However, a Qur'an-abiding Muslim can never kill another person simply because the other person doesn't follow Islam.

On the other hand, all around the world, murders are being committed and brutal acts are carried out in the name of Islam and the victims of these horrible acts are most typically Muslims. Scores of Muslims lose their lives everyday as a result of terrorist attacks carried out around the world.

tent of Charlie Hebdo and other similar publications
offended Muslims. However, what a Muslim should
s resorting to legal recourses. Better yet, he can
ly explain to the offenders that humour can be made
more elegant style, and encourage them to adopt a
e loving and compassionate attitude instead.

SURELY, ISLAM IS BEYOND THE PICTURES DEPICTED.

Islam is beyond these drawings. A Qur'an-abiding Muslim can never kill another person simply because the other person doesn't follow Islam.

It should be kept in mind that what these people live is not an Islam based on the Qur'an, but radicalism. The radicalism that emerged after the passing of the Prophet Muhammad (pbuh) has produced rules that are non-existent in religion and, using the name of God and the Prophet (pbuh), created a whole new religion. This system that developed based on fabricated hadiths has no room for love, compassion, friendship, respect for women, peace, beauty, art or science; in other words, for the things that bring joy to people. There is only room for oppression, coercion, cruelty and violence. The radical system virtually seeks to bury people alive and takes away everything beautiful using the name of Islam.

Therefore, it is of paramount importance that in the efforts to explain the fact that Islam is a religion of peace, their explanations must be based on the Qur'an. It is technically impossible for a person who defends a version of Islam that is full of the radicals' superstitions, fabricated hadiths and accounts to talk about peace and love.

This truth provides guidance not only to Muslims but also to the Western world that wishes to stop terrorism: The way to stop the so-called Islamic terrorism is intellectually eradicating the ideas that feed it. As long as the radical state of mind persists, bombing the Muslim world with drones, sending troops, or killing terrorist leaders, retaliating to violence with more violence, will not end terrorism. On the contrary, it will fuel it and make it even a bigger monster. Anything that would exacerbate hatred and hostility should be carefully avoided and an environment of ideas rather than one of weapons should be built.

Let us reiterate: terror is unacceptable in any form. In particular, equating Islam, which regards the killing of one person as equivalent to the killing of all mankind, with terror is one of the most terrible tragedies of our century. However, terror will not disappear by holding protest marches on the streets, nor through condemnations by politicians, nor through simply repeating, "Islam is a religion of peace." The fact that Islam is a religion of peace is in the Qur'an, and that fact needs to be proclaimed to the world, persistently and with full supporting evidence, through education. The Islamic world also needs to be purged of nonsense: Western support is of course important for that, but it is Muslims who need to do the job.

Why do they join the radical terrorist organisations?

Experts on terrorism, intelligence agents, writers, editors and analysts in the West are constantly seeking the answer to one question: Why do people join radical organisations?

They come up with numerous theories; they talk about poor kids from city suburbs, about uneducated and ignorant people and about bored young people looking for adventure. Some describe this phenomenon as "the attractive force of utopian politics", while others maintain that these people set out with the aim of "writing a story of their own".

However, these theories have been largely shelved as it has gradually been realized that many such groups contain large numbers of wealthy people, people with careers, academics, doctors and engineers, and that many of their members hail from well-off backgrounds.

Some have declared that those who join such organisations have "mental problems". The response to that came from John Horgan, a psychologist and a professor at the University of Massachusetts Lowell's Center for Terrorism and Security Studies: *"Because of what terrorists do, we assume that can be explained via the pathology of those people, but trying to explain terrorism as mental illness is misleading."*[5]

Horgan and others have had to eliminate all the possibilities they had hypothesized; neither poverty, nor boredom, nor mental illness can explain why people from almost every country in the world are so determined to overcome a good deal of difficulties to become part of a system in which people die and are killed with ease. Nobody would hurl himself into a war, leaving behind his family and all he owns for the sake of "writing a story". He would never accept death so swiftly and unconditionally.

People are joining radical groups from all over the world, from European countries to Kazakhstan, from Australia to Somalia and from Russia to Tunisia. The number of people joining such groups is rising all the time. European countries such as France and Germany head the lists of these figures.

Let us now look at the true answer to the disturbing question: Turning away from the Qur'an and the true teachings of Islam and the consequent adoption of a skewed interpretation of Islam has led some Muslims to turn their backs on liberty, art and science and has radicalised them to a significant extent. As the ideological infrastructure of radicalism has spread in an uncontrolled manner (and sometimes in a manner controlled by certain covert forces) it has begun threatening a wide swath of territory, including Europe. The radicalism that ensued triggered Islamophobia, though the proponents of Islamophobia fail to see that they are further encouraging radicalism in a manner they never desired.

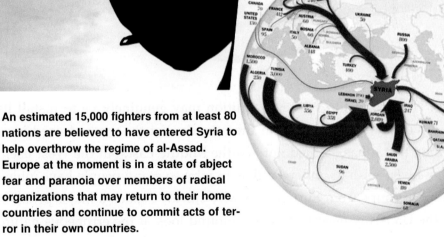

An estimated 15,000 fighters from at least 80 nations are believed to have entered Syria to help overthrow the regime of al-Assad. Europe at the moment is in a state of abject fear and paranoia over members of radical organizations that may return to their home countries and continue to commit acts of terror in their own countries.

As the numbers of those seeking a solution in destroying Islam and Muslims, who do not want Muslims in their country and who sit back and watch the oppression of Muslims in the world has grown, this further serves to incite hatred. The horrifying images left behind by the coalition forces' interventions in Afghanistan and Iraq were, for a good many, the final straw. Nobody could or did remain unmoved by the Western powers' indiscriminate killing of families and destruction of homes. Savagery inevitably incites hatred.

The aim of the Western coalition may genuinely be to install its own version of democracy in these lands. Yet the method used is so wrong that it has harmed not just the Middle East, but the West itself. Those who wish to understand as to why so many people have joined radical groups from Europe and why suicide is such a major problem in the US Army need to take a profound look at the erroneous nature of the policies being followed.

So what should the solution be? Radical groups follow a deviant ideology that many people in the world believe to be true. The followers of that ideology cannot oppose the groups in question because, at heart, they simply do not believe that they are on the wrong path. This deep-rooted problem can only be resolved by the Islamic world completely renouncing sources based on nonsense and turning to the Qur'an instead, and the person who will bring that about is Hazrat Mahdi (pbuh).

More than 1,000 foreign fighters are joining the fight in Syria each month. Even airstrikes do not seem to change this rate. The problem of radicalism can only be resolved by the Islamic world completely renouncing sources based on nonsense and turning to the Qur'an instead.

Radical groups manage to produce this effect to a large extent by way of the internet. They employ social media with a mastery of persuasive propaganda. They reach out to five continents and gather supporters. They win people over with perhaps only a few brief lines. In other words, through education.

Horgan summarizes that effect in these words: *"They have become so adept at social media that they are reaching out to disaffected individuals on a global scale."*

It is truly astonishing, given that education is so easy, that the Western coalition powers still insist upon reinforcing their bases in the Middle East with more weapons. What needs to be done is to set out using the same means and to show people the false nature of that religion of superstition with evidence from the Qur'an by making use of such a powerful communication tool as the internet. It is to prove, using Islam's own holy book, that Islam rejects savagery and teaches love and peace. If the West can do that, there is of course no need to remind anyone that it has greater means at its disposal than the radical groups. Just imagine that all the international media, which are generally under the control of the West, were to provide such education with a loud voice! It would take mere seconds for the world to hear the truth.

Europe at the moment is in a state of abject fear and paranoia over members of radical organisations that may return to their home countries. It believes that people who have fought in those regions and then come home will inevitably continue to commit acts of terror in their own countries, and those countries are taking extraordinary security precautions in order to preclude such a nightmarish possibility. Yet they never stop to think that the problem could be resolved at the root

What needs to be done in the face of radical groups is to prove, using Islam's own holy book, that Islam rejects savagery and teaches love and peace. It would take mere seconds for the world to hear the truth if the international media were to provide such education.

if they were to simply educate these people about the true Islam.

What they need to understand is this: If someone has set out to kill or die in a foreign land, the reason for that can only be an underlying belief. Since that belief is based on a deeply flawed interpretation of the Qur'an, there is a solution that can produce clear and certain results; to teach people the true belief from the true source, in other words, the Qur'an. However, if Western countries in particular continue to turn their backs on that education, the tragedy afflicting the world may well begin to threaten them even more. Bombs, guns and missiles are no solution to the problem; they are just a means of spreading hatred.

TV News Reports Must Not Give Terror Room to Breathe

Today, even the world's most developed countries are under the threat of terror. The most concrete example of this is France. This year, troops entered Paris for the first time since the Second World War. The stationing of 1,080 soldiers around the Eiffel Tower, in response to Paris terror attacks and against another potential attack, reveals the extent of this threat. However, even these precautions weren't enough and new terrorist acts were encountered in the city centre.

Fascist and extreme-right movements have been on the rise as of late in Europe, and attacks on migrants, and particularly Muslims, have increased. The tensions between

Russians and Chechens are unending. Fighting dating back decades persists in Africa and the Middle East. On the other hand the PKK, which claims to have halted its terrorist activities up in the mountains, continues with massacres in Turkish cities.

Various theories aimed at eradicating terrorism have been proposed over the years and various methods have been tried. Not only has none borne fruit, acts of terror have actually increased.

The clearest example of this was the killing of Osama Bin Laden. Did his death put an end to al-Qaeda? No.

Terrorist organisations wish to intimidate innocent people into loyalty to them in order to achieve control over society; they perform the most ruthless and bloodthirsty acts to that end. In perpetrating these acts, they seek to keep their own supporters' morale high and to give them the impression that they are strong and victory is at hand. We can clearly see this in Turkey in the activities of the terrorist PKK.

Terrorist organisations typically do careful planning before their atrocities. The attack on the World Trade Center and the Pentagon on September 11, the attacks on the London Underground, the train attack in Spain, the theatre bombing in Russia, the attacks in France and all the atrocities perpetrated by the PKK in Turkey were all the result of careful planning. The cold-blooded professional terrorists in the latest Paris attack laid bare this truth.

Almost all terrorist groups make active use of the media for publicity purposes. These groups are therefore quite keen for the anarchy and corruption they create to receive wide coverage in the media. In the view of terrorist organisations, the supposed success of their actions is directly proportional to their coverage in the media.

For example, when an action is repeated on TV many times over and is widely covered in social media, the multiplier effect is as if it had been committed hundreds of times over.

For this reason, one of the most important responsibilities in the fight against terror falls on the media. In its reports, the media must not directly - or indirectly - support terrorist organisations and must not allow them room to grow.

How and to what extent the media should cover acts of terror is an important subject of debate across the world. As a matter of fact, one of the main reasons why even the most advanced, powerful and modern countries have failed to put an end to terror is that the media feeds terror through thoughtless and hysterically insensible coverage. As a result of such coverage, the horror of terrorism is able to spread rapidly.

There is no doubt that the media has a duty to approach a news story in an objective manner but they must be even more cautious when it comes to terrorism: Human life must be held above all other values, and the media must be careful not to become part of this savagery by unwittingly disseminating terrorist propaganda in their typically sensationalist manner. In its coverage of acts of terror, the media must not be guided by ratings and competition.

For example, the American media after the September 11 attacks and the British media after the London Underground attack behaved in quite a circumspect fashion in their coverage. <u>Even in the recent incidents in Ferguson, Missouri, the U.S. media has shown very little of the violence that took place. However, the global media covered all the details of the Paris attack for day upon day without let-up.</u>

Care must be taken in news coverage not to broadcast close-ups of slaughter or anything that might create public panic and fear. Great circumspection is needed when making programs with the people concerned, even if they are politicians, and no statements that might be perceived as the propaganda of terrorist organisations must be allowed. No impression must be given, albeit unwillingly, that might suggest that a terror organisation is strong and influential.

The media is one of the most important weapons in the war against terror. It is very important for states to educate the accessible public through media. The powerful influence of the media over the public should be directed towards raising public awareness against terrorism. In the same way that terrorist organisations are always trying to impose their ideologies on people in the regions they seek to control, states must also constantly raise public awareness against terrorism through the media and ensure that programs that provide the intellectual basis for this are made. One way of doing this is to broadcast regular scientific criticisms of the bloodthirsty accounts of terrorist groups.

It must not be forgotten that terror cannot be defeated solely through arms and politics. What will really put an end to terror is to conduct intellectual studies that will undermine its intellectual infrastructure.

Islamophobia, the rise of the extreme right and xenophobic movements fuel radicalism

Although the fear known as "Islamophobia" emerged across the globe in the wake of the September 11, 2001, attacks, its roots go back to the Crusades, or even earlier.Islam has now spread across the world: Muslims represent 6 percent of the population of Europe, more than 45 million. By 2050, Muslims are estimated to make up some 20 percent of the population and one in five people in Europe will be a Muslim—one of the main reasons for the rise in Islamophobia among Europeans in recent years.

However, the real trigger behind the rise in Islamophobia is the radical terrorist groups that have emerged in the name of Islam.These

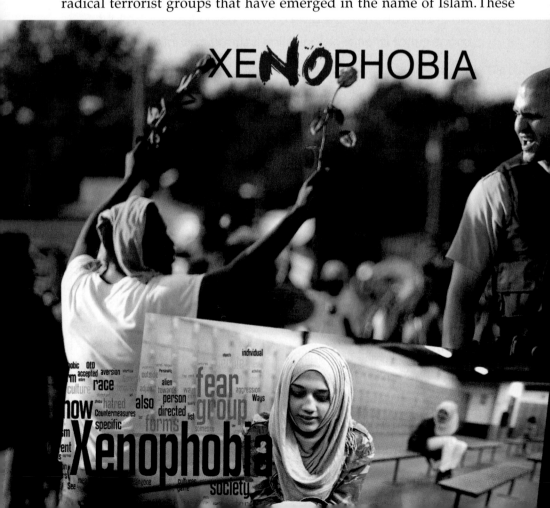

radical organisations, with their perverse mind-sets, far removed from the essence of Islam, have caused a great deal of fear and hatred of Islam.

Various circles opposed to Islam have also played a stunningly effective role in planting this fear into people's minds and this has led to a virtual cottage industry of Islamophobic talk and activities and to the emergence of a security, intelligence and industrial apparatus worth trillions of dollars. This industry is intended to prevent the rise of the Islamic world, which possesses economic and financial power centres, major energy resources and underground wealth.

The policies adopted by Western governments, especially after September 11th, which generally targeted Muslims, and the laws

XENOPHOBIA AND INTOLERANCE IN THE EU

HATE CRIME IN THE EU

→**47,210** RACIST CRIMES were reported in the EU in 2013

→ However, **only 33%** OF EU MEMBER STATES published hate crime statistics in 2013

→**Many hate crimes** GO UNREPORTED or uninvestigated (e.g. In the Czech Republic, and Italy, an estimated 40-60% of reported racist crimes are not fully investigated by police)

→**Up to 74%** OF RACIALLY-MOTIVATED INCIDENTS of assault or threat are not reported to the police (depending on the group surveyed)

VICTIMS OF DISCRIMINATION IN THE EU

→**17%** OF ALL EUROPEANS (*) personally experienced discrimination

→**1 in 3** JEWS surveyed have faced physical or verbal violence because they were Jewish in 2013

→**39%** OF EUROPEANS SURVEYED in 2012 said they believed that not being white was a disadvantage when looking for a job

→**27%** OF EUROPEANS FROM AN ETHNIC MINORITY

→**28%** OF PEOPLE WITH A DISABILITY

→**1 in 5** ROMA surveyed said they had been the victim of hate crime in 2013

As this chart shows, racially-motivated incidents and hate crimes against ethnic minorities are quite high in number and are a big threat facing the EU today. A cultural environment based on love, respect, friendship and brotherhood, without despising those who are not from it, is a basic value that should be sustained strongly.

Islamophobia is an existing form of racism and Europe is witnessing a growing trend of it. However, the real trigger behind the rise in Islamophobia is the radical groups that have emerged in the name of Islam. These groups, far removed from the essence of Islam, have caused a great deal of fear and hatred of Islam.

passed in that context, accelerated the growth of Islamophobia. Extreme right-wing parties played a major role in encouraging opposition to Islam. These parties use Islamophobic speech to gather votes, grow strong on the back of it and target Muslim migrants in particular.

Muslim migrants in Europe have to strive against xenophobia as well as Islamophobia. The ethnocentric mentality that regards them as different and excludes and despises them and subjects them to both physical and psychological attacks on the grounds that migrants threaten their cultural and social lives, is on the rise in many European countries. Attacks along the lines of physical beatings, stones thrown at mosques and workplaces, the throwing of Molotov cocktails, the beat-

ing of employers and workers, swastikas and insulting slogans being written on walls, the vandalism of cemeteries, attacks on homes and families being beaten and threatened with verbal harassment, are some of the things that Muslims in Europe are frequently subjected to.

However, like all other migrants, Muslims are people who leave their own homes and seek to integrate into the countries they go to, making great economic contributions to their new societies. Discrimination and hostility toward them is wholly incompatible with human rights and modern democracy, as well as being unjust and intolerant.

However, it would be equally wrong to consider hostility toward Islam and Muslims in Europe as a single category. People who think that Muslims are taking jobs and other benefits away from Westerners, those who deliberately play on these concerns to encourage hostility toward Islam and Muslims, or those who think that increasing numbers of Muslims will eliminate Christianity and/or degenerate Western culture and those who equate Islam with terror and radicalism must all be considered separately. There is only one way of overcoming all these fears; true Muslims must describe their faith with patience and moderation and explain and show that an Islam purged of all nonsense is modern, compatible with science, democracy and logic, enlightened, progressive, opposes terror and commands love, brotherhood and peace. They must explain that Muslims have no intention of doing away with Christianity and that the Qur'an praises Christians. They must explain that the mentality equated with terrorism, slaughter and suicide attacks, that is against art, science and all beauty and that is hostile to other faiths derives not from Islam, but from deluded and badly misguided fanatics. Under the influence of fringe-element fanatics, Westerners imagine that Islam rejects reason, tolerance and modernity and advocates terrorism and radicalism, and that Islamic values are thus incompatible with democracy and human rights. Muslims must therefore engage in a systematic consciousness-raising campaign,

In the Qur'an, there is no distinction between races; the Qur'an advises that people of different faiths live together in the same society in peace and happiness. A world can thus be established in which people will be able to live together in peace no matter to what race or religion they belong, in which every racist perversion will be rejected, everyone's rights will be regarded and everyone will be respected.

bearing in mind that misinformation is perhaps the main cause of Islamophobia, that many people who fear Islam in fact know very little about it and that much of what they think they know is, quite bluntly, untrue.

The West, which boasts of the importance it attaches to democracy and human rights and how it treats all beliefs equally, also has a major responsibility: The first thing the West needs to do is introduce legal measures against Islamophobic and racist activities. Islamophobia must be regarded as a hate crime in the same way that anti-Semitism is. The West's priority must be to develop a culture based on love, respect, friendship and brotherhood, without despising those who are not from it. Western countries, international organisations and civil society organisations must urgently demonstrate sensitivity on this subject. It is a matter of the greatest urgency in terms of world peace for new legislation to be introduced and for the public to be educated so new generations are freed of these prejudices.

Laws won't stop radical ideologies, but education will

In the wake of the Charlie Hebdo attack, the parliaments of the European countries embarked on some intense work. The European countries passed their own individual anti-terror laws[1] [2] [3] and swung into action to receive aid from NGOs. At this point, they need to pay attention to one important point; not to nurture the poisonous ideologies of radicals while combatting terror.

Radical terror long ago rose to a threat level that can change the world's demography. In the wake of the Charlie Hebdo attack proposals that may cause a radical change in the EU's structure have been brought forward. The idea of removing the Schengen Zone[4], a suggestion that may reduce Europeans' living standards in the spheres of tourism, trade and diplomacy, has been brought to the agenda. The countries in favour of putting border controls in place again are the ones that have had their share from terror threat; namely, Britain, Belgium, Denmark, France, Germany, Poland, Spain and Holland. Yet the question remains: To what extent can these countries obtain results with these laws that will disrupt the peace of these countries' citizens and cause further polarization in their societies?

Everyone must know that every step taken to make the lives of Muslim groups more difficult will simply butter the bread of radical groups; these groups are nourished by hatred and fury, and when it comes to dealing with these two feelings, laws alone remain insufficient.

You may thwart a terrorist's attempt to plant a bomb in a shopping mall by taking strict security measures and making life difficult for every citizen in that city: However, no law can change the opinion of a bigot who harbours hatred for the women wearing revealing clothes in that shopping mall.

The objective of Western society must be to raise generations considering everyone's life in that shopping mall as blessed and respectful to civil norms. Otherwise, counter-terrorism becomes a vortex both financially and in terms of time wasted, and this ultimately benefits terrorists.

French Interior Minister Bernard Cazeneuve's offer for border controls clearly reveals how the European countries fail to grasp the issue of radicalism. Cazeneuve proffered a law making it more difficult to enter the European countries[5] rather than adding checkpoints on the borders within the EU. The French Minister seems unaware of the fact that radical threats see no borders. Likewise, he seems unaware of the extent to which radicalism challenges European social structures, and that a young person born into a European family can also be radicalized. Today's means of communication makes it possible for radical terror groups to educate their followers entirely over the internet, and they thus have access to every corner of the world in the ideological sense.

The communist guerrilla movement that appeared in the 1950s in Cuba could recruit members by paying visits to the numerous and sundry mountain villages in Sierra Maestra; blockading these villages by the military could have slowed down the spread of the movement. Alternatively, preventing the circulation of Sun Tzu's writings could have caused a setback in the ideological training of guerrilla fighters in Far East countries. Yet today, by means of the internet, the highest mountain village in the world or the remotest island state is only a click away. It has also become evident that filtering the internet does not stop access to information. Once a website is closed, another one appears right away on another address. Today people who are called "lone wolves" direct terrorist acts from their individual cells and they are dispersed homogeneously in almost every society.

In the face of this threat, there exists only one workable method: Carrying out an intellectual struggle, thereby putting the internet, televisions and radios to better use than the radicals. If radicals have a thousand websites used for ideological purposes, we need to have tens of thousands of them that will propagate love, brotherhood and unity.

What the European states must do is to strive so that a mindset that follows only the true teachings of Islam based solely on the Qur'an is developed in the Muslim world. Turkey, a country which managed to establish a stable democratic foundation and a secular constitutional framework despite being one of the most populous Muslim nations, can help the West. If we consider Turkey's success in keeping its youth safe from recruitment to terror groups, in its integration to a Western lifestyle on a comparative study among the European countries, we can see the positive results of centuries-long Islamic tradition and experience in youth education. Even though the European countries only have a small minority of Muslims, their numbers of recruits to such groups far exceed the numbers from Turkey, with its 99% Muslim population. Turkey is certainly entitled to be Europe's partner in this endeavour against terrorism. Turkey is a country that will carry the virtues it has preserved from the past forward into the future.

1. http://www.theguardian.com/commentisfree/libertycentral/2009/jan/22/explainer-terrorism-legislation

2..http://www.christiantimes.com/article/david.cameron.wants.new.anti.terror.laws.in.cyberspace.after.paris.attacks/50351.htm

3. http://www.telegraph.co.uk/news/worldnews/europe/france/11335586/EU-pushing-for-new-anti-terror-powers-to-monitor-air-travel.html

4. http://europa.eu/rapid/press-release_MEMO-15-3140_en.htm

5.http://www.ft.com/cms/s/0/9f340c78-99af-11e4-93c1-00144feabdc0.html#axzz3PKGrqhaZ

Today's means of communication makes it possible for radical terror groups to educate their followers entirely over the internet, and they thus have access to every corner of the world in the ideological sense. In the face of this threat, there exists only one workable method: Carrying out an intellectual struggle, thereby putting the internet, televisions and radios to better use than the radicals.

Military Operations Do Not Produce a Solution to Terrorism

American soldiers always win in American films. The most complex operations take place, victory is won and the hostages are freed. American superiority is always symbolized. But is that how it is in the real world?

If we look back at history we will see that the facts do not always match fiction. Operation Eagle Claw is one example of this. The operation staged by the U.S. military in April 1980 to free the 52 U.S. citizens being held hostage in the U.S. Embassy in Iran ended in a debacle due to a sudden sandstorm. An accident during refuelling en route to the USS Nimitz, the centre of the operation, led to the destruction of a C-130 Hercules plane and a U.S. helicopter. The U.S. Army lost eight soldiers, two military planes and one transporter, and had to withdraw from the region without carrying out the operation.

Another instance took place in Somalia. An operation in 1994 under the command of Gen. William F. Garrison ended in a fiasco and the deaths of 24 Pakistani and 19 U.S. troops in fighting in Mogadishu. The U.N. peacekeeping force and U.S. troops withdrew from the region on March 3rd, 1995, in the wake of increasing losses.

The U.S. military history is full of such failed rescue operations, even if they are not always as notorious as these two. One such incident took place in mid-December, 2014, in the village of Dafaar in the Yemeni province of Abva. A rescue operation by U.S. special forces ended in two hostages, the 33-year-old American photojournalist Luke Somers and South African teacher Pierre Korkie, being shot to death by militants. A local al-Qaeda commander, various militants, a woman and a 10-year-old child also lost their lives.

U.S. Defense Secretary Chuck Hagel confirmed that this had happened during a hostage rescue operation. Somers and Korkie had been held hostage in Yemen for more than a year.

The U.S. had been conducting operations with drones in Yemen since 2002. Yet many of these operations ended in failure, with the deaths of many civilians. In 2014, 13 civilians died and 20 people were injured in an aerial attack on al-Qaeda targets in the Yemeni town of Rada.

So what should be done now as these countries are unable to stop the continuing terrorist activities in their lands and external military interventions are leading to the deaths of innocent people?

To reiterate, first and foremost, an intellectual struggle must be waged against terror organisations that use violence in the name of Islam. The distortions in the thinking of members of these organisations need to be explicitly stated. All leaders of opinion and politicians must emphatically state that in the Qur'an, it is explicitly stated that Muslims must invite people to the moral values of Islam simply with gentle words, not using force and compulsion. These people can be summoned to the true path only by telling them of the freedom of belief found in Islamic moral values.

All Muslims, Shiite or Sunni, must be told that violence is no way to seek their rights and that it is a flagrant violation of Islamic moral values. People need to be told that Islamic moral values cannot be espoused through acts of terror, that such acts will simply add to the numbers of the enemies of Islam and that they will invariably inflict even worse harm on Muslims.

Classes aimed at undermining the intellectual infrastructure of terror organisations need to be provided for students in schools; books and articles must be studied, and conferences and academic seminars must be held. That is the only way terrorism can be eradicated from the world. This method can dry up the swamp in which terror breeds.

Today there are radical organisations and their extensions operating in a wide range of territory from Central Asia to the Caucasus, from Africa to the Balkans, and from inside Europe to the U.S.

The only reason why radicalism is able to gather supporters from such different cultures and geographies is the education, instruction and propaganda techniques they implement on people who are mostly ignorant of religion and who approach matters emotionally, rather than with their intellect. The internet and social media are the global communication tools most commonly used by radical organisations for education and propaganda. Therefore, it is obvious that a different means against radicalism, other than the use of force and weapons, needs to be developed.

Yet the West's most popular strategic institutions, think tanks and political advisors have failed to come up with any alternative to constantly producing new military strategies. To be more accurate, the idea that there might be an alternative to mass slaughter has never even occurred to them. They have always ignored the factors of belief and ideology in the emergence of sociological phenomena such as radicalism.

The only way of putting an end to the terror, violence and killings that stem from a distorted conception of Islam based on superstitious references, distorted interpretations and false hadiths and commandments that are totally at odds with the Qur'an is to inform the entire Islamic world of the true Islam based on the Qur'an, in the finest manner possible, and to correct those false beliefs and understandings in the light and under the guidance of the Qur'an.

All Muslims must totally reject an angry, unbending argumentative attitude which goes against the very nature of the Qur'an and in its place adopt a friendly, gentle, affectionate, calm and compassionate one. Muslims must set an example to the world and be admired for their maturity, compassion, moderation, modesty and peacefulness. Muslims must live Islam in the best possible way and introduce to the world the Islamic morality, not only in these things, but also by their achievements in the fields of science, culture, art, aesthetics and social order and others.

The System of the Mahdi Is the Only Force That Can Halt ISIL

ISIL, which has been active since 2013, first assumed a prominent place on the global agenda with its simultaneous advances in Syria and Iraq in 2014. The United States of America applied its strategy of fighting terror, a strategy that has remained little changed since September 11, and initiated military operations against ISIL. The essential difference between that operation and those in Iraq and Afghanistan was that there would be no American boots on the ground. America had lost thousands of troops in Iraq and Afghanistan and was unwilling to see its own people dying in the fight against ISIL; it therefore wanted "Muslims to wipe out one another" to solve the problem, as certain circles explicitly put it. That perspective, which involved major problems in respect of humanity and good conscience, was clearly never going to bring peace and stability to the region or bestow any success on America. There was one very important fact that America ignored in developing its strategy against ISIL: the truths revealed by our Prophet (pbuh) in the hadiths. If America and the coalition forces genuinely want to see peace, tranquility and democracy in the region, they must grasp the perspective of destiny set out in the hadiths of our Prophet (pbuh) and develop a parallel strategy to it.

ISIL is an organisation that our Prophet (pbuh) described in detail in the hadiths. He described both the coming of ISIL and the solution to it. The violence perpetrated by ISIL in a manner incompatible with the Qur'an will come to an end when they pledge allegiance to the Mahdi (pbuh) and abide by the Qur'an, and that will mean the end of the terror and violence in the region. To put it another way, the only power that can put an end to the violence committed by ISIL is the system of the Mahdi.

Let us now have a look at how the coming, the growth and the end of ISIL are described in the hadiths:

1. THOSE WITH BLACK BANNERS WILL APPEAR FROM THE EAST

WHEN THOSE BLACK BANNERS APPEAR IN THE (EAST) in Khorasan... *(al-Ghaybah Nomani, p. 228)*

This hadith refers to a community who will appear with black banners from the East. As is known, al-Qaeda appeared with large black banners.

2. AGAIN FROM THE EAST, THIS TIME A GROUP WITH SMALLER BLACK BANNERS WILL APPEAR

... Once they proceed for a while, **AGAIN FROM THE EAST, THIS TIME SMALL BLACK BANNERS APPEAR**... *(Hadith from the Compilation of Jalal al-din al-Suyuti, The Portents of the Mahdi of the End Times, p.61, hadith no. 7.77)*

ISIL (Islamic State of Iraq and the Levant) was once affiliated with al-Qaeda, but then they went their own separate way. Following the large black banners of al-Qaeda, this time ISIL appeared as a group with smaller black banners.

3. BEFORE THE APPEARANCE OF THOSE WITH BLACK BANNERS THERE WILL BE CONFLICTS IN SYRIA

"Following the three portents await the appearance of Imam Qaim (Mahdi)."

They asked him: "What are these portents?"

"DISAGREEMENTS BETWEEN SYRIANS, the appearance of black banners from Khorasan and fear in the month of Ramadan." *(Bihar al-Anwar, 14)*

4. THOSE WITH BLACK BANNERS WILL BE IN SYRIA

...And again when **A MAN WITH A SMALL BLACK BANNER IS SEEN IN DAMASCUS (SYRIA)...** *(Hadith from the Compilation of Jalal al-din al-Suyuti, The Portents of the Mahdi of the End Times, p.61, hadith no. 7.8)*

... Another portent of the (appearance of Mahdi) is that **THE SOLDIERS OF THE ARMY WITH BLACK BANNERS TIE THEIR HORSES TO THE OLIVE TREES IN DAMASCUS...** *(Al-Qawl al-Mukhtasar fi `Alamat al-Mahdi al-Muntazar, p. 23)*

5. THEY WILL FIGHT AGAINST AL-ASSAD

... **THEY FIGHT AGAINST A MAN FROM THE LINEAGE OF ABU SUFYAN (BASHAR ASSAD)...** *(Al-Qawl al-Mukhtasar fi `Alamat al-Mahdi al-Muntazar, p. 29)*

Several other hadiths suggest that Hafez al-Assad, who wreaked the most terrible slaughters on Muslims during his time in power, was the Sufyan. Consequently the person referred to in the hadith as the man from the lineage of Abu Sufyan, against whom those with black banners would fight, is Bashar al-Assad.

6. THEY WILL HEAD FOR IRAQ AFTER SYRIA

BLACK BANNERS OF BEN AL-'ABBAS (IRAQ) appear... *(Nuaym bin Hammad, Qitab al-Fitan)*

IN THEIR CITIES ON THE BANKS OF EUPHRATES, THEY (those with black banners) WILL KILL THEM [THOSE WHO OPPOSE THEM] ON LAND AND IN THE SEA. *(al-Ghaybah al-Nomani, p. 327)*

7. THEY WILL OBTAIN RESULTS VERY RAPIDLY

While they are in that situation, banners will come from Khorasan, **THEY WILL ACT SWIFTLY.** *(al-Ghaybah al-Nomani, p. 327)*

They will come back from there with an army and will **SEIZE** Kufa and Basra **IN ONE NIGHT...** *(Qitab al-Haft al-Sharif, p.174)*

8. THE CITIES THEY ENTER WILL ALMOST BE PRESENTED TO THEM

Once it is not presented to them, they will gain a victory by waging war and **WHAT THEY DESIRE WILL BE PRESENTED TO THEM.** *(Majlisi, Bihar al-Anwar, v.51, p.87)*

9. THEIR HAIR AND MOUSTACHES WILL BE LONG

His (the commander of those with black banners) **SOLDIERS' HAIR AND MOUSTACHES WILL BE VERY LONG,** their clothes are black and **THEY ARE THE MEN OF BLACK BANNERS.** *(al-Ghaybah al-Nomani, p. 303)*

10. THEY WILL COMMIT MASS MURDERS

God will send someone hard-hearted and whose lineage is not known and he will have victories... **THEY WILL MASSACRE THEM** (those opposing them) **WITHOUT MAKING ANY DIFFERENTIATION.** *(al-Ghaybah al-Nomani, p. 303)*

11. THEY WILL PROCEED TOWARDS KUFA

THOSE WITH BLACK BANNERS appearing from Khorasan **WILL COME DOWN TO KUFA**...*(Hadith from the Compilation of Jalal al-din al-Suyuti, The Portents of the Mahdi of the End Times, p.61, hadith no. 7.12)*

12. BECAUSE OF AN INCREASE IN VIOLENCE AND CONFLICT, PEOPLE WILL START ASKING FOR THE MAHDI

A great war occurs. Ultimately the black banners gain victory. The forces of Sufyan run away. **THEN PEOPLE WILL START TO ASK FOR THE MAHDI AND LOOK FOR HIM.** *(Hadith from the Compilation of Jalal al-din al-Suyuti, The Portents of the Mahdi of the End Times, p.61, hadith no. 7.26)*

13. THOSE WITH BLACK BANNERS WILL EVENTUALLY ABIDE BY THE MAHDI

... and **THEY WILL COME UNDER THE OBEDIENCE OF THE MAHDI.** *(Imam al-Suyuti)*

But they will not accept it and **GRANT IT TO THE MAHDI WHO IS FROM MY LINEAGE...***(Majlisi, Bihar al-Anwar, v.51, p.87)*

As revealed in the hadith, ISIL will eventually pledge allegiance to Hazrat Mahdi (pbuh). One of the most distinguishing features between the real Mahdi (pbuh) and the various false mahdis is that he is a student of the Qur'an, takes love as his guide and never sheds so much as even a single drop of blood. When ISIL aligns itself with the Mahdi (pbuh), it will abandon its evil ways, which are deeply rooted in superstitions, and will abide by the Qur'an, thereby putting an end to its violence.

14. AT THE TIME OF THE MAHDI, WARS WILL COME TO A COMPLETE END AND NOT A SINGLE DROP OF BLOOD WILL BE SHED

One of the main attributes of Hazrat Mahdi (pbuh) is his never shedding a single drop of blood. He who sheds blood, wages war or oppresses people is not the Mahdi. Such false mahdis are all doomed to failure.

Such is his (the Mahdi's) vast justice that, **A SLEEPING PERSON WILL NOT BE WAKENED AND NOT EVEN A SINGLE DROP OF BLOOD WILL BE SHED.** *(Majlisi, Bihar al-Anwar, v.51, p.87)*

THE PARTIES TO A WAR LAY DOWN THEIR BURDENS [THEIR ARMS ETC.] No enmity will remain among anyone. All enmities, conflicts and envy will absolutely come to an end. *(Imam as-Sharani, Death-Doomsday-Hereafter and the Portents of the End Times, p. 496)*

At the root of the current turmoil in the Islamic world lies the sad fact of the abandonment of the Qur'an and people living instead by a religion based largely on false knowledge that does not appear in the Qur'an. Indeed, the Prophet Muhammad's (pbuh) only complaint about Muslims in the Qur'an is that **"...they treat this Qur'an as something to be ignored"** (Qur'an, 25:30).

The violence perpetrated by ISIL has no place in the Qur'an. However, many of the values it espouses do exist in some basic Islamic works. Careful examination of the basic works of Sunni Islamic culture, such as those of Bukhari, Muslim, Abu Dawud and Tirmidhi, shows that they do refer to primitive and barbaric methods of punishment such as "decapitation and stoning", even though these are not in the Qur'an. First and foremost, it is imperative that these remarks be removed from Islamic sources and there must be a return to the essence of the faith; to the Qur'an, in other words. The whole Islamic world must be told, in great detail, that there is no violence in the Qur'an and that such interpretations are incompatible with the Qur'an. That is only possible through the system of the Mahdi. Our Prophet (pbuh) has revealed that one of the most important characteristics of Hazrat Mahdi (pbuh) is that he will nullify the superstitions that have been added on to Islam and lighten and ease the faith. Lightening and easing the faith means Islam being restored to its origin. This means living in complete compliance with the Qur'an. The whole world will then witness how Islam is indeed a religion of love and peace.

If we want a spirit based on love, compassion, pluralism, understanding and affection to prevail across the Islamic world, the way to bring this about is a return to the moral values of the Qur'an, which have been ignored for centuries, and the establishment of the system of the Mahdi. The Islamic world will never accept such a transition without a spiritual leader such as Hazrat Mahdi (pbuh). Those who want

ISIL to renounce its violence must therefore seek out Hazrat Mahdi (pbuh).

What needs to be done under these conditions is clear; first, to expose the invalidity of the information that ISIL and other groups use as supposed evidence and that appears in various Islamic sources, with evidence from the Qur'an; secondly, to search for the Mahdi (pbuh) and to communicate the system of the Mahdi. Winning over the thousands of young Europeans, Americans and others who have joined ISIL is only possible through education and by replacing misguided notions with the truth, not by killing tens of thousands of people in the Middle East and raining bombs down upon them. It goes without saying that the West can only succeed in that endeavour with the system of the Mahdi.

Happiness, justice, economic well-being and welfare can only be attained through peace and unity.

Divine religions all command love.

It is time for everyone to realize that peace lies in adopting a humane approach based on the morals of religion.

Adnan Oktar (Harun Yahya)

Examples of Compassion, Affection and Humanity in the History of Islam

To sum up the facts we have seen so far, the faith of Islam as described in the Qur'an is a religion of peace, love and compassion. This truth is accepted by many non-Muslim historians and theologians too. One of these is the British historian Karen Armstrong, a former nun and an expert on Middle East history. In her book *Holy War*, which examines the history of the three Divine religions, she makes the following comments:

... The word 'Islam' comes from the same Arabic root as the word 'peace' and the Qur'an condemns war as an abnormal state of affairs opposed to God's will... Islam does not justify a total aggressive war of extermination... Islam recognizes that war is inevitable and sometimes **a positive duty in order to end oppression and suffering. The Qur'an teaches that war must be limited and be conducted in as humane a way as possible.**

Mohammad had to fight not only the Meccans but also the Jewish tribes in the area and Christian tribes in Syria who planned on offensive against him in alliance with the Jews. Yet this did not make Mohammed denounce the People of the Book. His Muslims were forced to defend themselves but they were not fighting a 'holy war' against the religion of their enemies. When Mohammad sent his freedman Zaid against the Christians at the head of a Muslim army, he told them **to fight in the cause of God bravely but humanely.** They must not molest priests, monks and nuns nor the weak and helpless people who were unable to fight. There must be no massacre of civilians nor should they cut down a single tree nor pull down any building.[3]

The Caliphs who succeeded the Prophet Muhammad (pbuh) were also very sensitive in exercising justice. In conquered countries, both the indigenous people and the newcomers led their lives in peace and security. Abu Bakr (ra), the first Caliph, demanded his people adopt just and compassionate attitudes in these lands. All these attitudes were in compliance with the values of the Qur'an. Abu Bakr gave the following command to his army before the first Syrian expedition:

> Stop, O people, that I may give you ten rules to keep by heart: Do not commit treachery, nor depart from the right path. You must not mutilate, neither kill a child or aged man or woman. Do not destroy a palm tree, nor burn it with fire and do not cut any fruitful tree. You must not slay any of the flock or herds or the camels, save for your subsistence. You are likely to pass by people who have devoted their lives to monastic services; leave them to that to which they have devoted their lives. You are likely, likewise, to find people who will present to you meals of many kinds. You may eat; but do no forget to mention the name of God.[4]

Omar ibn al-Khattab, who succeeded Abu Bakr, was famous for the way he exercised justice and made contracts with the indigenous people of the conquered countries. Each one of these contracts proved to be an example of compassion and justice. For instance, in his declaration granting protection to Christians in Jerusalem and Lod, he ensured that churches would not be demolished and guaranteed that Muslims would not worship in churches in groups. Omar granted the same conditions to the Christians of Bethlehem.

During the conquest of Medain, the declaration of protection given to the Nestorian Patriarch Isho'yab III (650 - 660 AD) again guaranteed that churches would not be demolished and that no building would be converted into a house or a mosque.[5] The letter written by the patriarch to the bishop of Fars (Persia) after the conquest is most striking, in the sense that it depicts the understanding and compassion shown by Muslim rulers to the People of the Book in the words of a Christian:

Jerusalem, which is sacred to Muslims, Jews and Christians, must be a place where all believers can remember God with joy and love.

The Arabs to whom God has given at this time the government of the world... do not persecute the Christian religion. Indeed, they favour it, honour our priests and the saints of the Lord and confer benefits on churches and monasteries.[6]

The following document by Omar shows us the kind of under-standing and concept of justice God grants to man, provided that he adopts the character traits described in the Qur'an:

This is the security which 'Umar, the servant of God, the com-mander of the faithful, grants to the people of Ælia. He grants to all, whether sick or sound, security for their lives, their pos-sessions, their churches and their crosses, and for all that concerns their religion. Their churches shall not be changed into dwelling places, nor destroyed, neither shall they nor their appurtenances be in any way diminished, nor the crosses of the inhabitants nor aught of their possessions, nor shall any constraint be put upon them in the matter of their faith, nor shall any one of them be harmed.[7]

All these are very important examples revealing the understanding of justice and compassion of true believers. In a verse God commands the following:

> **God commands you to return to their owners the things you hold on trust and, when you judge between people, to judge with justice. How excellent is what God exhorts you to do! God is All-Hearing, All-Seeing. (Qur'an, 4:58)**

Canon Taylor, one of the mission leaders of the Anglican Church, expresses the beauty revealed by the Islamic morality in one of his speeches as follows:

> It [Islam] brought out the fundamental dogmas of religion – the unity and greatness of God, that He is merciful and righteous, that He claims obedience to His will, resignation and faith. It proclaimed the responsibility of man, a future life, a day of judgment, and stern retribution to fall upon the wicked; and enforced the duties of prayer, almsgiving, fasting and benevolence. It thrust aside the artificial virtues, the religious frauds and follies, the perverted moral sentiments, and the verbal subtleties of theological disputants... It gave hope to the slave, brotherhood to mankind, and recognition to the fundamental facts of human nature.[8]

The false assertion that people in conquered countries converted to Islam under threat has also been disproved by Western researchers, and the justice and compassionate attitude of Muslims has been con-

At the time of the Prophet Muhammad (pbuh), a just and compassionate policy was practised in relation to the People of the Book.

firmed. L.Browne, a Western researcher, expresses this situation in the following words:

> Incidentally these well-established facts dispose of the idea so widely fostered in Christian writings that the Muslims, wherever they went, forced people to accept Islam at the point of the sword.[9]

In his book *The Prospects of Islam*, Browne goes on to say that the

The Ottoman Empire, a Muslim state, granted its subjects religious freedom. Thus a peaceful multi-cultural mosaic was to be found in Ottoman lands. The state protected its citizens in accordance with Muslim moral teaching, providing for its poor no matter what religion they practised.

real motive behind the Muslims' conquests was the brotherhood of Islam. The vast majority of Muslim administrators who have reigned over the Muslim lands throughout history continued to treat the members of other religions with the utmost compassion and respect. Within the borders of all Islamic states, both Jews and Christians lived in safety and enjoyed freedom.

The reign of the Seljuk Turks and that of the Ottoman Empire were also marked by the just and compassionate outlook of Islam. In his book, *The Preaching of Islam*, Thomas Arnold explains the Christians' willingness to come under Seljuk rule because of this attitude:

> This same sense of security of religious life under Muslim rule led many of the Christians of Asia Minor, also, about the same time, to welcome the advent of the Saljuq Turks as their deliverers... In the reign of Michael VIII (1261-1282), the Turks were often invited to take possession of the smaller towns in the interior of Asia Minor by the inhabitants, that they might escape from the tyranny of the empire; and both rich and poor often emigrated into Turkish dominions.[10]

Malik Shah, the ruler of the Islamic Seljuk Empire during its brightest age, approached the people in the conquered lands with great compassion and justice and thus was remembered with respect and love by them. All objective historians refer to the justice and compassion of Malik Shah in their works. His compassion also kindled feelings of love towards him in the hearts of the People of the Book. For this reason, unprecedented in history, many cities came under Malik Shah's rule of their own free will. Sir Thomas Arnold also mentions Odo de Diogilo, a monk of St. Denis, who participated in the Second Crusade as the private chaplain of Louis VII, refers in his memoirs to the justice administered by Muslims regardless of the subjects' religious affiliation. Based on the graphic account of Odo de Diogilo, Sir Thomas Arnold writes:

> The situation of the survivors would have been utterly hopeless, had not the sight of their misery melted the hearts of the Muhammadans to pity. They tended the sick and relieved the poor and starving with open-handed liberality. Some even bought up the French money which the Greeks had got out of

the pilgrims by force or cunning, and lavishly distributed it samong the needy. So great was the contrast between the kind treatment the pilgrims received from [them] . and the cruelty of their fellow-Christians, the Greeks, who imposed forced labour upon them, beat them, and robbed them of what little they had left, that many of them voluntarily embraced the faith of their deliverers. As the old chronicler [Odo de Diogilo] says: "Avoiding their co-religionists who had been so cruel to them, they went in safety among the infidels who had compassion upon them, and, as we heard, more than three thousand joined themselves to the Turks when they retired."[11]

These statements by historians reveal that Muslim administrators who truly adopted the morality of Islam always ruled with compassion and justice. Likewise, the history of the Ottoman Empire which ruled lands on three continents for centuries abounds with examples of justice.

The way the Jews settled in Ottoman lands during the time of Sultan Beyazid II, after being subjected to massacre and exile in the Catholic kingdoms of Spain and Portugal, is a fine example of the compassion that Islamic morality brings with it. The Catholic monarchs who ruled much of Spain at the time brought grave pressure to bear on the Jews who had formerly lived in peace under Muslim rule in Andalusia. While Muslims, Christians and Jews were able to live side by side in peace in Andalusia, the Catholic monarchs tried to force the whole country to become Christian, and declared war on the Muslims while oppressing the Jews. As a result, the last Muslim ruler in the Granada region of southern Spain was overthrown in 1492. Muslims were subjected to terrible slaughter, and those Jews who refused to change their religion were sent into exile.

One group of these Jews without a homeland sought shelter in

In 1492, the Jews who refused to convert were exiled from Spain by King Ferdinand and Queen Isabella (on the left). The Jews were accepted by the Ottoman Empire, a haven of Islamic justice and compassion.

the Ottoman Empire, and the state allowed them to do so. The Ottoman fleet, under the command of Kemal Reis, brought the exiled Jews, and those Muslims who had survived the slaughter, to the land of the Ottomans.

Sultan Beyazid II has gone down in history as a most pious believer, and in the spring of 1492 he settled these Jews who had been expelled from Spain in certain parts of his empire, around Edirne, and Thessalonica in present-day Greece. Most of the 25,000 Turkish Jews living in Turkey today are the ancestors of those Spanish Jews. They practice their religion and customs, which they brought from Spain some 500 years ago and continue to live most comfortably with their own schools, hospitals, old people's homes, cultural associations and newspapers. In the same way that they have traders and businessmen, they also have representatives in numerous professions, from technical subjects to advertising, with increasingly developing intellectual circles. While Jewish communities in many countries in Europe have for

Sultan Beyazid II was a devout Muslim. He welcomed the Jews who were fleeing from Spanish persecution, and afforded them the freedom to practise their religion in Muslim lands.

centuries been exposed to the fear of anti-Semitic racist attacks, those in Turkey have lived in peace and security. This example alone is enough to demonstrate the compassion that Islam brings with it and its understanding of justice.

The compassion and affection exhibited by Sultan Beyazid II applied to all the Ottoman sultans. When Sultan Mehmet the Conqueror conquered Istanbul, he allowed the Christians and the Jews to live freely there. André Miquel, who is known for the valuable works he has written about the just and compassionate practices of Muslims and the world of Islam, says:

> The Christian communities lived under a well administered state that they did not have during the Byzantine and Latin periods. They were never subjected to systematic persecution. On the contrary, the empire and especially Istanbul had become a refuge for Spanish Jews who were tortured. People were

Sultan Mehmet the Conqueror granted many concessions to the Patriarchate. The Patriarch enjoyed autonomy for the first time in history, under Turkish rule. In the picture we see Sultan Mehmet the Conqueror receiving the Patriarch.

never Islamized by force; the movements of Islamization took place as a result of social processes.[12]

The non-Muslims were granted many rights also in the pre-Ottoman Islamic states. Georgetown University's Professor of Religion and International Relations John L. Esposito describes how Jews and Christians who came under the administration of Muslim states met with enormous understanding:

> For many non-Muslim populations in Byzantine and Persian territories already subjugated to foreign rulers, Islamic rule meant an exchange of rulers, the new ones often more flexible and tolerant, rather than a loss of independence. Many of these populations now enjoyed greater local autonomy and often paid lower taxes... Islam proved a more tolerant religion, providing greater religious freedom for Jews and indigenous Christians.[13]

Those who believe and do not mix up their belief with any wrongdoing, they are the ones who are safe...
(Qur'an, 6:82)

THE REAL FACE OF THE TERRORISTS WHO ACT IN THE NAME OF RELIGION

*A*ll these examples reveal that organising acts of terror against innocent people is utterly against Islam and no Muslim who takes as his guide the verses of the Qur'an and the practices of the Prophet Muhammad (pbuh) could ever commit such crime. On the contrary, Muslims are responsible for stopping these people, that is removing "mischief on earth" and bringing peace and security to all people all over the world.

It is not possible to talk about "Christian terror", "Jewish terror" or "Islamic terror". Indeed, an examination into the background of the perpetrators of these acts, regardless of their faith, reveal that the terrorism in question is not a religious but a social phenomenon.

Crusaders: Barbarians Who Trampled Their Own Religion

As mentioned earlier, the true message of a religion or a system of belief can be at times distorted by its own pseudo-adherents. The Crusaders, whose period constitutes a dark episode in Christian history, are an example of this type of distortion.

The Crusaders were European Christians who undertook expeditions from the end of the 11th century onwards to recover the Holy Land (Palestine and the surrounding area) from the Muslims. They set out with a so-called religious goal, yet they laid waste to each acre of land they entered spreading fear wherever they went. They subjected civilians along their way to mass executions and plundered many villages and towns. Their conquest of Jerusalem, where Muslims, Jews and Christians lived under Islamic rule in peace, became the scene of immense bloodshed. They massacred all the Muslims and Jews in the city without mercy.

In the words of one historian, **"They killed all the Saracens and the Turks they found... whether male of female."**[13] One of the Crusaders, Raymond of Aguiles, in his own eyes boasted of this violence:

> Wonderful sights were to be seen. Some of our men (and this was more merciful) cut off the heads of their enemies; others shot them with arrows, so that they fell from the towers; others tortured them longer by casting them into the flames. **Piles of heads, hands and feet were to be seen in the streets of the city.** It was necessary to pick one's way over the bodies of men and horses. But these were small matters compared to what happened at the Temple of Solomon, a place where religious services are normally chanted ... in the Temple and porch of Solomon, **men rode in blood up to their knees and bridle reins.**[14]

In two days, the Crusader army killed some 40,000 Muslims in the barbaric ways just described.[15]

The Crusaders' barbarism was so excessive that, during the Fourth Crusade, they plundered Constantinople (present-day Istanbul), a Christian city, and stole the golden objects from the churches.

Of course, all this barbarism was utterly against the essence of Christianity. Christianity, in the words of the Gospel, is a **"message of love"**. In the Gospel according to Matthew, it is said that the Prophet Jesus (pbuh) said to his followers, **"Love your enemies and pray for those who persecute you"** (Matthew, 5:44). In the Gospel according to Luke, it is said that the Prophet Jesus (pbuh) said, **"To him who strikes you on the cheek, offer the other also."** (Luke, 6:29) In no part of the Gospels is there any reference to the legitimacy of violence; thus murdering innocent people is unimaginable. You can find the concept of "murdering the innocent" in the Bible; but only in the cruel King Herod's attempt to kill the Prophet Jesus (pbuh) while he was a baby.

If Christianity is a religion based on love that accommodates no violence, how did Christian Crusaders carry out some of the most violent acts in history? The major reason for this was that the Crusaders were mainly made up of ignorant people. These masses, who knew almost nothing about their religion, who had probably never read or even seen the Bible once in their lifetime, and who were for the most part completely unaware of the moral values of the Bible, were led into barbarism under the conditioning of Crusaders' slogans which presented this violence falsely as "God's Will". Employing this fraudulent method, many were encouraged to commit dreadful acts strictly forbidden by God.

It is worth mentioning that in that period, Eastern Christians – the people of Byzantium, for instance – who were culturally far ahead of Western Christians, espoused more humane values. Both before and after the Crusaders' conquests, Orthodox Christians managed to live together with Muslims. According to Terry Jones, the BBC commentator, with the withdrawal of the Crusaders from Middle East, "civilized life started again and members of the three monotheistic faiths returned to peaceful coexistence."[16]

The example of the Crusaders is indicative of a general phenome-

non. The more the adherents of an ideology are uncivilised, intellectually underdeveloped and ignorant, the more likely they are to resort to violence. This also holds true for ideologies that have nothing to do with religion. All communist movements around the world are prone to violence. Yet the most savage and bloodthirsty of them were the Khmer Rouge in Cambodia. This was because they were the most ignorant.

In the same way ignorant people can carry every idea espousing violence to the point of madness, so they can also involve violence in the Divine religions, which are absolutely opposed to violence. As in the Christian and Jewish worlds, examples of this have also taken place in the Islamic world and are still taking place today.

It is essential to refer to the character of the Bedouins in the time of our Prophet (pbuh) in order to see the true face of those who commit terror in the name of religion:

Christianity is a religion based on love, yet Crusaders carried out some of the most violent acts in history. These masses, who knew almost nothing about their religion, and who had probably never read the Bible once in their lifetime, were led into barbarism under the conditioning of slogans which presented this violence falsely as "God's Will".

The Bedouin Character in the Qur'an

In the period of the Prophet Muhammad (pbuh), there existed two basic social structures in Arabia. City-dwellers and Bedouins (desert Arabs). A sophisticated culture prevailed in Arab towns. Commercial relations linked the towns to the outer world, which contributed to the formation of good manners among Arabs dwelling in cities. They had refined aesthetic values, enjoyed literature and especially poetry. Desert Arabs, on the other hand, were the nomad tribes living in the desert who had a very crude culture. Utterly unaware of arts and literature, most of them developed an unrefined character.

Islam was born and developed among the inhabitants of Mecca, the most important city of the peninsula. However, as Islam spread to the rest of the peninsula, all the tribes in Arabia embraced it. Among these tribes were also desert Arabs, who were somehow problematic: their cultural background prevented some of them from grasping the profundity and noble spirit of Islam. Of this God states the following in a verse:

> **The desert Arabs are the worst in disbelief and hypocrisy, and more fitted to be ignorant of the limits which God has sent down to His Messenger. But God is Knowing, Wise. (Qur'an, 9:97)**

Some among the desert Arabs who were "worst in disbelief and hypocrisy" and prone to disobey God's commands, became a part of the Islamic community in the Prophet's (pbuh) time. But in subsequent periods, due to erroneous interpretations and attitudes, some of them have given rise to bodies incompatible with the moral values of Islam.

The sect called "Kharijites" that emerged among the Bedouins was an example. The most distinctive trait of this perverse sect (which was called "Kharijites", literally "those who leave", because they greatly deviated from Sunni practices), was their wild and fanatical nature. The "Kharijites", who had little understanding of the essence of Islam

Bedouins were nomadic tribes of the desert at the time of the Prophet Muhammad (pbuh). Because of the harsh conditions in which they lived, they came to possess a hard and rough culture.

or of the virtues and the values of the Qur'an, waged war against all other Muslims basing this war on a few Qur'anic verses about which they made distorted interpretations. Furthermore, they carried out "acts of terrorism". Hazrat Ali (ra), who was one of the closest companions of the Prophet (pbuh) and was described as the "gate of the city of knowledge", was assassinated by a Kharijite.

In other words, just as the Crusaders distorted and misinterpreted Christianity as a teaching of brutality, some perverted groups emerging in the Islamic world misinterpreted Islam and resorted to brutality. What is common to these sects and the Crusaders was their ignorant, unrefined and uncultivated nature, lacking a true understanding of their religion. The violence they resorted to resulted from this lack of understanding, rather than from the religion they claimed to espouse. They didn't even know the basic sources of their religion and acted on the superstitious beliefs they invented.

It would be completely wrong to think that the Bedouin character was limited to that time and no longer exists. The presence of people with the same character today is notable. These people, who like nobody apart from themselves or the group to which they belong, and even seek to portray the use of violence against those who do not share their faith as a religious requirement, harbour numerous flaws of logic. Denouncing people as unbelievers and misinterpretation of retaliation in kind are examples of these:

The corrupted rationale of those who shed blood in the name of Islam

In the Islamic world, some Muslims who believe in the same God, who accept the Prophet Muhammad (pbuh) as His messenger and the Qur'an as the true Book accuse one another of divorcing themselves from the faith and of infidelity and kill one another. The mass killings of Shias and the destruction of Shia mosques that have recently cropped up have drawn attention to a radical deviance in the Islamic world. The attacks of some Shia groups against Sunnis in some regions such as Iraq have also contributed to this picture: However, this sanguinary mindset is not limited to these radical organizations only nor it is a new ailment.

What is responsible for those Muslims being killed in Egypt only because they are Shias, or those murdered and dragged through the streets of Iraq only because they are Sunnis are the rulings, or fatwas, issued by some so-called scholars who claim to speak on behalf of Islam. These so-called scholars speak in their mosques or appear on TV channels and drag mostly ignorant people into such brutality with their fatwas. In the Middle East, this flawed concept of religion based on superstitions is seen in the fierce struggle between Shia and Sunni groups within the same country. Meanwhile they are also seen in sectarian wars between countries that are waged by means of proxy groups and organizations. Of course the violence perpetrated by these groups is wrong. But that mistake cannot be corrected without a return to the Qur'an, the essence of the faith.

Denouncing People as Unbelievers

This ruthless spirit of dissention considers shedding the blood of the innocent as an "act of worship", it refuses to grant the right to life for those who do not adhere to their own understanding of faith and it causes the spread of this sedition which incessantly sheds blood in the Islamic countries. One of the problems at the base of this deviant ideology is "takfir":

"Takfir" means declaring a person [or a group] an unbeliever (kafir), accusing him of divorcing himself from the faith of Islam. When

wait (the Imam Ja'far as-Sadiq Mosque bombing)

Attack on a mosque in Yemen

Camp Speicher massacre, where some 1,700 Shia Iraqi Air Force cadets were killed

the groups referred to as "takfiri" arrive at this verdict about a person or a group, they also declare it obligatory for these people to be killed in line with their bigoted un-Islamic understanding based on superstitions. However in the Qur'an, God does not grant any human being the right to reject or not accept one's adherence to Islam. On the other hand, even if a person swerves to irreligion after his faith his punishment is for God to decide.

> **The judgment concerning anything you differ about is God's concern... (Qur'an, 42:10)**
> **... God alone is qualified to judge. His order is to worship none but Him. That is in truth the straight and upright religion, but most of mankind simply do not know. (Qur'an, 12:40)**

In our day, some Sunni groups declare Shias unbelievers while Shias declare Sunnis unbelievers. We see that they mention one another's name with hatred, that they do not pray together and in many regions they kill one another in a fierce struggle. The rationale of takfir that has entered into the religion of Islam has no place in the Qur'an; this sedition is based on a so-called hadith known as the "'al-Firqat al-

In our day, some Sunni groups declare Shias unbelievers while Shias declare Sunnis unbelievers. We see that they do not pray together. The rationale of takfir that has entered into the religion of Islam, however, has no place in the Qur'an.

Najiyah" (the Saved Sect) ascribed to our Prophet (pbuh). The most widely referred to part of this fabricated hadith – one that is part of various narrations but has no foundation in the verses of the Qur'an – is as follows:

"My nation will split-up into seventy-three sects, all of them in the Fire save one: that which I and my Companions are upon."

This line of reasoning takes place in different narrations with various additions or deletions. For instance, in at-Tirmidhi there is no mentioning of *"All of them in the Fire save one."* In Hakim, this hadith is narrated very briefly saying, **"My nation will be divided into some seventy sects; the largest one acts of its own accord and makes what is lawful unlawful, and makes that which is unlawful lawful."** *(Al-Mustadrak, 4/430)*

The disintegration and fragmentation we see in the Islamic world is the outcome of a mindset that does not find the Qur'an to be sufficient, and attempts bringing about a different form of Islam through superstitions, bigotry and fabricated hadiths and traditions. Instead of following the example of the Muslims at the time of our Prophet (pbuh), such bigoted and fanatical groups make up their own fabrications of what is lawful and unlawful and believe only in their own conjectures; they declare other Muslims who practice Islam in a different way to be apostates. However, God has precluded the grounds for such a mindset quite clearly in the Qur'an:

You who believe! When you go out to fight in the Way of God verify things carefully. Do not say, "You are not a believer, to someone who greets you as a Muslim, simply out of desire for the goods of this world. With God there is booty in abundance. That is the way you were before but God has been kind to you. ... (Qur'an, 4:94)

In the hadiths, we see that our Prophet (pbuh) guided Muslims to shy away from accusing one another with disbelief:

... he who labelled anyone with unbelief or called him the enemy of God, and he was in fact not so, it rebounded on him. (Sahih Muslim, Book 1, Hadith 118)

... cursing a believer is like murdering him, and whoever accuses a believer of disbelief, then it is as if he had killed him." (Sahih Bukhari, Book 73, Hadith 126)

Whoever prays like us and faces our Qibla and eats our slaughtered animals is a Muslim and is under God's and His Apostle's protection. So do not betray God by betraying those who are in His protection. (Sahih Bukhari, Book 8, Hadith 386)

Any person who called his brother: O unbeliever (has in fact done an act by which this unbelief) would return to one of them. If it were so, as he asserted (then the unbelief of man was confirmed but if it was not true), then it returned to him (to the man who labelled it on his brother Muslim). (Sahih Muslim, Book 1, Hadith 117)

When a man calls his brother an unbeliever, it returns (at least) to one of them. (Sahih Muslim, Book 1, Hadith 116)

At the time of our Prophet (pbuh), there were hypocrites, those who did not have faith in their hearts and of course deviators: God has informed us in many verses in the Qur'an that there were people who were not pleased with the judgment of the Prophet (pbuh), who displayed abnormalities in their conduct and morals, and even some who were covertly in disbelief. However, our Prophet (pbuh) pursued communicating religion and made efforts to strengthen the faith of everyone without exception, and never indicted them for disbelief. It is not possible for a servant of God to judge any person regarding his faith or punish him on the basis of this.

God informs us that Muslims' differing among themselves or being in dispute is an error that must be accounted for in the hereafter:

As for those who divide up their religion and form into sects, you have nothing whatsoever to do with them. Their affair will go back to God and then He will inform them about what they did. (Qur'an, 6:159)

In the Qur'an, we are informed that Muslims should be united, that they should live as brothers, that they must not separate and they must be friends and be in ranks like well-built walls and not quarrel:

Obey God and His Messenger and do not quarrel among yourselves lest you lose heart and your momentum disappear. And be steadfast. God is with the steadfast. (Qur'an, 8:46)

Do not be like those who split up and differed after the clear signs came to them. They will have a terrible punishment. (Qur'an, 3:105)

Instead of contributing to the unity of Muslims, those who make statements of separation and hatred or give fatwas declaring others to be in a state of disbelief incite Muslims to violence and bloodshed. Those who wage a so-called jihad against their fellow Muslims based on the pronouncements of their sect leaders are in grave error, which they will not be able to account for in the hereafter. God commands making peace between Muslims as follows:

The believers are brothers, so make peace between your brothers and have fear of God so that hopefully you will gain mercy. (Qur'an, 49:10)

Misinterpretation of Qisas (retaliation in kind)

The commandments in the Qur'an are intended to eliminate the arbitrary punishments resulting from personal vengeance and grudges, a common occurrence in Arab society of the time of the Prophet Muhammad (pbuh). The principle of deterrence prevalent throughout the Qur'an is also visible in the commandment of "qisas" and protects life by preventing and eliminating crime:

"You who believe! Retaliation is prescribed for you in the case of people killed: free man for free man, slave for slave, female for female. But if someone is absolved by his brother, blood-money should be claimed with correctness and

paid with good will. That is an easement and a mercy from your Lord. Anyone who goes beyond the limits after this will receive a painful punishment. (Qur'an, 2:178)

The noteworthy point about this verse concerning retaliation in kind is that it encourages forgiveness and pardoning, and says that these are better forms of behavior. In this sense, there is life in retaliation for us.

There are some requirements for retaliation as to the manner of its application – and by whom as well as to whom. In the Qur'an, God explains that the ones who are entitled to retaliation are the "next of kin":

Do not kill any person God has made inviolate, except with the right to do so. If someone is wrongly killed **We have given authority to his next of kin.** But he should not be excessive in taking life.... (Qur'an, 17:33)

In addition to that, as explained in the Qur'an 5/178, the said next of kin has the option to waive retaliation and ask for compensation, which is favouring forgiveness. In another verse, God explains that forgiving is preferable:

> The repayment of a bad action is one equivalent to it. But if someone pardons and puts things right, his reward is with God. Certainly He does not love wrongdoers. (Qur'an, 42:40)

As is clear in the verses of the Qur'an, the best course of action is forgiving and improving. It is explained that this is a behaviour that God favoured even before Islam:

> We prescribed for them in it [the Torah]: a life for a life, an eye for an eye, a nose for a nose, an ear for an ear, a tooth for a tooth, and retaliation for wounds. But if anyone forgoes that as a sadaqa, it will act as expiation for him. Those who do not judge by what God has sent down, such people are wrongdoers. (Qur'an, 5:45)

In the eyes of the Qur'an, it is wrong to respond to evil with evil

When the leaders of the terrorist organizations that abuse the religion of Islam, or the clergy that seek to legitimize them, are asked why they issue fatwas allowing such massacres and suicide bombings, they will say that it is in retaliation for attacks on Muslims. It is true that Muslims have been massacred in various parts of the world, wronged, oppressed and treated unfairly; nonetheless, God forbids responding to tyranny with tyranny. The way that forgiveness is recommended in the commandments concerning retaliation in kind is a reflection of this fact.

In the eyes of Islam, guilt is personal, and retaliation in kind must not be applied out of arbitrary feelings of revenge

God forbids wickedness in the Qur'an. Furthermore, Islam states the principle of the "individuality of crime." Bombing people, attacking them regardless of them being innocent civilians, children, women or elderly is nothing but sheer murder. Likewise, killing people merely for the reason of their nationality, faith, or sect or taking revenge based on such reasons, is also completely against Islam.

At the basis of the law of war in Islam is being just, and always aiming to establish peace, compromise and forgive. The goal is always ensuring the continuance of life for oneself as well as for others. For these reasons, the principle of "retaliation" that God allowed only as a deterrent principle against deliberate killing, and only through certain restrictions and conditions and over which forgiveness should be chosen, cannot be applied against individuals or societies based on personal thoughts of vengeance.

The commandments in the Qur'an are perfectly clear, but the existence of people who seek to perpetrate terror in the name of religion makes it essential to investigate the psychology of terror:

Terrorist Methods and Diseased Psychology

The concept of terror has a wider meaning in today's language. Generally it refers to the armed conflict carried on by radical ideological groups. In general, terror means intimidation. But this intimidation encompasses a broad field including the whole lives of people who feel the intense threat of fear and violence. Terror includes intense and systematic intimidation designed to make people adopt a certain way of thinking and behaviour, as well as every kind of violent act carried out to produce this intimidation. But in every situation, the target of terrorism is directly or indirectly the citizens themselves.

Terror organisations use terror to rally support. The intimidation they use is calculated to increase their strength and so to gain the support of some or all the citizens.

The first thing that people think of when we mention the word "terror" is generally the kind known as "leftist terror", but there is also a kind of terror found in Third World countries and practiced by dictatorial regimes. Actually the reality here is nothing other than a massive implementation of leftist terror tactics. A dictator or a group in power is oppressive, using their power only for personal gain and for this reason they experience various kinds of social opposition. In this situation, the dictatorial regime always resorts to the same formula to show that it is stronger than the opposition; they inaugurate the use of terror so that citizens will be afraid and their own power is consolidated.

For terrorists, killing people, wreaking destruction and havoc is a way of life. For them, bloodshed is a deliberate act. They can shoot innocents, throw a bomb at children or blow up a house without any feeling of compassion.

Terror organisations, on the other hand, in accordance with the ideologies they espouse, claim that their aim is to remove a government and its administrators which they regard as illegitimate and cruel and, in so doing, that they will reach their goal of establishing a happier and more just way of life. However, this is not a realistic claim. In the Qur'an, in the first verses of Surat al-Baqara, God issues this command to those who think in this way:

When they are told, "Do not cause corruption on the earth," they say, "We are only putting things right." No indeed! They are the corrupters, but they are not aware of it. (Qur'an, 2:11-12)

For terrorists, killing people is a way of life. They may shoot innocent people without pity and throw bombs at children. For them shedding blood is a pleasure. They have ceased to be human beings and turned into raving savage beasts. If there is anyone among them who shows the least feeling of compassion, they brand him as a coward or a traitor and demote him. Often they use their guns against one another and carry out bloody purges against internal factions in their own organisation.

Terrorism is nothing other than a totally diabolical source of bloodshed. Whoever supports this cycle of savagery is defending a satanic system. If a terrorist uses religious language and symbols, this must not deceive anyone. Terrorists who hide under the cloak of false religion are doubly guilty, both of the blood they have shed and for the anti-religious propaganda they have spread while committing these crimes in the name of religion.

Terror and religion are completely opposed to each other. Terrorism adopts the way of aggression, murder, conflict, cruelty and misery. But according to the Qur'an, all these things are kinds of oppression. God enjoins peace, harmony, goodwill and compromise. He forbids terror and every kind of act that does not promote peace, and, condemns those who commit such acts:

But as for those who break God's contract after it has been agreed and sever what God has commanded to be joined, and cause corruption in the earth, the curse will be upon them. They will have the Evil Abode. (Qur'an, 13:25)

The basic quality that terror and those who are infected by its cruelty have in common is that the fear and love of God is something completely alien to them. Their hearts have become hardened and they are spiritually ill.

A Terrorist Is Without Pity, Whose Only Purpose Is to Destroy

The founder of Russian Anarchism, Michael Bakunin and his disciple Nechayev define an "ideal" terrorist in this way:

The whole work of his [a revolutionist's] existence, not only in words, but also in deeds, is at war with the existing order of society, and with the whole so-called civilized world, with its laws, morals and customs, he is an uncompromising opponent... He knows only one science; the science of destruction.[17]

As understood from these words of Bakunin and Nechayev, terrorists are people who sever their relationship with every material and spiritual institution thereby rejecting every moral value, and who view these institutions as impediments to their designs. Bakunin also said, "Day and night dare he [a revolutionist] have only one thought, one aim: the unmerciful destruction; while he, cold-blooded and without rest, follows that aim, he himself must be ready to die at any time and ready to kill with his own hands any one who seeks to thwart his aims." In his *Ground-Work for the Social Revolution*, there is this description of what kind of person a terrorist must be:

Stringent with himself he must also be to others. All weak sen-

timent towards relation, friendship, love and thankfulness must be suppressed through the only cold passion of the revolutionary work.[18]

These words lay bare the dark face of terrorism and show that it is completely opposed to the religion of Islam which is founded on peace, compassion and love.

Terrorists see their destructive acts as a means of propaganda; they hope to spread fear by destroying people and property.

Islam Condemns All Acts of Terror and Violence, and So It Does With The Boston Attack

The horrible terrorist attack on the Boston Marathon in the USA in 2013 was condemned by all true Muslims, just like 9/11 and other terrorist attacks were.

This terrorist act, in which three people lost their lives and hundreds were injured, was a savage act of misguided foolishness designed to set the Western and Islamic worlds against one another. Such ruthless acts have been used many times in different countries to try and give the West the impression that Islam is a faith that regards violence and terror as legitimate. Those acts have been successful in no small measure. As a matter of fact, in the wake of the Boston attack statements were made by some media organizations in the USA encouraging violence against Muslims and their isolation from society. There have always been such provocations and they will continue to happen. However, Muslims have a very important duty amidst this setting: not limiting themselves to condemning terrorist attacks and talking about the real Islamic morality to the entirety of humanity.

Whoever claims to be a Muslim and says that the faith advocates acts of terror or violence is either an agent provocateur claiming to be a Muslim, or someone who is

In the moral teaching of the Qur'an, to kill an innocent person is an act of immense cruelty. God forbids terrorist acts and condemns those who commit them.

wholly ignorant of the faith. Someone who says such things out of ignorance will mend his ways if told what the Qur'an truly says. People can only be properly informed about Islam if no credence is attached to provocation. If everyone knows that Islam views violence and hatred as unacceptable there will be no more issues for provocateurs or extremists to rage about.

There are people trying to incite hostility toward Islam in the Christian and Jewish world, and there are also people trying to incite hostility toward Christianity and Judaism in the Islamic world. These people are bigoted fanatics who issue provocative statements based not on the Qur'an, but on hadiths they fabricate themselves. This is a very serious and a very real problem in the Islamic world, and we cannot simply dismiss it. All true Muslims are deeply uneasy at such people being regarded as members of the Islamic world and representatives of the faith because these people have nothing to do with the values espoused by Islam. They have deprived themselves of fine feelings such as love, affection and compassion. They are filled with hatred and rage, not only for members of other faiths, but also for most Muslims from different sects. They may hate someone they have never met solely because he belongs to a different group. This is a perverse and unacceptable perspective for Muslims.

Causing members of different faiths and/or ethnicities to fall out and inciting conflict among them has been a technique successfully employed by those wishing to spread war throughout the course of history. Yet this world is wide and fertile enough for everyone to live in happiness and peace and well-being. There is no real reason for conflict or resorting to violence. All the supposed reasons for war and conflict are hollow ruses.

It is much, much easier to live in peace and love than in conflict and war. For example, it is unacceptable for either Palestinians or Israelis to have to live behind walls in fear of bombs, rockets and other weapons. This plight of these two peoples, one descended from the Prophet Ishmael and the other from the Prophet Jacob (peace be upon them both), is a disgrace on all mankind.

Our hope is that people with radical views will ultimately fade away within the moderate, loving and respectful views held by rational people – historically, radical movements inevitably burn out or destroy themselves – but for that to happen it is absolutely essential for sensible people in the Islamic, Christian and Judaic worlds to act as one in a spirit of solidarity. An alliance of good people is essential. This alliance must be brought about, not solely between Muslims, but also with the People of the Book. Otherwise, neither terror nor acts of violence can ever be entirely overcome.

*God calls to the Abode of
Peace and He guides whom
He wills to a straight path.
(Qur'an, 10:25)*

THE OUTLOOK OF ISLAM
ON THE PEOPLE OF
THE BOOK

*A*nother important topic that has been on the agenda with the acts of terrorism against the United States is the relation between the Western and Islamic world. As is known, by the 90s, some intellectuals were falsely suggesting that a struggle would take place between the West and Islamic world in the near future. This is the basic theme of Samuel Huntington's well-known thesis "The Clash of Civilisations". However, this thesis – better called as "The Clash of Ignorance" by Edward W. Said – rests on an imaginary scenario generated by the exaggeration of the influence of some radical and ignorant factions to be found in these two civilisations. Huntington's idea of "clashes of civilisations" is a theory without any scientific, intellectual or conscientious basis. Various civilisations have always existed in different parts of the world throughout the history and these civilisations interacted with each other socially and culturally, and took part in an "exchange of civilisations." Every race, every nation, every community has a different civilisation and every civilisation has their unique qualities and people get something from all civilisations in line with the principles of mutual understanding and reconciliation.

This idea of conflict was tested in recent history through communism, which culminated in the bloody losses of the 20th century. However, what the world needs at the moment is not war, but total peace.

Moreover, policies which favour conflict can never benefit anyone and besides there can be no clash between Western civilisation and Islamic civilisation, because the beliefs of Judaism and Christianity, the tenets upon which Western civilisation is based, are in perfect harmony with Islam.

In the Qur'an, Jews and Christians are called the "People of the Book". This is because the members of these two religions abide by the Divine Books revealed by God. The outlook of Islam on the People of the Book is extremely just and compassionate.

This attitude towards the People of the Book developed during the years of the birth of Islam according to the principles in the Qur'an. At that time, Muslims were a minority, struggling to protect their faith and suffering oppression and torture from the pagans of the city of Mecca. Due to this persecution, some Muslims decided to flee Mecca and shelter in a safe country with a just ruler. The Prophet Muhammad (pbuh) told them to take refuge the Christian king of Ethiopia. The Muslims who went to Ethiopia found a very fair administration that embraced them with love and respect. The King refused the demands of the pagan messengers who had travelled to Ethiopia and asked him to surrender the Muslims to them, and announced that Muslims could live freely in his country.

These Christian attitudes of compassion, mercy, and justice, are referred to in a verse of the Qur'an which states:

... You will find the people most affectionate to those who believe are

those who say, "We are Christians." That is because some of them are priests and monks and because they are not arrogant. **(Qur'an, 5:82)**

Common Beliefs and Values Shared by Muslims and the People of the Book

Christian and Muslim beliefs have many aspects in common. Judaism too shares many beliefs with Islam. In the Qur'an, God relates that Muslims share the same faith with the People of the Book and that they say to them **"We have faith in what has been sent down to us and what was sent down to you. Our God and your God are one and we submit to Him."** (Qur'an, 29:46)

When Muslims, Christians and Jews unite around a common word, when they understand that they are friends, not enemies, the world will be a very different, beautiful place.

All true adherents of these three great religions:

❏ believe that God has created the entire universe out of nothing and that He dominates all that exists with His omnipotence.

❏ believe that God has created man and living things in a miraculous way and that man possesses a soul granted him by God.

❏ believe in resurrection, heaven and hell and angels, and that God has created our lives with a certain destiny.

❏ believe that God sent many prophets such as the Prophet Noah (pbuh), the Prophet Abraham (pbuh), the Prophet Isaac (pbuh), the Prophet Joseph (pbuh) and the Prophet Moses (pbuh) throughout history, and they love all these prophets.

In one verse, that Muslims make no distinction among prophets is related as follows:

> **The Messenger believes in what has been sent down to him by his Lord, and so do the believers. Each one believes in God and His angels and His Books and His Messengers. We do not differentiate between any of His Messengers. They say, "We hear and we obey. Forgive us, our Lord! You are our journey's end." (Qur'an, 2:285)**

The beliefs of the People of the Book are in harmony with Muslims, not only in terms of faith-related issues, but also of moral values. Today, in a world where such immoralities as adultery, drug addiction and a model of egoism and self-seeking cruelty have grown widespread, the People of the Book and Muslims share the same virtues: Honour, chastity, humility, self-sacrifice, honesty, compassion, mercy and unconditional love.

Even though such concepts like "The End of History" and the "Clash of Civilisations" started to be popular from the 90's onwards, one fact looms in these harsh times; these concepts have no validity whatsoever and they fail to deliver any solutions. Experience has taught us that we cannot build bliss upon the misery of others. This being the case, we need to find the way of binding up these wounds together and "recovering" as soon as possible. One means to this is to understand the value that the Qur'an attaches to the People of the Book.

Today both the Muslims and the People of the Book are engaged in a broadening struggle against immoralities such as sexual perversions or drug addiction. Each of these three religions accepts chastity, honesty and self-sacrifice as the greatest virtues.

The Value Placed on the People of the Book in the Qur'an

Today all good things have been made halal [lawful] for you. <u>And the food of those given the Book [Jews and Christians] is also halal for you and your food is halal for them.</u> So are chaste women from among the believers and <u>chaste women of those given the Book before you</u> [Jews and Christians], once you have given them their dowries in marriage, not in fornication or taking them as lovers. But as for anyone who rejects faith, his actions will come to nothing and in the hereafter he will be among the losers. (Qur'an, 5:5)

This verse describes the value that Muslims place on the People of the Book with various pieces of important detail. According to this verse, a Muslim man is allowed to marry a woman of the People of the Book. This is a significant permission, because as commanded in the verse, **"Corrupt women are for corrupt men and corrupt men are for corrupt women, good women are for good men and good men are for good women..."** (Qur'an, 24:26), Muslims have a responsibility to marry good, clean people. This indicates that Jews and Christians are also good, clean people.

In addition, there is a very important criterion in this verse. A Muslim will intend to take a Jewish or Christian woman as his wife, to call her "darling" or "beloved," to start a family with her, to spend his life with her and even to spend eternal life with her. This is the sole person throughout his life with whom he will share all his troubles and all his happiness. These two look after one another when they are ill, and trust one another.

According to the fanatics' way of thinking, however, a person should feel enmity toward the woman he calls "beloved," with whom he spends his life and entrusts his own life to, the mother of his children, and declare her to be cursed only because she is a Christian or a Jew. One would have to be profoundly psychologically disturbed to do that. This verse describes the love to be shown to a Jew or Christian by a rational Muslim who heeds the Qur'an.

The verse also bestows a special authorization on Muslims: the authority to eat food prepared by the People of the Book. This is very important. As we know, Muslims have to pay great attention to certain prohibitions when preparing food; pork, and meat from an animal that has not been slaughtered in the name of God, is prohibited in Islam. The fact that food prepared by Jews and Christians is made lawful shows that these people are to be trusted. The same thing also applies to Christians and Jews, and the verse makes food prepared by Muslims lawful for them.

It will also be useful to refer to another expression of friendship here. The People of the Book and Muslims can eat together under the same roof, be one another's guests, sit down at the same table and play host to one another. This is a description of friendship. What is being described is not an environment based on hatred and killing, but one of love, friendship and brotherhood.

In the Qur'an, Christians and Jews are defined as the People of the Book, and there is a command to show respect, mercy and kindness to them. Both Christians and Jews believe in God and share the same moral values as Muslims.

This is not the only verse to set out the position of the People of the Book. God praises the People of the Book in many of the Qur'an's verses. The related verses include:

Among the people of Moses there is a group who guide by the truth and act justly in accordance with it. (Qur'an, 7:159)

They are not all the same. **There is a community among the People of the Book who are upright. They recite God's signs throughout the night, and they prostrate. They have faith in God and the Last Day, and enjoin the right and forbid the wrong, and compete in doing good. They are among the righteous ones. They will not be denied the reward for any good thing they do.** God knows those who have fear of God. (Qur'an, 3:113-115)

Among the people of the Book there are some who have faith in God and in what has been sent down to you and what was sent down to them, and who are humble before God. They do not sell God's signs for a paltry price. Such people will have their reward with their Lord. And God is swift at reckoning. (Qur'an, 3:199)

As these verses clearly show, pure and sincere Jews and Christians are praised with fine words in the Qur'an and are promised a fine reward by God; God says that He will take these people into paradise. This is an expression of His love. How can a Muslim be the enemy of someone whom God loves, is pleased with and welcomes into paradise? That is impossible according to the Qur'an. Such enmity is a crime according to the Qur'an. Therefore, the fanatics who adopt false hadiths as their guide – despite the verses of the Qur'an clearly demonstrating the contrary – are committing an offense in the view of Islam by spreading hostility toward the People of the Book.

What needs to be done is to invite the People of the Book to Islam using pleasant words, and then to leave the decision up to them.

Muslims Invite the People of the Book to the "Oneness of God"

Only argue with the People of the Book in the kindest way – except in the case of those of them who do wrong – saying, <u>"We have faith in what has been sent down to us and what was sent down to you. Our God and your God are One and we submit to Him."</u> (Qur'an, 29:46)

Say, <u>"People of the Book! Come to a proposition which is the same for us and you – that we should worship none but God and not associate any partners with Him and not take one another as lords besides God."</u> If they turn away, say, "Bear witness that we are Muslims." (Qur'an, 3:64)

These verses show that the duty of Muslims is not to disparage the People of the Book, force them into a corner, feel hatred for or kill them, as some fabricated hadiths suggest. It is simply to summon them to the oneness of God in the most pleasant manner. Monotheism is the fundamental doctrine in all three faiths. Muslims can meet with and speak to the People of the Book, preach to them and call on them to believe in the oneness of God and all the sacred scriptures that have been sent down. Communication, preaching and friendship exist among them. According to the Qur'an, a Muslim has a responsibility to speak kindly to a Jew or a Christian when he sees one and to invite him to believe in the oneness of God using very kind words, rather than jostling him into a corner.

The Jews Enjoy the Right to Live in the Holy Land in the Qur'an

Since some Muslim communities are unaware of the verses of the Qur'an and are exceedingly ignorant on the subject of Islam, they strive to remove the Jews from the Holy Land or to wipe the state of Israel off the map. They are unaware that in doing this they are rebelling against the Qur'an.

According to the Qur'an, the Jews have the right to live in the Holy Land. Verses on the subject read:

> **Remember when <u>Moses said to his people</u>, "My people! Remember God's blessing to you when He appointed prophets among you and appointed kings for you, and gave you what He had not given to anyone else in all the worlds! My people! <u>Enter the Holy Land which God has ordained for you.</u> Do not turn back in your tracks and so become transformed into losers." (Qur'an, 5:20-21)**

> **We said to the <u>tribe of Israel</u> after that, "<u>Inhabit the land</u> and, when the promise of the hereafter comes, We will produce you as a motley crowd." (Qur'an, 17:104)**

As clearly shown in the verses of the Qur'an, both the Torah and the Qur'an state that Jews must exist in the Holy Land. Indeed it is a good thing for there to be Jews in the Holy Land, and that is a source of joy for true Muslims. It is an exceedingly fine thing to see a promise

Muslims want Jews, Christians and themselves to live in peace and contentment, treating each other with understanding, friendship, respect and compassion.

made by God 3,000 years ago coming true and witnessing what was foretold by the Prophet Abraham (pbuh) and the Prophet Moses (pbuh). God revealed that, "The Jews will be in those lands" thousands of years ago, and we can see that miracle manifested now. This is a wonderful state of affairs to be observed with fervour and joy.

It is of great importance to state that God imposes one essential condition on sincere believers, both in the Qur'an and the Torah – "Peace." There will be Jews in the Holy Land; there will also be Muslims and Christians there, and they will altogether ensure that love and peace prevail across the region. They will live in brotherhood. There is plenty of room for all. Nobody will be forced from his home or driven away. That will not happen. This is a religious service for Jews, Christians and Muslims all. God always wants peace for all of us.

Monasteries, Churches and Synagogues Must Be Respected according to the Qur'an

Another important fact we learn from the Qur'an is that Muslims must respect Jewish and Christian places of worship. In the Qur'an, the places of worship of the People of the Book, ie. monasteries, churches and synagogues, are mentioned as places of worship protected by God.

... if God had not driven some people back by means of others, monasteries, churches, synagogues and mosques, where God's name is mentioned much, would have been pulled down and destroyed. God will certainly help those who help Him – God is All-Strong, Almighty. (Qur'an, 22:40)

This verse shows every Muslim the importance of respecting and protecting the holy places of the People of the Book.

Indeed, the Prophet Muhammad (pbuh) also made contracts with pagans as well as the People of the Book. Pagans were always treated with justice, and when they asked to be taken under protection, their requests were readily accepted by the Prophet (pbuh). This meant that these communities sought the protection of the Messenger of God (pbuh) in the face of an attack or a wrongful accusation. Throughout his life, many non-Muslims and pagans requested protection from the Prophet Muhammad (pbuh), and he took them under his protection and ensured their security. In the Qur'an God advises that requests of pagans seeking protection be accepted by believers. Of this, God says the following:

> If any of the idolaters ask you for protection, give them protection until they have heard the words of God. Then convey them to a place where they are safe... (Qur'an, 9:6)

Jews and Christians, due to their shared commonalities with Muslims are much closer to Muslims than those who have no faith in God. Each of these religions has its book, that is, they are subject to a book sent down by God. They know what is right and what is wrong, what is lawful and what is unlawful according to their scriptures, and all revere the prophets and messengers that accompanied them. They all believe in a hereafter, and afterlife where they will have to give an account to God for all their actions. So, there is a shared foundation from where we all can unite upon.

Mosques, churches and synagogues are special places of prayer where the name of God is revered. In the Qur'an, God says that all these sanctuaries must be respected and preserved.

Rallying to a Common Formula

Concerning the People of the Book, God gives Muslims a command in the Qur'an; to rally to a common formula:

Say, "O People of the Book! Let us rally to a common formula to be binding on both us and you: That we worship none but God; that we associate no partners with Him; that we erect not, from among ourselves, Lords and patrons other than God." (Qur'an, 3:64)

This is indeed our call to Christians and Jews: As people who believe in God and follow His revelations, let us rally to a common formula – "faith". Let us love God, Who is our Creator and Lord, and follow His commands. And let us pray to God to lead us to an even straighter path.

When Muslims, Christians and Jews rally to a common formula this way; when they understand that they are friends not enemies, then the world will become a very different place. The wars in many parts of the world, enmities, fears and terrorist attacks will come to an end, and a new civilisation based on love, respect and peace will be established upon this "common formula" once an intellectual struggle is waged against radical ideas and ideologies that lead to denial of God.

There are important facts to consider for Muslims. What God teaches us in the Qur'an about different peoples and creeds is clear: The morality of the Qur'an excludes every kind of racism.

It is evident that some of the Jews who lived in the past have committed many errors which are stated and criticized in the Qur'an. But all this must not be taken by Muslims as a cause to feel hostility against all Jews. The crime committed by some Jews cannot be ascribed to Judaism and the Jewish nation.

Again a basic vantage point prescribed in the Qur'an is not to make judgements about people just because they belong to a particular

The evils in the world will come to an end when Muslims, Christians and Jews all worship God in unity, respecting their differences.

race, nation or religion. In every community, there are good people as well as wicked people. This differentiation is stated in the Qur'an. For instance, right after mentioning the rebellious nature – against God and His religion – of some people among Jews and Christians, there is reference to an exception and, said thus:

> [However] They are not all alike. Among the People of the Book there is an upright community who recite the revelation of God during the night and fall prostrate before Him. They believe in God and the Last Day, enjoin what is right and forbid what is evil, and vie with one another in good works. They are of the righteous and whatever good they do, its reward will not be denied them. God knows those who fear [Him]. (Qur'an, 3:113-115)

God revealed to all messengers that He is the Unique and that there is no one but Him Whom people must worship, serve and obey. The Divine message, conveyed to the people by God through His messengers, has been communicated to people since the creation of man. Some societies have accepted the message and followed the right path while others have denied and swerved from it. This also holds true for the present day. Some people will side with the righteous, whereas some others will plunge into mischief. This is the law of God. Those who believe should also adopt such an outlook and never forget that there may be sincere, pious people who have fear of God among the members of all religions as well as those who are far removed from the religious tenets.

Our hope is that a world will be established in which people will be able to live together in peace, no matter what race or religion they belong to, in which every racist perversion will be rejected, everyone's rights will be safeguarded and everyone will be respected. The struggle that will have to take place on intellectual grounds against radicalism and anti-religious ideologies will hopefully establish the peace that has been longed for. Of this God relates the following in the Qur'an:

> **Those who disbelieve are the friends and protectors of one another. If you do not act in this way (be friends and protectors of one another) there will be turmoil in the land and great corruption. (Qur'an, 8:73)**

> **Would that there had been more people with a vestige of good among the generations of those who came before you, who forbade corruption in the earth, other than the few among them whom We saved. ... (Qur'an, 11:116)**

Why Should the Muslims and the People of the Book Act Together?

Another important fact that draws Christianity, Judaism and Islam together and necessitates them to act together is the atheist philosophies that are so influential in our time. There is also the damage caused by various radical notions that were later made a part of the three Divine religions.

Among the best-known and most harmful philosophies of our age can be cited materialism, communism, fascism, anarchism, racism, nihilism and existentialism. Many people who believed in the false diagnoses, deceptive descriptions and explanations of these ideas on the universe, society and man, have lost their faith or doubted it. What is more, these ideologies have dragged people, societies and nations into great crises, conflicts and wars. Their share of the blame for the pain and troubles that humanity suffers from today is immense.

While they deny God and creation, all the above-mentioned ideologies are based on a so-called scientific basis; Charles Darwin's theory of evolution. Darwinism constitutes the basis of atheist philosophies. This theory briefly claims – without having any scientific basis – that living beings have evolved as a result of coincidences and by means of a struggle for life. Therefore, Darwinism sends this deceptive message to people:

"You are not responsible to any-one, you owe your life to coinci-dences, you need to struggle, and if necessary to oppress oth-ers to succeed. This world is one of conflict and self-interest".

The social messages put across by Darwinist concepts such as "Natural selection", "struggle for life", "survival of the fittest" are a means of dangerous indoctrination. This evil morality advises people to be egoistical, self-seeking, cruel and oppressive. It destroys such virtues as mercy, com-passion, self-sacrifice and humility, the moral values of the three great monotheistic religions and presents this as if it is a necessity of "the rules of life."

This Darwinist indoctrination is just the opposite of the beliefs of the People of the Book and the morality of the Qur'an. Consequently, the Darwin-ist indoctrination constitutes the foun-dation of a world which inherently opposes all the three Divine religions.

This being the case, it is necessary for the People of the Book and Muslims to co-operate, since they believe in God and accept the morality that He teach-es. The followers of these three religions should expose to the world the fallacy of Darwinism, which has no scientific basis, but which people are trying to preserve for the sake of materialist philosophy. They should co-operatively carry out an intellectual struggle against all other deceptive ideas (communism, fascism, racism) that serve atheism. They need to make an effort to explain that the radical ideas that were later made a part of every religion are wrong and tell the truth instead. Once these are realized, the world will, in a very short time, embrace peace, tranquillity and justice.

The Cruelty of Anti-Semitism Must be Stopped

Our world has seen its fair share of brutality.

From Hulagu Khan, who boasted about killing 200,000 Muslims during his violent week-long rampage in the city of Baghdad, which also resulted in the complete destruction of centuries-old heritage, to Vikings that took what they deemed desirable by force, to the modern-day Syrian regime targeting its own people, we can say that our world has witnessed some unspeakable acts of violence and still does in such places as East Turkestan, Kashmir and Iraq among many others.

However, throughout history, some groups were targeted more than others. Like the Jewish people: Their ordeal started at the hands of Pharaoh, who killed their boys and let only their girls live. The oppression against Jews continued throughout antiquity, at the hands of the Assyrians, Babylon and the Romans, who massacred and exiled Jews and destroyed their temples and cities. In medieval times, Jews were once again targeted, labelled, discriminated against and chased away from wherever they took shelter. The oppression continued in recent history when six million Jews were slaughtered by Nazis.

Today, the persecution still goes on.

Anti-Semitism in Europe lingers in the form of harassment in public areas, offensive remarks and discriminatory behaviour in social life and more terrifyingly, in the form of brutal assaults; the vandalizing and looting of Jewish businesses, burning of cars, hundreds chanting "gas the Jews," "kill the Jews," in violent protests, shootings and fire-bomb attacks against synagogues, and the recent Creteil attack in France in which a Jewish couple was brutally attacked in their home. That incident was a horrible reminder of the 2006 incident – again in France – that involved a young Jewish man being captured, tortured for weeks and then left naked to die.

France is not the only place that witnesses anti-Semitism. From Argentina to Tunisia, from Ireland to Spain, Jews seem to be caught up in a constant cycle of hatred targeting their communities. Even in the US, which is certainly well-known for its unwavering support for Israel, Jewish people are wary of divulging their identities, or practicing their religious duties in public. An unprovoked attack on a 24-year-old Jewish man wearing a kippa by four men in Brooklyn, New York;

the assault of a 12-year-old Jewish girl, who had a bottle thrown at her by a group of girls, including one who yelled, "You dirty Jew"; and the attack on a Jewish man in Los Angeles, California, who was surrounded by five male suspects who yelled "Heil Hitler!" before striking him, can be listed among the disturbing recent incidents in the US.

The Middle East is home to the worst cases of anti-Semitism, however. Especially after the recent Gaza war, hatred toward Jewish people regardless of age, gender or involvement in the conflict has risen in a disturbingly fast manner.

The persecution of Jews throughout history was basically a consequence of racist prejudices, which are definitely contrary to Islam. No Muslim should condone unjust or cruel treatment of innocent Jewish people and children.

Jews as underhanded conspirators who segregated themselves from the societies they lived in due to widespread
anti-Semitic propaganda, such as The Protocols of the Elders
of Zion. The sentiment was further fuelled with notorious lies
like the blood libel, portraying Jews as the veritable embod-
iment of evil. Today, the conflict between Israelis and Palestinians is the driving force behind this ubiquitous hatred, and
often used as a cloak to justify violence against ordinary
Jews on the streets.

Surely political administrations or individuals within a community might make mistakes. However, persecuting an
entire community based on the acts of a few would be neither Qur'anic nor moral. The Jewish people are known for
their calm and modest demeanour. They are a quiet people
that like to occupy themselves with their daily routine and
religious practices. Therefore it is even more shocking that

such a calm and reserved people have been on the receiving end of such persecution throughout the history.

Any disagreement with the policies of the Israeli government should be voiced in a civil manner, without putting the blame on the entire community. God prohibits Muslims from such a behaviour. In the Qur'an, God warns believers as such:

"O you who have believed, be persistently standing firm for God, witnesses in justice, and do not let the hatred of a people prevent you from being just. Be just; that is nearer to righteousness. And fear God; indeed, God is Acquainted with what you do." (Qur'an, 5:8)

It is most natural for there to be good and bad people in every group, community or nation. Just like there are countless murderers, liars and criminals in Muslim communities, it is natural for Jewish communities to include people whose actions are less than commendable. Yet, it is patently absurd and utterly ridiculous to feel antipathy toward a group in its entirety for the actions of a few. Most importantly, it is opposite to the teachings of the Qur'an.

According to the Qur'an, Jews are People of the Book and are to be respected, protected and approached with love. God praises Jews in many verses for their devotion and piety and indeed, the Jewish people serve as a great example to Muslims with their unwavering loyalty to the Prophet Moses.

All these facts make it abundantly clear that there is no basis, either in Islam or in Judaism, that could lead to such hostility. Once everyone realizes that God created this world for love and it is against God's wishes to harbour hostile feelings toward each other, brotherhood and peace will prevail.

Our Prophet's (pbuh) Relations with the People of the Book

• *There are accounts of our Prophet (pbuh) attending wedding feasts of the People of the Book, visiting them when they were sick and giving them presents.*

• *When the Christians of Najran visited him, the Prophet Muhammad (pbuh) spread out his robe on the ground for them to sit on and welcomed them in that fashion.*

• *One of the wives of our Prophet (pbuh) was Marya bint Sham'ûn (also known as Maryam al-Qubtiyyah), a Coptic Christian from Egypt.*

• *Our mother Safiyya bint Huyayy, one of the wives of the Prophet (pbuh), was the daughter of the chief of the Jewish tribe Banu Nadir of Medina, Huyayy ibn Akhtab.*

• *The Prophet Muhammad (pbuh) allowed the Jews to become a party to the Constitution of Medina signed with the clans of the Aws and Khazraj, thus ensuring the survival of the Jews as a separate religious group among the Muslims.*

• *Under the article, "The Jews of Banu Awf are a community along with the believers. To the Jews their religion, and to the Muslim their religion," of the Consti-*

tution of Medina, the foundation of the respect that Muslims have for the Jews' traditions and beliefs was laid in the time of our Prophet (pbuh). Articles 26-33 of the same constitution state that members of the People of the Book enjoy the same rights as Muslims, while article 16 states that no injustice is to be inflicted on them.

• In the year 630 A.D., our Prophet (pbuh) issued the following command to envoys of the King of Himyar who came to Medina to announce that they had become Muslims: "If a Jew or Christian becomes a Muslim, he becomes equal to believers [enjoys the same legal rights with Muslims]. Whoever wants to remain as a Jew or Christian, he is not interfered." (Ibn Hisham, as-Seera, II, 586)

• The Christians of Najran sent a delegation of 60 members to Medina. When the delegation arrived at Medina they entered the presence of our Prophet (pbuh), and when the time for prayer came they desired to visit the mosque. The people objected to this, but the Prophet (pbuh) made the mosque available for them. They turned to the East and prayed. (Ibn Hisham, as-Seera, Beirut, I, 573-574; Hamidullah, The Prophet of Islam, I, 619-620.)

• The rights of the People of the Book were placed under protection in the time of the Prophet (pbuh) under treaties made with Jews and Christians. Whenever a disagreement arose in later times, the People of the Book would point to these treaties. For example, when the Christians of Damishq had a problem, they showed their treaty to Hazrat Umar, the caliph of the time, and requested a solution. This is a known fact appearing in history books.

• The text of a covenant of our Prophet (pbuh) with the Christian Ibn Harith ibn Ka'b and his people contains the passages; "To Sayyid Ibn Harith ibn Ka'b, his co-religionists, and all those who profess the Christian religion, be they in East or West, in close regions or faraway regions, be they Arabs or foreigners, known or unknown. ... I commit myself to support them, to place their persons under my protection, as well as their churches, chapels, oratories, the monasteries of their monks, the residences of their anchorites, wherever they are found, be they in the mountains or the valleys, caves or inhabited regions, in the plains or in the desert. I will protect their religion and their Church wherever they are found, be it on earth or at sea, in the West or in the East, with utmost vigilance on my part, the People of my House, and the Muslims as a whole. ... No Christian will be made Muslim by force: And dispute ye not with the People of the Book, except with means better (29:46). They must be covered by the wing of mercy. Repel every harm that could reach them wherever they may find themselves and in any country in which they are."

• The charters given by our Prophet (pbuh) to the People of the Book from Adruh, Makna, Khaybar, Najran and Aqaba' also show that the lives and property of the People of the Book were under the protection of

Muslims and recognized their freedom of belief and worship.

• When our Prophet (pbuh) first started preaching he first encountered a number of Christians in Mecca. Indeed, one of the first people to speak to our Prophet (pbuh) and Hazrat Khadija in the first days of the revelation was Waraqa bin Naufal, a Christian with handwritten copies of the Gospel. (Sahih Bukhari)

• Churches that were destroyed in the time of the caliphs were restored by Muslims, and permission was given for new synagogues and churches to be built. For example, the Monastery of St. Sergios that had been burned by Patriarch Mar Amme was rebuilt in the time of Hazrat Uthman.

• Muslims used to perform the Friday prayer in the Church of St. John in Damascus after the conquest of Syria. Christians performed their own religious observances there on Sundays. Members of both faiths used the same place of worship in peace.

Our Prophet's (pbuh) Practices concerning the Torah and the Gospel

Narrated Abu Huraira: The people of the Book used to read the Torah in Hebrew and then explain it in

Arabic to the Muslims. *(Sahih Bukhari, Book 92, Hadith 460)*

Al-Hafiz al-Zahabi related that Abdullah ibn Salam, a convert to Islam from Judaism, came to the Prophet (pbuh) and said "I read the Qur'an and the Torah (last night)." He replied, "Read one in one night and the other on another night." (al-Thalabi, Al-Iman al-Thalabi Tathkarar al-Huffadh, Vol. 1, p. 27)

Abdullah ibn Amr, one of the close companions of the Prophet (pbuh), would frequently read the Torah. One night he dreamed that he was holding oil in one hand and honey in the other, and that he sometimes ate from one hand and sometimes from the other. Abdullah ibn Amr described his dream to the Prophet (pbuh). The Prophet (pbuh) interpreted his dream as meaning the two books, and his reading sometimes from the one and sometimes from the other. (Sahih Bukhari, Vol. 6, Hadith 987, p. 439)

From Abu Sa'id al-Khudri: We asked the Prophet (pbuh): "O the Messenger of God! May we relate accounts from the Children of Israel?" He said, "Yes, you may relate accounts from the Children of Israel. There is no problem. Know that if you relate accounts from them, there is more interesting information as well." (Musnad of ibn Hanbal, 111/12, Hadith 11034)

Our Prophet (pbuh) always favoured peace

Our Prophet (pbuh) never desired war and over the years he made great efforts to spread Islam by peaceful means. He was patient in the face of severe assaults and pressure. Only when dealing with such pressure became imperative did he give permission for war, in the light of a revelation from God. He never declared war so long as there was still the slightest possibility of peace, and as long as an enemy's attacks and pressure represented no mortal danger.

During our Prophet's (pbuh) lifetime, the Mu'tah Expedition was the bloodiest and most difficult waged by the Muslims. He appointed Zayd ibn Harithah to command the army and admonished the troops:

"Wage war in the name of God, on the path of God, against those who deny God. Engage in no treachery. Do not cut off ears and noses and other parts of the body. Do not kill women and children, the elderly, and men of religion in their places of worship. Do not cut down date and other trees, and do not tear down buildings." *(Bukhari)*

Based on the prophetic orders on war, the following principles, which may be called "The Islamic Principles of Combat", are outlined by Muslim scholars:

1. War is to be waged only against those who encourage and engage in it.

2. Priests in churches, children, women and the elderly must never be harmed.

3. Sown fields must not be damaged.

4. Treaties and agreements must not be broken.

5. Animals must not be harmed.

6. There must be no cruelty and torture.

7. Towns must not be destroyed. *(Ahmet Hamdi Akseki, Abdurrahman Azzam Pasa'nin "Allah'in Peygamberlerine emanet ettigi ebedi risalet", Diyanet Isleri Baskanligi Nesriyat, Ankara, 1948)*

One reason why the time of the Prophet (pbuh) was blessed with peace and security was his position of justice, so in line with the morality of the Qur'an. Foreign writers, too, have been impressed by his superior character and praise our Prophet's (pbuh) morality in their works.

In his book *The Genuine Islam*, George Bernard Shaw described these superior traits:

> "I have always held the religion of Muhammad in high estimation because of its wonderful vitality. It is the only religion which appears to me to possess that assimilating capacity to the changing phase of existence which can make itself appeal to every age. I have studied him ... he must be called the Savior of Humanity. I believe that if a man like him were to assume the dictatorship of the modern world, he would succeed in solving its problems in a way that would bring it the much needed peace and happiness..." *(Sir George Bernard Shaw in 'The Genuine Islam,' 1936, http://www.geocities.com/Athens/Forum/9192 /mainquote2.html#shaw)*

In our own time as well, abiding by the Qur'an's morality, purified of bigotry, is the only answer to all the conflicts, fighting, and instability of the world. Like our Prophet (pbuh), never we should depart from the path of justice, and should always respect the rights of different communities and individuals, whatever their beliefs and identities may be.

Our Prophet (pbuh) bestowed many agreements on the People of the Book

Various agreements made at the time of our Prophet (pbuh) granted the Jewish and Christian communities certain privileges that guaranteed their rights and existence. The privileges granted to the monks of the St. Catherine Monastery at Mt. Sinai are examples of this. These documents guaranteed the legal, religious, and social rights of those Jews and Christians who came under Muslim rule or acknowledged Islam's sovereignty. Problems were resolved by referring to these documents. For example, the history books mention that the Christians in Damascus presented the documents recording their privileges to Caliph Umar when they encountered a problem and asked him to resolve the issue accordingly.

You who believe! Enter Islam totally. Do not follow in the footsteps of satan. He is an outright enemy to you.
(Qur'an, 2:208)

ISLAM HAS BROUGHT PEACE AND HARMONY TO THE MIDDLE EAST

*H*istory witnessed peace, justice and love in the lands ruled by Muslim administrators who followed the guidance of Qur'an. The practices in the lands conquered during the lifetime of the Prophet Muhammad (pbuh) are very important examples, and just administrators succeeding him, who followed in the footsteps of God's messengers and never swerved from the morality of the Qur'an established peaceable societies. The true justice, righteousness and honesty described in the Qur'an persisted in the time of these administrators, thereby providing a role model for the succeeding generations to follow.

The land of Palestine and its capital Jerusalem, where members of the three Divine religions reside together, are important in the sense that they show how Muslims bring peace and stability to the lands they rule. Indeed, for most of the last 1,400 years, Muslim rule has brought peace to Jerusalem and Palestine.

The Peace and Justice Brought to Palestine by the Caliph Omar

Jerusalem was the capital of the Jews until A.D. 71. In that year, the Roman Army made a major assault on the Jews, and exiled them from the area with great savagery. As the time of the Jewish diaspora began, Jerusalem and the surrounding area was becoming an abandoned land.

However, Jerusalem once again became a centre of interest with the acceptance of Christianity during the time of the Roman Emperor Constantine. Roman Christians built churches in Jerusalem. The prohibitions on Jews settling in the region were lifted. Palestine remained Roman (Byzantine) territory up until the 7th century. The Persians conquered the region for a short time, but the Byzantines later reconquered it.

An important turning point in the history of Palestine came in the

Citadel of Jerusalem, Coloured lithograph by L. Haghe after D. Roberts, 1841.

year 637, when it was conquered by the armies of Islam. This meant new peace and harmony in Palestine, which had for centuries been the scene of wars, exile, looting and massacre, and which saw new brutality every time it changed hands, a frequent occurrence. The coming of Islam was the beginning of an age when people of different beliefs could live in peace and harmony.

Palestine was captured by Hazrat Omar, the second Caliph after the Prophet (pbuh) himself. The entry of the Caliph into Jerusalem, the compassion, maturity and kindness he showed towards people of different beliefs, introduced the beautiful age that was beginning. Karen Armstrong describes the capture of Jerusalem by Hazrat Omar (ra) in these terms in her book *Holy War*:

> The Caliph Omar entered Jerusalem mounted on a white camel, escorted by the magistrate of the city, the Greek Patriarch Sophronius. The Caliph asked to be taken immediately to the Temple Mount and there he knelt in prayer on the spot where his friend Mohammed had made his Night Journey. The Patriarch watched in horror: this, he thought, must be the Abomination of Desolation that the Prophet Daniel had foretold would enter the Temple; this must be Antichrist who would herald the Last Days. Next Omar asked to see the Christian shrines and, while he was in the Church of the Holy Sepulchre, the time for Muslim prayer came round. Courteously the Patriarch invited him to pray where he was, but Omar as courteously refused. **If he knelt to pray in the church, he explained, the Muslims would want to commemorate the event by erecting a mosque there, and that would mean that they would have to demolish the Holy Sepulchre.** Instead Omar went to pray at a little distance from the church, and, sure enough, directly opposite the Holy Sepulchre there is still a small mosque dedicated to the Caliph Omar.

The other great mosque of Omar was erected on the Temple Mount to mark the Muslim conquest, together with the mosque al-Aqsa which commemorates Mohammed's Night Journey. **For years, the Christians had used the site of the ruined Jewish Temple as the city rubbish dump. The Caliph helped his Muslims to clear the garbage with his own hands** and there Muslims raised their two shrines to establish Islam in the third most holy city in the Islamic world.[19]

With the Muslim conquest of Jerusalem, the city became a safe haven in which all three religions could co-exist in peace. John L. Esposito writes:

When the Arab armies took Jerusalem in 638, they occupied a center whose shrines had made it a major pilgrimage site in Christendom. Churches and the Christian population were left unmolested. Jews, long banned from living there by Christian rulers, were permitted to return, live, and worship in the city of Solomon and David.[20]

The agreement - mentioned in previous pages - that Caliph Omar had signed with the Patriarch of Jerusalem when he entered Jerusalem is a result of his compassion.

In short, Muslims brought civilisation to Jerusalem and all of Palestine. Instead of beliefs that showed no respect for other peoples' sacred values, and which killed them simply out of differences of faith, there reigned the just, tolerant and moderate culture of Islam. After its capture by Hazrat Omar, Muslims, Christians and Jews lived together in peace and harmony in Palestine. Muslims never tried to use force to make people convert, although some non-Muslims who saw that Islam was the true religion did so of their own free will.

The peace and harmony in Palestine lasted as long as Muslim rule in the region. However, at the end of the 11th century, a conquering force entered the region from abroad, and the civilised land of Jerusalem was barbarically and savagely plundered, in a way never before seen. These were the Crusaders.

Mosque of Omar

The Savagery of the Crusaders in Palestine

While members of all three religions were living peaceably together in Palestine, the Christians in Europe decided to organise a crusade. Following a call by Pope Urban II on 27 November 1095 at the Council of Clermont, more than 100,000 people from all over Europe set out for Palestine to free the Holy land from the Muslims and find the fabled wealth of the East. After a long and wearying journey, and much plundering and slaughter along the way, they reached Jerusalem in 1099. The city fell after a siege of nearly five weeks, and the Crusaders moved in. And they carried out a savagery the like of which the world has seldom seen. All Muslims and Jews in the city were put to the sword.

The peace and harmony in Palestine, which had lasted since Hazrat Omar, ended in terrible slaughter. The Crusaders violated all

The Muslims and Jews of Jerusalem were brutally massacred by the Crusaders.

the ethical laws of Christianity, a religion of love and compassion, and spread terror in the name of Christianity.

The Justice of Saladin Ayyubi

The barbaric Crusader army made Jerusalem their capital, and established a Latin Kingdom whose borders stretched from Palestine to Antioch. However, the Crusaders who brought savagery to Palestine did not last long. Saladin gathered all the Muslim kingdoms, and defeated the Crusaders at the battle of Hattin in 1187. After the battle, the two leaders of the crusader army, Reynald of Chatillon and King Guy, were brought into Saladin's presence. Saladin executed Reynald of Chatillon, who had become infamous for the terrible savagery he had committed against Muslims, but he let King Guy go, as he had not committed the same crimes. Palestine once again saw the true meaning of justice.

Immediately after Hattin, and on the very same day that the Prophet Muhammad (pbuh) had been taken from Mecca to Jerusalem in one night, the day of the Ascent, Saladin entered Jerusalem and freed it from 88 years of Crusader occupation. When the Crusaders had taken the city 88 years earlier, they had killed all the Muslims inside it, and for that reason they were afraid that Saladin would do the same thing to them. However, he did not touch even one Christian in the city. Furthermore, he merely ordered the Latin (Catholic) Christians to leave it. The Orthodox Christians, who were not Crusaders, were allowed to live in the city and worship as they chose. In the words of John L. Esposito, "The Muslim army was as magnanimous in victory as it had been tenacious in battle. Civilians were spared; churches and shrines were generally left untouched... Saladin was faithful to his word and compassionate toward noncombatants."[21]

Karen Armstrong describes the second capture of Jerusalem in these words:

On 2 October 1187 Saladin and his army entered Jerusalem as conquerors and for the next 800 years Jerusalem would remain a Muslim city. Saladin kept his word, and conquered the city according to the highest Islamic ideals. **He did not take revenge for the 1099 massacre, as the Qur'an advised (16:127), and now that hostilities had ceased he ended the killing (2:193-194).** Not a single Christian was killed and there was no plunder. The ransoms were deliberately very low... Saladin... released many of them freely, as the Qur'an urged.... His

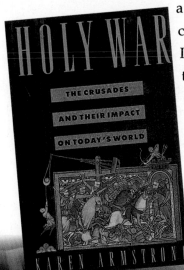

brother al-Adil was so distressed by the plight of the prisoners that he asked Saladin for a thousand of them for his own use and then released them on the spot... All the Muslim leaders were scandalised to see the rich Christians escaping with their wealth, which could have been used to ransom all the prisoners... [The Patriarch] Heraclius paid his ten-dinar ransom like everybody else and was even provided with a special escort to keep his treasure safe during the journey to Tyre.[22]

In short, Saladin and the Muslims in his command treated the Christians with great mercy and justice, and even showed them more compassion than their own leaders had. Not only the Christians but

Saladin entered Jerusalem in 1187 and freed it from 88 years of Crusader occupation. While best known for this military triumph, Saladin was also very forgiving and just toward the Crusaders as well as all other Christians. Even though the Crusaders had inflicted unspeakable cruelty on the Muslims, Saladin exacted no revenge upon them, and no civilian was harmed when he freed Jerusalem.

also Jews attained peace and security with the conquest of Jerusalem by Muslims. The well-known Spanish-Jewish poet Yehuda al-Harizi expressed his feelings thus in one of his works:

> God ...decided that the sanctuary would no longer rest in the hands of the sons of Esau... Thus in the year 4950 of Creation [AD 1190] God aroused the spirit of the prince of the Ishmaelites [Salah al-Din], a prudent and courageous man, who came with his entire army, besieged Jerusalem, took it and had it proclaimed throughout the country that he would receive and accept the race of Ephraim, wherever they came from. And so we came from all corners of the world to take up residence here. We now live in the shadow of peace.[23]

After Jerusalem, the Crusaders continued their barbarity and the Muslims their justice in other cities in Palestine. In 1194, Richard the Lionheart, who is portrayed as a great hero in British history, had 3,000

Saladin and Guy de Lusignan after battle of Hattin in 1187

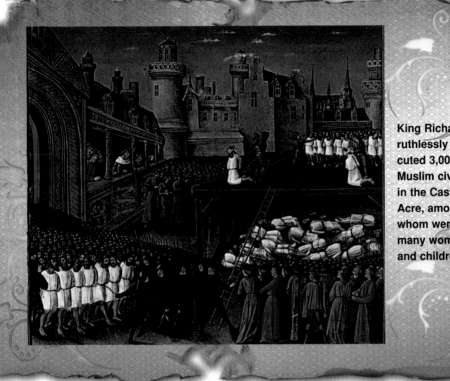

King Richard ruthlessly executed 3,000 Muslim civilians in the Castle of Acre, among whom were many women and children.

Muslims, among whom were many women and children, basely executed in Castle Acre. Although the Muslims witnessed this savagery, they never resorted to the same methods. They abided by God's command **"Let not the hatred of a people [who once] obstructed you from the Sacred Mosque lead you to transgress..."** (Qur'an, 5:2) and never used violence against innocent civilians. They never employed unnecessary violence, not even against the Crusader armies they defeated.

The savagery of the Crusaders and the justice of the Muslims once more revealed a historic truth: **An administration built on the principles of Islam allowed people of different faiths to live together**. This fact continued to be demonstrated for 700 years after Saladin, particularly during the Ottoman period.

God is Ever-Gentle

with His servants.

(Qur'an, 3:30)

THE BASIC FOUNDATION OF TERRORISM: DARWINISM AND MATERIALISM

*E*arlier, we explained that there are two important sources of terrorism. We showed with examples and evidence that one of them is radical terrorism, which misinterprets Divine religions and takes superstitious references that were fabricated over time as a basis. We demonstrated in the light of Qur'anic verses that the actions of the terrorist organizations which claim to act in the name of Islam are actually in violation of Islam. The other source of terrorism is the materialist and Darwinist worldview.

Most people think the theory of evolution was first proposed by Charles Darwin, and rests on scientific evidence, observations and experiments. However, the truth is that Darwin was not its originator, neither does the theory rest on scientific proof. The theory consists of an adaptation to nature of the ancient dogma of materialist philosophy. Although it is not backed up by scientific discoveries, the theory is blindly and fanatically supported in the name of materialist philosophy. (see Harun Yahya, *The Atlas of Creation* and *The Evolution Deceit.*)

This fanaticism has resulted in all kinds of disasters. Together with the spread of Darwinism and the materialist philosophy it supports, the answer to the question "What is a human being?" has changed. People who used to answer: "Human beings were created by God and have to live according to the beautiful morality He teaches", have now begun to think that "Man came into being by chance, and is an animal who developed by means of the fight for survival." There is a heavy price to pay for this great deception. Violent ideologies such as racism, fascism and communism, and many other barbaric world views based on conflict have all drawn strength from this deception.

This part of the book will examine the disaster Darwinism has visited on the world and reveal its close connection with terrorism, one of the most important problems of our time.

The Darwinist Lie: "Life Is Conflict"

Darwin set out with one basic fallacy when developing his theory: **The development of living things depends on the fight for survival. The strong win the struggle. The weak are condemned to defeat and oblivion.**

According to Darwin's unscientific ideas, there is a ruthless struggle for survival and an eternal conflict in nature. The strong always overcome the weak, and this enables development to take place. The subtitle he gave to his book *The Origin of Species, "The Origin of Species by Means of Natural Selection or the Preservation of Favoured Races in the Struggle for Life"*, encapsulates his deviant and unscientific view.

Furthermore, Darwin proposed the lie that the "fight for survival" also applied between human racial groups. According to that mythical claim, favoured races were victorious in the struggle. Favoured races, in Darwin's view, were white Europeans. African or Asian races had lagged behind in the struggle for survival. Darwin went further, and suggested that these races would soon lose the struggle for survival entirely, and thus disappear:

> At some future period, not very distant as measured by centuries, the civilised races of man will almost certainly exterminate and replace the savage races throughout the world. At the same time the anthropomorphous apes ... will no doubt be exterminated. The break between man and his nearest allies will then be wider, for it will intervene between man in a more civilised state, as we may hope, even than the Caucasian, and some ape as low as a baboon, instead of as now between the negro or Australian and the gorilla.[24]

The Indian anthropologist Lalita Vidyarthi explains how Darwin's theory of evolution imposed racism on the social sciences:

> His [Darwin's] theory of the survival of the fittest was warmly welcomed by the social scientists of the day, and they believed mankind had achieved various levels of evolution culminating in the white man's civilization. By the second half of the nineteenth century racism was accepted as fact by the vast majority of Western scientists.[25]

Darwin's Source of Inspiration: Malthus' Theory of Ruthlessness

Darwin's source of inspiration on his unscientific, dark and dangerous ideas was the British economist Thomas Malthus' book *An Essay on the Principle of Population*. Left to their own devices, Malthus calculated that the human population increased rapidly. In his view, the main influences that kept populations under control were disasters such as war, famine and disease. In short, according to this brutal claim, some people had to die for others to live. Existence came to mean permanent war.

In the 19th century, Malthus' deviant ideas were widely accepted. European upper class intellectuals in particular supported his cruel ideas. In the article **"The Scientific Background of the Nazi "Race Purification" Programme,"** by T.D. Hall, the importance 19th-century Europe attached to Malthus's views on population is described in this way:

In the opening half of the nineteenth century, throughout Europe, members of the ruling classes gathered to discuss the newly discovered "Population problem" and to devise ways of implementing the Malthusian mandate, to increase the mortality rate of the poor: **"Instead of recommending cleanliness to the poor, we should encourage contrary habits. In our towns we should make the streets narrower,**

Europe Since 1870 by the English professor of history, James Joll

crowd more people into the houses, and court the return of the plague. In the country we should build our villages near stagnant pools, and particularly encourage settlements in all marshy and unwholesome situations," and so forth and so on.[26]

As a result of this cruel policy, the weak, and those who lost the struggle for survival would be eliminated, and as a result the rapid rise in population would be balanced out. This so-called "oppression of the poor" policy was actually carried out in 19th-century Britain. An industrial order was set up in which children of eight and nine were made to work sixteen hours a day in the coal mines and thousands died from the terrible conditions. The struggle for survival demanded by Malthus's theory led to millions of Britons leading lives full of suffering.

Thomas Malthus and Charles Darwin

The implementation in the 19th century of Malthus's thesis of the necessity of the struggle for life brought misery to the helpless and poor children in England. Religion, however, ensures the protection of children. A life of goodness and virtue, without any misery and suffering, is only possible if the moral teachings of religion are practiced.

Influenced by these wild ideas, Darwin applied this concept of conflict to all of nature, and proposed that the strong and the fittest emerged victorious from this war of existence. Moreover, he claimed that the so-called struggle for survival was a justified and unchangeable law of nature. On the other hand, he invited people to abandon their religious beliefs by denying the creation, and thus undermined all ethical values that might prove to be obstacles to the ruthlessness of the struggle for survival.

Humanity has paid a heavy price in the 20th century for the dissemination of these callous views which led people to ruthlessness and cruelty.

The Role of Darwinism in Preparing the Ground for World War I

As Darwinism dominated European culture, the effects of the fallacy of struggle for survival began to emerge. Colonialist European nations in particular began to portray the nations they colonized as so-called "evolutionary backward nations" and looked to Darwinism for justification.

The bloodiest political effect of Darwinism was the outbreak of World War I in 1914.

In his book *Europe Since 1870*, the well-known British professor of history James Joll explains that one of the factors that prepared the ground for World War I was the belief in Darwinism of European rulers at the time:

> ...it is important to realise how literally the doctrine of the struggle for existence and of the survival of the fittest was taken by the majority of the leaders of Europe in the years preceding the First World War. The Austro-Hungarian chief of staff for example, Franz Baron Conrad von Hoetzendorff, wrote in his memoirs after the war:

> Philanthropic religions, moral teachings and philosophical doctrines may certainly sometimes serve to **weaken mankind's struggle for existence** in its crudest form, but they will never succeed in removing it as a driving motive of the world... **It is in accordance with this great principle that the catastrophe of the world war came about as the result of the motive forces in the lives of states and peoples, like a thunderstorm which must by its nature discharge itself.**

> Seen against this sort of ideological background, Conrad's insistence on the need for a preventive war in order to preserve the

Austro-Hungarian monarchy becomes comprehensible.

We have seen too how these views were not limited to military figures, and that Max Weber for example was deeply concerned with the international struggle for survival. Again Kurt Riezler, the personal assistant and confidant of the German chancellor Theobald von Bethmann-Hollweg, wrote in 1914:

Eternal and absolute enmity is fundamentally inherent in relations between peoples; and **the hostility which we observe everywhere...** is not the result of a perversion of human nature but is **the essence of the world and the source of life itself.**[27]

Friedrich von Bernhardi, a World War I general, made a similar connection between war and the laws of war in nature. **"War"** declared Bernhardi **"is a biological necessity"**; it "is as necessary as the struggle

of the elements of nature"; it "gives a biologically just decision, since its decisions rest on the very nature of things."[28]

As we have seen, World War I broke out because of European thinkers, generals and administrators who saw warfare, bloodshed and suffering as a kind of development, and thought they were an unchanging law of nature. The ideological root that dragged all of that generation to destruction was nothing else than Darwin's concepts of the "struggle for survival" and "favoured races."

World War I left behind it 8 million dead, hundreds of ruined cities, and millions of wounded, crippled, homeless and unemployed.

The basic cause of World War II, which broke out 21 years later and left 55 million dead behind it, was also based on Darwinism.

Fascism, which has Darwinist concepts at its heart, caused the death of millions of innocent people. This dreadful ideology drew many countries of the world into a maelstrom of destruction and misery.

World War II caused the deaths of 55 million people, leaving many others wounded and homeless, their lives in ruins. The war devastated cities and caused economies to collapse.

Nazism, a blend of Social Darwinism and neo-paganism, has killed millions and spread horror into the hearts of many others.

What "The Law of the Jungle" Led to: Fascism

As Darwinism fed racism in the 19th century, it formed the basis of an ideology that would develop and drown the world in blood in the 20th century: Nazism.

A strong Darwinist influence can be seen in Nazi ideologues. When one examines this theory, which was given shape by Adolf Hitler and Alfred Rosenberg, one comes across such concepts as "natural selection", "selective mating", and "the struggle for survival between the races", which are repeated dozens of time in the works of Darwin. When calling his book *Mein Kampf* (My Struggle), Hitler was inspired by the Darwinist struggle for survival and the principle that victory went to the fittest. He particularly talks about the struggle between the races:

> History would culminate in a new millennial empire of unparalleled splendour, based on a new racial hierarchy ordained by nature herself.[29]

> In the 1933 Nuremberg party rally, Hitler proclaimed that "a higher race subjects to itself a lower race... a right which we see in nature and which can be regarded as the sole conceivable right".[30]

That the Nazis were influenced by Darwinism is a fact that almost all historians who are expert in the matter accept. Peter Chrisp, the author of the book *The Rise of Fascism*, expressed this fact as follows:

> Charles Darwin's theory that humans had evolved from apes was ridiculed when it was first published, but was later widely accepted. The Nazis distorted Darwin's theories, using them to justify warfare and racism.[31]

The historian Hickman describes Darwinism's influence on Hitler as follows:

THE RISE OF FASCISM

L MATTINO ILLUSTRATO

Un grande fuori-testo a colori con i ritratti dei due Condottieri HITLER e MUSSOLINI è allegato a questo numero del giornale

Anno XV - N. 19 - NAPOLI
16 Maggio 1938 - Anno XVI

[Hitler] was a firm believer and preacher of evolution.

Whatever the deeper, profound, complexities of his psychosis, it is certain that [the concept of struggle was important because] ... his book, *Mein Kampf*, clearly set forth a number of evolutionary ideas, particularly those emphasizing struggle, survival of the fittest and the extermination of the weak to produce a better society.[32]

Communist leaders, whose ideas of human society were also based on Darwinism, will go down in history as having caused terrible suffering with their cruel policies.

Communism applied the Darwinian idea of conflict to the class conflict, and thus accepted murder and bloodshed as legitimate methods of control.

Hitler, who emerged with these views, dragged the world to violence that had never before been seen. Many ethnic and political groups, and especially the Jews, were exposed to terrible cruelty and slaughter in the Nazi concentration camps. World War II, which began with the Nazi invasion, cost 55 million lives. What lay behind the greatest tragedy in world history was Darwinism's concept of the "struggle for survival."

The Bloody Alliance: Darwinism and Communism

While fascists are found on the right wing of Social Darwinism, the left wing is occupied by communists. Communists have always been among the fiercest defenders of Darwin's theory.

This relationship between Darwinism and communism goes right back to the founders of both these "isms." Marx and Engels, the founders of communism, read Darwin's *The Origin of Species* as soon as it came out, and were amazed at its dialectical materialist attitude. The correspondence between Marx and Engels showed that they saw Darwin's theory as "containing the basis in natural history for communism." In his book *The Dialectics of Nature*, which he wrote under the influence of Darwin, Engels was full of praise for Darwin, and tried to make his own contribution to the theory in the chapter "The Part Played by Labour in the Transition from Ape to Man."

Russian communists who followed in the footsteps of Marx and Engels, such as Plekhanov, Lenin, Trotsky and Stalin, all agreed with Darwin's theory of evolution. Plekhanov, who is seen as the founder of Russian communism, regarded Marxism as **"Darwinism in its application to social science."**[33]

Trotsky said, **"Darwin's discovery is the highest triumph of the dialectic in the whole field of organic matter."**[34]

Darwinist education had a major role in the formation of communist cadres. For instance, historians note the fact that **Stalin was religious in his youth, but became an atheist primarily because of Darwin's books.**

Mao, who established communist rule in China and killed millions of people, openly stated that **"Chinese socialism is founded upon Darwin and the theory of evolution."**[35]

The Harvard University historian James Reeve Pusey goes into great detail regarding Darwinism's effect on Mao and Chinese communism in his research book *China and Charles Darwin*.

In short, there is an unbreakable link between the theory of evolution and communism. The theory claims that living things are the product of chance, and provides a so-called scientific support for atheism. Communism, an atheist ideology, is for that reason firmly tied to Darwinism. Moreover, the theory of evolution proposes that development in nature is possible thanks to conflict (in other words "the struggle for survival") and supports the concept of "dialectics" which is fundamental to communism.

If we think of the communist concept of "dialectical conflict", which killed some 120 million people during the 20th century, as a "killing machine", then we can better understand the dimensions of the disaster that Darwinism visited on the planet.

Dialectical Conflict Does Not Foster the Development of Societies, It Destroys Them

As we learned earlier, Darwinism proposed that the struggle between living things is the cause of their development and gained so-called scientific currency for the philosophy of dialectical materialism.

As can be understood from its name, dialectical materialism rests on the idea of "conflict". Karl Marx, the founder of this philosophy, propagated the idea that **"if there were no struggle and opposition, everything would stay as it is."** In another place he said, **"Force is the midwife of every old society pregnant with a new one."**[36] By saying this, he called people to violence, war and bloodshed in order that they could develop.

The first to apply Marx's theory in the realm of politics was Lenin. Fostering the idea that **"progress comes about as a result of the conflict of opposites"**, Lenin advocated that people with opposing ideas should be in constant conflict. Lenin also repeatedly stated that this conflict would require bloodshed, that is, terrorism. A piece by Lenin titled **"Guerrilla Warfare"** which was first published in *Proletary* in 1906, eleven years before the Bolshevik Revolution, shows the terrorist methods he had adopted:

> **The phenomenon in which we are interested is the armed struggle.** It is conducted by individuals and by small groups. Some belong to revolutionary organisations, while others (the majority in certain parts of Russia) do not belong to any revolutionary organisation. Armed struggle pursues two different aims, which must be strictly distinguished: in the first place, **this struggle aims at assassinating individuals, chiefs and subordinates in the Army and police; in the second place, it aims at the confiscation of monetary funds both from the government and from private persons.** The confiscated funds go partly into the treasury of the party, partly for the special purpose of arming and preparing for an uprising, and partly for the maintenance of persons engaged in the struggle we are describing.[37]

In the 20th century, one of the most well-known ideologies to oppose communism was fascism. The interesting thing is that, although fascism declared itself opposed to communism, it believed just as much as communism did in the concept of struggle. Commu-

It is natural that disagreements occur, but they should not be the cause of conflict and wars between people. Mutual respect and compassion can ensure agreement and co-existence between parties in disagreement. The moral teaching of the Qur'an offers to people a life of contentment and joy, whereas the dialectical struggle always brings unhappiness, destruction and death.

nists believed in the necessity of the class struggle; the fascists simply changed the arena of the struggle concentrating on the idea of the struggle between races and nations. For example, the German historian Heinrich Treitschke, one of the most important sources for Nazi ideas and a prominent racist, wrote, **"nations could not prosper without intense competition, like the struggle for survival of Darwin."**[38] Hitler also said that he had taken inspiration from Darwin's understanding of struggle:

> **The whole world of Nature is a mighty struggle between strength and weakness–an eternal victory of the strong over the weak.** There would be nothing but decay in the whole of nature if this were not so. He who would live must fight. He who does not wish to fight in this world where permanent struggle is the law of life, has not the right to exist.[39]

These two social Darwinist ideologies believed that, for a society to grow strong, struggle and bloodshed are necessary; what they created in the 20th century is well known. Countless numbers of innocent people died; countless others were wounded or maimed; national economies crumbled; money that used to be spent on health, research, technology, education and art was spent on arms, on bandages to bind the wounds caused by those arms and to restore ruined cities. It became evident as time went on that struggle and terror did not promote human development but rather caused destruction.

Differences of opinion do not necessitate conflict. On the contrary, good things can emerge from them

Certainly there are contradictions in the world. Just as in nature there are light and darkness, day and night, hot and cold, so there are also contradictions in putting ideas into practice. But a contradiction in ideas does not necessitate conflict. On the contrary, if contradictions are approached with peace, understanding, love, compassion and mercy, good results may be achieved. Everyone who compares his own idea with another's may develop his own or see its deficiencies and remedy them. Those who defend opposing opinions could have an exchange of ideas in conversation or engage in a constructive critique. Only the kind of sincere, forgiving, peaceful and humble person who conforms to the moral teaching of the Qur'an can develop this approach.

To kill a person or do him harm because he has different ideas, believes in a different religion or belongs to a different race is an immense act of cruelty. For this reason only, throughout history and all over the world, sons and daughters of the same fatherland have struggled with one another to the death, murdering one another without pity. Or people of different race or nationality, women and children included, have been indiscriminately slaughtered. The only person who could do such a thing is someone who has no respect for a human being, and who regards the person in front of him just as an intelligent animal; it is someone who does not believe that he will have to give an account to God for what he has done.

The best and truest attitude to have towards opposing ideas is revealed in the Qur'an. Clashes of ideas have arisen throughout history and one of the most well-known examples of this is the opposition between Moses (pbuh) and his contemporary Pharaoh. Despite all Pharaoh's cruelty and aggressiveness, God sent the Prophet Moses to invite him to God's religion, and He explained the method the Prophet Moses was to use:

Go to Pharaoh; he has overstepped the bounds. But speak to him with gentle words so that hopefully he will pay heed or show some fear. (Qur'an, 20:43-44)

The Prophet Moses (pbuh) obeyed God's command and explained true religion to him. In order to stop Pharaoh's denial of God and his cruelty to people, the Prophet Moses patiently explained every matter.

However, Pharaoh showed a hostile attitude toward the Prophet's noble character and patience, threatening to kill him and those who shared his ideas. But it was not Pharaoh's attitude that prevailed; on the contrary, he and his people were drowned. The Prophet Moses and his people were victorious.

As this example shows, the victory of an idea or the struggle for development does not come about by hostility or aggression. The meeting between the Prophet Moses and Pharaoh offers a lesson from history: it is not those on the side of contention and cruelty who are victorious, but those who are on the side of peace and justice. The exercise of fine moral principles receives its reward both in this world and in the hereafter.

The Link between Darwinism and Terrorism

As we have so far seen, Darwinism is at the root of various ideologies of violence that have spelled disaster to mankind in the 20th century. The fundamental concept behind this understanding and method is "fighting whoever is not one of us." There are different beliefs, worldviews and philosophies in the world. It is very natural that all these diverse ideas have traits opposing one another. However, these different stances can look at each other in one of two ways:

1) They can respect the existence of those who are not like them and try to establish dialogue with them, employing a humane method. Indeed, this method conforms with the morality of the Qur'an.

2) They can choose to fight others, and to try to secure an advantage by damaging them, in other words, to behave like a wild animal. This is a method employed by materialism, that is, irreligion.

The horror we call "terrorism" is nothing other than a statement of the second view.

When we consider the difference between these two approaches, we can see that the idea of **"man as a fighting animal"** which Darwinism has subconsciously imposed on people is particularly influential. Individuals and groups who choose the way of conflict may never have heard of Darwinism and the principles of that ideology. But at the end of the day they agree with a view whose philosophical basis rests on

Darwinism. What leads them to believe in the rightness of this view is such Darwinism-based slogans as "In this world, the strong survive", "Big fish swallow little ones", "War is a virtue", and "Man advances by waging war". Take Darwinism away, and these are nothing but empty slogans.

There may be disagreement between states or societies, but conflict and war can never solve the problems. As we are told in the Qur'an, all disagreements must be solved by mutual patience, compassion and understanding.

Actually, when Darwinism is taken away, no philosophy of conflict remains. The three Divine religions that most people in the world believe in, Islam, Christianity and Judaism, all oppose violence. All three religions wish to bring peace and harmony to the world, and oppose innocent people being killed and suffering cruelty and torture. Conflict and violence violate the morality that God has set out for man, and are abnormal and unwanted concepts. However, Darwinism sees and portrays conflict and violence as natural, justified and correct concepts that have to exist. Therefore, it is this twisted ideology that lies behind the terrorist activities in the world, as it sees struggle and violence as the shortest way to achieve a goal.

Every Person Who Desires Peace Must Recognise the Danger of Darwinism

The solution in the fight against a particular problem lies in doing away with the ideas this problem fundamentally depends on. For instance, no matter how hard one endeavours to keep the surroundings of a stinking garbage bin clean, the garbage will keep on stinking. All solutions will prove to be short-lived. The real solution lies in a thorough cleaning of the garbage's source, removing the trash altogether. Otherwise, it is like spending years raising poisonous snakes on a farm, then letting them go, wondering why they start to bite people and trying to round them all up again. The important thing is not to breed them in the first place.

Consequently, in the fight against terrorism, searching for terrorists one by one and trying to render them ineffectual does not provide a viable and permanent solution. **The only way of totally eradicating the scourge of terrorism from the face of the earth is to identify the basic sources that breed terrorists and remove them. The main source of terrorism, on the other hand, is erroneous ideologies and the education received in the light of these ideologies.**

In our day, in almost all countries of the world, Darwinism is incorporated into school curricula and is considered to be scientific fact. Young people are not taught that they are created by God, that they are endowed with a spirit, wisdom and conscience. They are not told that they will have to give account of their deeds on the Day of Judgement and accordingly be punished in hell or rewarded with paradise for all eternity. On the contrary, they are taught the lies that they are creatures whose forefathers were animals that somehow came into existence by some random coincidences. Under such indoctrination, they assume themselves to be stray beings who are not answerable to God and see their future – that is their survival – in being victorious through struggle. After this stage, it becomes rather easy to brainwash these people, who have been already indoctrinated all through their school lives, and to turn them into enemies of humanity cruel enough to murder innocent children. Such young people can be readily attracted by any strayed ideology; they can act under the influence of the terrorists' conditioning and engage in inconceivably cruel and violent

SCIENCE REFUTES DARWINISM

acts. The communist, fascist and racist terrorist groups that have been in existence since the 19th century are the products of this kind of education system.

The second great harm this education system does is to entirely distance education from religion, thereby limiting the sphere of religion to the world of uneducated people. Thus, while those who have access to education are totally removed from religion as a result of Darwinist-materialist instillation, religion becomes something peculiar to the uneducated. This causes the development of superstitious and erroneous ideas and allows those who put forward ideas totally contrary to religion in the name of religion to take control easily.

To conclude, the way to stop acts of terrorism is to put an end to Darwinist-materialist education, which is one of the most significant sources of terrorism, to educate young people in accord with a curricula based on true scientific findings and to instil in them the love and fear of God and the desire to act wisely and scrupulously. The fruits of such an education will be a community made up of peaceable, trustworthy, forgiving, compassionate, kind and humane people.

The Damaging Effects of One-Sided Darwinist Education that Lead to Violence

By spreading the lie that there is no purpose to human life, Darwinist education turns people into psychologically sick individuals, pessimistic and psychopathic, devoid of all hope and joy.

One of the examples of this is the Norwegian Anders Behring Breivik. Breivik admitted to perpetrating twin terror attacks in Norway on 22 July, 2011. One of these was a bomb attack on the government building in Oslo in which 8 people died. The other was an attack on a Labour party youth camp on the island of *Utøya*. Sixty-nine people lost their lives in that attack.

Before the attacks, Breivik set out his views in his "European Independence Manifesto." On page 1518, he stated that he regarded himself as a champion of the scientific world view and modern biology. Among the books he *"most valued"* was Charles Darwin's *Origin of Species*.[1] According to Breivik, "a perfect Europe" must include the laws of social Darwinism.[2]

On page 1202, Breivik says that he entirely agrees with the Darwinist biologist from Princeton University Lee Silver regarding the re-implementation of eugenics. He agrees with Silver's view that radical policies will have to be applied in the future if the world population is to be reduced to less than half of the current figure, or 3.8 billion.[3] On the same page, Breivik makes it clear that he has signed up to Darwin's argument that "genocide and natural selection ... go hand in hand ":

Terrorists aim to damage people both physically and psychologically to attain a certain goal. The morality of religion, however, is opposed to terrorism in that it aims to foster love, well-being, compassion, joy and hope in society.

"Even if the second and third world countries ignores the call of this "hegemony" (to stop having babies), nature will correct their suicidal tendencies as they are unable to feed their populations."[4]

Breivik goes on to say that there must be no intervention in this natural process, or famine:

"If starvation threatens the countries who have failed to follow our (population capacity) guidelines we should not support them by backing their corrupt leaders or send any form of aid."[5]

"Food aid to 3rd world countries must stop immediately as it is the primary cause of overpopulation."[6]

These words written by Breivik in person clearly show that he had lost all moral values because of his Darwinist education, as a result of which he cold-bloodedly perpetrated his terrorist attacks that cost the lives of dozens of people.

Another example of the moral collapse and savagery caused by Darwinist education is the American serial killer Jeffrey Dahmer, who killed and ate 17 children before he was caught. In a last interview with the Dateline NBC channel immediately before he was put to death, Dahmer made the following statement:

"If a person doesn't think that there is a God to be accountable to, then what's the point of trying to modify your behavior to keep it within acceptable ranges? That's how I thought anyway. **I always believed the theory of evolution as truth, that we all just came from** the slime (by chance). When we died, you know, that was it, there was nothing."[7]

Darwin's superstition that has poisoned vast numbers, turns people into serial killers and even makes them psychopathic enough to eat human flesh. That is what comes of this false religion that seeks to indoctrinate people with the idea they have no responsibility to a Creator, that convinces them they are purposeless, irresponsible and aimless entities, that regards human beings as animals and that seeks to turn people away from the fact of the hereafter by portraying death as the end.

Darwinism was the worst deception and scourge of the last century, and was behind the killing, oppression, terror, mass slaughter, degeneration and afflictions of all kinds for the last 200 years. DARWINISM WAS THE WORST DECEPTION AND SCOURGE OF THE LAST CENTURY, and was behind the world wars and the communism and fascism that led to irreligion, racism and mass slaughter in societies at one time.

The unfortunate effects on society of this dark scourge initiated by Darwin have persisted down to the present day. The latest book by Richard Dawkins, one of the most committed devotees of Darwinism today, contains suggestions far removed from belief in God that will inevitably lead to pessimism and despair. One of the most significant instances of this was the way that Jesse Kilgore, a 22-year-old student in America, committed suicide under the effect of Dawkins' book he was recommended by a teacher.[8]

The effect of Dawkins' terrifying views based on the sinister ideology of Darwinism are by no means limited to that example. In the foreword to his book *Unweaving the Rainbow*, Dawkins himself admits that fact:

"A foreign publisher of my first book confessed that he could not sleep for three nights after reading it, so troubled was he by what he saw as its cold, bleak message. Others have asked me how I can bear to get up in the mornings. A teacher from a distant country wrote me reproachfully that a pupil had come to him in tears after reading the same book, because it had persuaded her that life was empty and purposeless. He advised her not to show the book to any of her friends, for fear of contaminating them with the same nihilistic pessimism."[9]

This sinister scourge, Darwinism, is a perverse religion that inflicts death, murder, despair, lack of feeling, terror and savagery and encourages people to think they are nothing more than animals that came into being by chance. The few remaining representatives of that faith are still striving with all their might to turn people away from belief in God. That is why they strenuously oppose the teaching of the weaknesses of Darwinism in schools, hide away fossils that prove Creation, and never admit that protein cannot come into being by chance and that more than 450 million fossils totally refute Darwinism. Yet despite all these measures, people in the 21st century are no longer taken in by lies. All the efforts made to keep Darwinism propped up after it was exposed as a fraud have been in vain.

1-http://www.darwinthenandnow.com/2011/07/breivik-a-darwinist/?cb=09394448816310614

2- Anders Behring Breivik, A European Declaration of Independence, p.1386

3-http://www.darwinthenandnow.com/2011/07/breivik-a-darwinist/?cb=09394448816310614

4- Anders Behring Breivik, A European Declaration of Independence, p.1202

5- Anders Behring Breivik, A European Declaration of Independence, p.1202

6- Anders Behring Breivik, A European Declaration of Independence, p.1203

7- Kelly J. Coghlan, Houston Chronicle Sunday-15 February 2009

8- http://www.worldnetdaily.com/index.php?fa=PAGE.view&pageId=81459

9- Richard Dawkins, Unweaving The Rainbow New York: Houghton Mifflin Company, 1998, p. ix.

Darwinist Education at Schools Leads to People Inclined to Violence and Terrorism

Nothing in this world is a coincidence, and neither was the darkness that the world was dragged into in the 20th and 21st centuries. God, through these painful stages in history, showed a very important example to humanity and He still wants them to see it. The people need to understand: If they forget that they were created for love, brotherhood, friendship and altruism, and if they choose to be divided and fight instead of uniting and getting stronger, and if they get carried away by false ideologies and movements and believe that "killing and fighting is necessary to improve", they will get what they want: fighting and suffering. And they will ultimately see that conflicts will not bring improvement, but only destruction.

Darwinism and Its Derivative Communism Is Based on a So-called Need to Fight and Conflict

Dialectics which first originated in ancient Greece and meant "debate" was described by Heraclitus (576-480) with the following words: "...all things come into being by a conflict of opposites." To Heraclitus, conflict is the father of everything. Therefore, there has to be a conflict between the thesis and the anti-thesis. If the defenders of a thesis are going to be defeated by the other side, it has to be through war and blood and the other side must be destroyed at all costs. Then the synthesis will turn into a new thesis and the same fight and war should continue at full speed.

Hegel and Marx, who followed centuries after him, called it "conflict," if not directly war and it certainly didn't take long before the bloody communist leaders perceived it as war and massacre. They believed in the necessity of war and considered it the basic condition for Marxism. Even though the green communists today reject this concept of war, communism requires brutal ambushes, guerrilla war, and massacres without any reservations. The current massacres in Syria, the bloodshed by the communist PKK in the South-eastern Anatolia is proof enough of that.

Communism: One of the most fundamental foundations of the terrorist organizations

Countries that are suffering from terrorism, including Turkey, most frequently have various and sundry communist terrorist or insurgent groups as their primary opponents. Communism is very much alive today, and even if it's not officially recognized; it's controlling parts of North America, Northern Europe and almost the whole of the Middle East. Then there are the countries which are officially under communist rule such as many South America countries, China and of course, North Korea. This communist, Marxist rule brings terrorism to the whole world. Those who shut their eyes to this very obvious Marxist threat are still looking for solutions to terrorism with never-ending TV debates. However, at the same time, they continue to teach their students dialectics in their schools. Their own children's minds are filled with lies that two opposing ideas need to fight each other and the history is full of such conflicts, and that only such conflicts can bring improvement and benefit to societies. Terrorists themselves are also indoctrinated with the same lies. Ironically, both communist countries and capitalist countries provide this education; the Marxist state of mind therefore continues to progress in every country with secretive but very firm steps.

There is another point that has to be kept in mind: Capitalism is not a blow dealt to Marxism. On the contrary, according to Marx, capitalism is an important requirement for societies to move forward to communism. Communism is simply lying in ambush, waiting to ensnare people and societies which became selfish under capitalism, which have abandoned their moral, religious and human values, thinking about themselves alone. The latest economic crisis played into the hands of communism. According to Marxists and communists, everything is now ready. Anyone wishing to understand this phenomenon better can take a closer look at the many problems in the world.

The Existence of Opposites Does Not Require Wars

There have always been opposites. The conflict between good and evil has existed since the beginning of the world. However, this conflict has to be defined accurately. The existence of opposites does not require war. The opposites can stand up for themselves through communication, and intellectual debate, presentation of evidence, all within the bounds of love and respect; no one can be forced to accept any idea and no one should be killed simply because he doesn't want to accept it. No war has ever brought about definitive improvement to any society so far. The bloody wars and conflicts of the 20th century, the endless fights of today, just help the armaments industry which makes money over weapons production and destroys people, civilisations, technology, cities and entire economies.

There can be no progress or improvement with people who live in fear. There can be no going forward when people keep getting hungrier, more malnourished, less educated, less productive. The cities won't be better when their infrastructure and technology is destroyed with bombs and jetfighters. No society can move forward with the younger generation dying out. The atom bombs dropped on Hiroshima and Nagasaki did not bring anything other than wholesale destruction that lingered through generations. The bloody dialectics introduced by Marxism never brought that imaginary progress to societies and it will not do so in the future. If we allow that, the world will be engulfed with even worse disasters, and everywhere will be drowning in blood.

Darwinism is the philosophical background of many conflicts in the world. The theory of evolution claims that all species evolved from a single cell (whose origin Darwinists can never explain) as a result of a rather nebulous string of coincidences. According to them, fighting is one of the elements of this imaginary evolutionary process. The basis of this brutal ideology, which claims that the living things can evolve only through fighting, is about the survival of the fittest. Introducing the deception of Darwinism as a scientific theory and including it in curriculums all around the world has brought upon a mass public deception and those twisted Darwinist ideas found a fertile breeding ground, which ultimately led to loss of millions of lives through various wars.

The Sole Solution against Bloody Ideologies Is Ending the One-Sided Education Favouring Darwinism

Opposing ideas can give rise to something better only through love and compassion, respect, freedom of thought and scientific evidence. Not through force or violence. It is high time for everyone to understand the reason behind the disasters handicapping the world. Marxism provides the rationale for war; Marxist societies set the stage for that in a covert manner. The most effective way to stop that is through showing that this bloody dialectics is a false scientific rationale to justify the wars. It should be said all around that the so-called dialectics of nature is pure nonsense, and as much as there are predators in nature, there are living things that act in a very selfless and altruistic manner too. A fast way to achieve this would be swiftly amending the education system that teaches young minds this bloody dialectic idea all around the world. This world is not a battlefield, neither for us, nor for other beings. The world will be beautiful only with love, as revealed by God in all the Divine religions. God wants love from us. God wants us to be one, brothers and sisters. God loves to love and to be loved. This world will change only if we follow God's orders and **"love."**

Bediuzzaman Points to the Importance of Intellectual Struggle Against Darwinism and Materialism

The great Islamic scholar Bediuzzaman, who devoted his entire life to an intellectual struggle against disbelief, explained in his works that disbelief was sustained by Darwinism and materialism. He, therefore, said that an intellectual struggle against such ideologies would play a vital role.

Bediuzzaman explains the impact of materialism on unbelievers trying to ambush him and his friends:

"And thirdly: To corrupt them with the enticing vices and stupefying, pleasurable poisons of materialist philosophy and civilization; and destroy their solidarity; and disparage their leaders with treacherous lies; and discredit their ways with some of the principles of science and philosophy..." *(Bediuzzaman, The Treatise of Light Collection, The Rays, Thirteenth Ray)*

As very wisely put by Bediuzzaman, the unbelievers sought to cheat believers with temporary and tempting worldly pleasures to nullify the intellectual works of Bediuzzaman, and with the encouragement from materialistic culture, tried to impair the unity and solidarity of the believers and slandered Bediuzzaman repeatedly. However they invariably failed.

Bediüzzaman says that Darwinism and materialism will get stronger especially in the End Times and that disbelief will be more widespread propelled by these two ideologies; however the Prophet Jesus (pbuh) and Hazrat Mahdi (pbuh) will put an end to this trouble through an effective intellectual struggle. As Bediüzzaman explained, Hazrat Mahdi (pbuh) will carry out this duty perfectly, and will intellectually end Darwinism and materialism and help save people's faith.

"The first: Under the influence of science and philosophy, and the spread of the materialist and naturalist epidemic into humanity, the first duty (of Hazrat Mahdi) is first of all to save faith as to entirely silence philosophy and materialistic thinking." *(Bediuzzaman, The Treatise of Light Collection, Emirdag Addendum, p. 259)*

Bediuzzaman says that Darwinism and materialism are the mainstays of the antichrist, and that the Prophet Jesus (pbuh) will carry out a great intellectual struggle against that mischief, effectively ending it:

"... at the end of time the religion of Christianity will be purified and divest itself of superstition in the face of the current of unbelief and atheism born of naturalist philosophy, and will be transformed into Islam. At this point, the collective personality of Christianity will kill the fearsome collective personality of irreligion with the sword of heavenly revelation; so too, representing the collective personality of Christianity, Jesus (pbuh) will (spiritually) kill the antichrist, who represents the collective personality of irreligion, that is, he will kill atheistic thought (he will intellectually eliminate it)." *(Bediuzzaman, The Treatise of Light Collection, The Letters, First Letter, p. 22)*

"... will (intellectually) kill the gigantic collective personality of materialism and irreligion which the antichrist will form – for the antichrist will be killed by Jesus' (pbuh) sword (of knowledge) – and destroy his ideas and disbelief, which are atheistic." *(Bediuzzaman, The Treatise of Light Collection, Flashes, 5ᵗʰ Flash, p. 589)*

Bediuzzaman Said Nursi makes it very clear that it is Darwinism and materialism that push people away from the moral values of religion and lead them to disbelief. He explains that Muslims will carry out a great intellectual struggle against these two twisted ideas under the leadership of the Prophet Jesus (pbuh) and Hazrat Mahdi (pbuh). By the grace of God, these ideologies will be ended by these two blessed personages and the moral values of Islam will come to reign throughout the world.

It is He Who sends down clear signs to His servant to bring you out of the darkness to the light.

(Qur'an, 57:9)

CONCLUSION: RECOMMENDATIONS TO THE WESTERN WORLD AND MUSLIMS

*T*here is an unchanging fact even if decades - or centuries - pass: Terrorism continues to destroy. People in many regions of the world live in fear of terrorism. Moreover, this fear is not limited to threats from other nations. In many countries people face threats in their own lands from their fellow citizens or co-religionists. The updated information given in the foreword to this new edition reveals the terrifying extent terrorism has reached today. This is evidence enough to prove that the political or military measures taken thus far to solve the problem of terrorism have all failed.

Today, the Western world is seriously concerned about the radical organisations that use terror under the guise of Islam and this concern is not misplaced. It is obvious that those carrying out terror and their supporters should be tried according to international judicial criteria. However, more effective strategies have to be pursued to discover viable solutions to these problems. The erroneous education system that underlies terrorism should be taken seriously, and the truths should be explained at every opportunity to replace the mistaken ideas that originate from Darwinist-materialist education as well as from bigotry.

The assessments above reveal that terror has no place in any of the Divine religions and that it is a crime committed against humanity. Revealing the inherently contradictory nature of the concept of "Islamic terror" provides us with an important vantage point:

1) The time ahead requires all countries to act with caution, sensitivity and wisdom. The world community at large must take the opportunities to live side by side in peace and must be open to all suggestions and works to this end. This is possible only if they know each other better, and study history, religion, art, literature, philosophy, science, technology, and culture.

2) That Islam is a religion of love, friendship, peace and brotherhood must be explained in all aspects and Islamic communities must be encouraged to understand this fact. The solution to combat radical factions in Islamic countries should not be "compulsory secularisation". On the contrary, such a policy will simply serve to incite a reaction from the masses. The solution is to abandon the radical mindset blended with Darwinist education and to speak about Islam in accordance with the Qur'an. This results in the embracing of the values of the Qur'an such as human rights, democracy, freedom, high morality, science, spirituality, and aesthetics, and in the appearance of a Muslim model which offers meaningful happiness and bliss to humanity.

Muslims must explain and live by the moral values com-

manded by the Qur'an. Muslims have the responsibility to take the Prophet (pbuh) as their model, who lived by the teachings of the Qur'an in the best manner, not those who misapply the faith and lead to a misunderstanding of Islam.

3) One of the sources of terrorism lies in bigotry and the solution to it is education. As explained in detail in previous sections, bigotry presents an erroneous, dreadful, loveless and hateful understanding of faith. To the circles who feel sympathy with terror, it must be made clear that terrorism stands in diametric opposition to Islam and that it only serves to harm Islam, Muslims and humanity at large; these people should be educated so that they are cleansed of bigotry.

4) Long-term cultural solutions must be devised to combat terrorism which has its roots in communist, fascist, racist and other false ideologies. Today in countries all over the world, Darwinist precepts form the basis of the education system. However, as we stressed earlier, Darwinism is an erroneous ideology that sees man as an animal who developed only by fighting for survival – something which constitutes the underlying basis of all forms of terrorism. An ideology that predicts only those holding power will survive and considers war as a virtue is like a huge morass that will never cease to visit disaster on the world. This being the case, beside the judicial and other measures that will be introduced to combat terrorism, there is also a need for a vigorous educational campaign to be launched all over the world. Disclosure of the real face of

the deception of Darwinism and materialism and instruction in the values God has revealed for people must be the fundamentals of this education. Peace and stability are attainable only through living by the good values of true religion. Without draining the morass, it is not possible to rid the world of disaster.

Our hope is that these measures will help the world to get rid of terrorism and all other such bigoted, brutal and barbarous notions. When they properly abide by the peaceful Christian culture they represent, countries such as the United States, which defines itself as "one nation under God", will become a friend of Muslims. In the Qur'an, God draws attention to this fact and informs us that Christians are those who are **"most affectionate to those who believe"**. (Qur'an, 5:82)

In history, some ignorant people misinterpreted this fact and caused conflicts and fighting between these two religions. To prevent the repetition of terrifying scenarios in our era, which have been propagated with nonsensical mottos like "The Clash of Civilisations" or "Holy War against the West", true Christians and Muslims need to come together and cooperate.

Indeed, the developments which took place in the aftermath of recent grievous events indicate that the seeds of this co-operation have already been sowed. Such grave acts of terrorism as 9/11, which has drawn the Christian and Muslim communities closer, led many Christians to come to know more about the religion of Islam and encouraged Muslims to make greater efforts to communicate the true Islamic morality described in the Qur'an.

All these developments are the glad tidings that people will understand Islamic values better and be able to rid themselves of any prejudices they had held. By the will of God, the 21st century will be the time when people will truly acknowledge that the dissemination of the values of Islam is the unique way of achieving a much longed-for peace on the planet.

He is God – the Creator, the Maker, the Giver of Form. To Him belong the Most Beautiful Names. Everything in the heavens and earth glorifies Him. He is the Almighty, the All-Wise. (Qur'an, 59:24)

Appendix

THE DECEPTION
OF EVOLUTION

*D*arwinism, in other words the theory of evolution, was put forward with the aim of denying the fact of Creation, but is in truth nothing but failed, unscientific nonsense. This theory, which claims that life emerged by chance from inanimate matter, was invalidated by the scientific evidence of miraculous order in the universe and in living things, as well as by the discovery of more than 300 million fossils revealing that evolution never happened. In this way, science confirmed the fact that God created the universe and the living things in it. The propaganda carried out today in order to keep the theory of evolution alive is based solely on the distortion of the scientific facts, biased interpretation, and lies and falsehoods disguised as science.

Yet this propaganda cannot conceal the truth. The fact that the theory of evolution is the greatest deception in the history of science has been expressed more and more in the scientific world over the last 20-30 years. Research carried out after the 1980s in particular has revealed that the claims of Darwinism are totally unfounded, something that has been stated by a large number of scientists. In the United States in particular, many scientists from such different fields as biology, biochemistry and paleontology recognize the invalidity of Darwinism and employ the fact of Creation to account for the origin of life.

We have examined the collapse of the theory of evolution and the proofs of Creation in great scientific detail in many of our works, and are still continuing to do so. Given the enormous importance of this subject, it will be of great benefit to summarize it here.

The Scientific Collapse of Darwinism

As a pagan doctrine going back as far as ancient Greece, the theory of evolution was advanced most extensively in the nineteenth century. The most important development that made it the top topic of the world of science was Charles Darwin's *The Origin of Species*, published in 1859. In this book, he opposed, in his own eyes, the fact that God created different living species on Earth separately, for he erroneously claimed that all living beings had a common ancestor and had diversified over time through small changes. Darwin's theory was not based on any concrete scientific finding; as he also accepted, it was just an "assumption." Moreover, as Darwin confessed in the long chapter of his book titled "Difficulties on Theory," the theory failed in the face of many critical questions.

Darwin invested all of his hopes in new scientific discoveries, which he expected to solve these difficulties. However, contrary to his expectations, scientific findings expanded the dimensions of these difficulties. The defeat of Darwinism in the face of science can be reviewed under three basic topics:

1) The theory cannot explain how life originated on Earth.

2) No scientific finding shows that the "evolutionary mechanisms" proposed by the theory have any evolutionary power at all.

3) The fossil record proves the exact opposite of what the theory suggests.

In this section, we will examine these three basic points in general outlines:

The First Insurmountable Step: The Origin of Life

The theory of evolution posits that all living species evolved from a single living cell that emerged on Earth 3.8 billion years ago, supposed to have happened as a result of coincidences. How a single cell could generate millions of complex living species and, if such an evolution really occurred, why traces of it cannot be observed in the fossil record are some of the questions that the theory cannot answer. However, first and foremost, we need to ask: **How did this "first cell" originate?**

Since the theory of evolution ignorantly denies Creation, it maintains that the "first cell" originated as a product of blind coincidences within the laws of nature, without any plan or arrangement. According to the theory, inanimate matter must have produced a living cell as a result of coincidences. Such a claim, however, is inconsistent with the most unassailable rules of biology.

"Life Comes From Life"

In his book, Darwin never referred to the origin of life. The primitive understanding of science in his time rested on the assumption that living beings had a very simple structure. Since medieval times, spontaneous generation, which asserts that non-living materials came together to form living organisms, had been widely accepted. It was commonly believed that insects came into being from food leftovers, and mice from wheat. Interesting experiments were conducted to prove this theory. Some wheat was placed on a dirty piece of cloth, and it was believed that mice would originate from it after a while.

Louise Pasteur

Similarly, maggots developing in rotting meat was assumed to be evidence of spontaneous generation. However, **it was later understood that worms did not appear on meat spontaneously, but were carried there by flies in the form of larvae, invisible to the naked eye.**

Even when Darwin wrote *The Origin of Species*, the belief that bacteria could come into existence from non-living matter was widely accepted in the world of science.

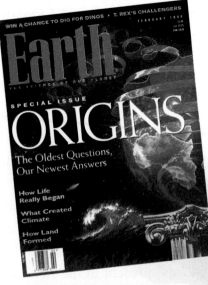

As accepted also by the latest evolutionist theorists, the origin of life is still a great stumbling block for the theory of evolution.

However, **five years after the** publication of Darwin's book, Louis Pasteur announced his results after long studies and experiments, that **disproved spontaneous generation,** a cornerstone of Darwin's theory. In his triumphal lecture at the Sorbonne in 1864, **Pasteur said: "Never will the doctrine of spontaneous generation recover from the mortal blow struck by this simple experiment."** (Sidney Fox, Klaus Dose, *Molecular Evolution and The Origin of Life*, W. H. Freeman and Company, San Francisco, 1972, p. 4.)

For a long time, advocates of the theory of evolution resisted these findings. However, as the development of science unraveled the complex structure of the cell of a living being, the idea that life could come into being coincidentally faced an even greater impasse.

Inconclusive Efforts of the Twentieth Century

The first evolutionist who took up the subject of the origin of life in the twentieth century was the renowned Russian biologist Alexander Oparin. With various theses he advanced in the 1930s, he tried to prove that a living cell could originate by coinci-

Alexander Oparin's attempts to offer an evolutionist explanation for the origin of life ended in a great fiasco.

dence. These studies, however, were doomed to failure, and Oparin had to make the following confession:

> Unfortunately, however, the problem of the origin of the cell is perhaps the most obscure point in the whole study of the evolution of organisms. (Alexander I. Oparin, Origin of Life, Dover Publications, New York, 1936, 1953 (reprint), p. 196.)

Evolutionist followers of Oparin tried to carry out experiments to solve this problem. The best known experiment was carried out by the American chemist Stanley Miller in 1953. Combining the gases he alleged to have existed in the primordial Earth's atmosphere in an experiment set-up, and adding energy to the mixture, Miller synthesized several organic molecules (amino acids) present in the structure of proteins.

Barely a few years had passed before it was revealed that **this experiment, which was then presented as an important step in the name of evolution, was invalid, for the atmosphere used in the experiment was very different from the real Earth conditions.** ("New Evidence on Evolution of Early Atmosphere and Life," *Bulletin of the American Meteorological Society*, vol 63, November 1982, 1328-1330)

After a long silence, **Miller confessed that the atmosphere medium he used was unrealistic.** (Stanley Miller, *Molecular Evolution of Life: Current Status of the Prebiotic Synthesis of Small Molecules*, 1986, p. 7)

All the evolutionists' efforts throughout the twentieth century to explain the origin of life ended in failure. The geochemist Jeffrey Bada, from the San Diego Scripps Institute accepts this fact in an article published in *Earth* magazine in 1998:

> Today as we leave the twentieth century, we still face the biggest unsolved problem that we had when we entered the twentieth century: How did life originate on Earth? (Jeffrey Bada, Earth, February 1998, p. 40)

The Complex Structure of Life

The primary reason why evolutionists ended up in such a great impasse regarding the origin of life is that even those living organisms Darwinists deemed to be the simplest have outstandingly complex features. The cell of a living thing is more complex than all of our man-made technological products. **Today, even in the most developed laboratories of the world, no single protein of the cell, let alone a living cell itself, can be produced by bringing organic chemicals together.**

The conditions required for the formation of a cell are too great in quantity to be explained away by coincidences. However, there is no need to explain the situation with these details. Evolutionists are at a dead-end even before reaching the stage of the cell. That is because the probability of just a single protein, an essential building block of the cell, coming into being by chance is mathematically "0."

The main reason for this is the need for other proteins to be present if one protein is to form, and this completely eradicates the possibility of chance formation. This fact by itself is sufficient to eliminate the evolutionist claim of chance right from the outset. To summarize,

1. Protein cannot be synthesized without enzymes, and enzymes are all proteins.

2. Around 100 proteins need to be present in order for a single protein to be synthesized. There therefore need to be proteins for proteins to exist.

3. DNA manufactures the protein-synthesizing enzymes. Protein cannot be synthesized without DNA. DNA is therefore also needed in order for proteins to form.

4. All the organelles in the cell have important tasks in protein synthesis. In other words, in order for proteins to form a perfect and fully functioning cell needs to exist together with all its organelles.

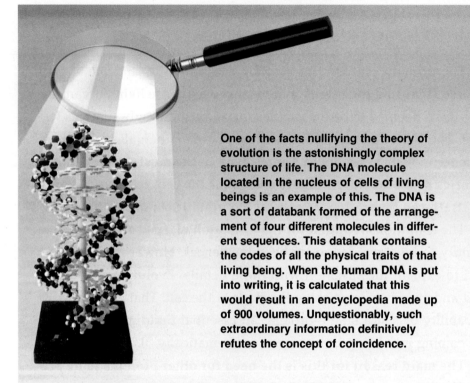

One of the facts nullifying the theory of evolution is the astonishingly complex structure of life. The DNA molecule located in the nucleus of cells of living beings is an example of this. The DNA is a sort of databank formed of the arrangement of four different molecules in different sequences. This databank contains the codes of all the physical traits of that living being. When the human DNA is put into writing, it is calculated that this would result in an encyclopedia made up of 900 volumes. Unquestionably, such extraordinary information definitively refutes the concept of coincidence.

The DNA molecule, which is located in the nucleus of a cell and which stores genetic information, is a magnificent databank. If the information coded in DNA were written down, it would make a giant library consisting of an estimated 900 volumes of encyclopedias consisting of 500 pages each.

A very interesting dilemma emerges at this point: DNA can replicate itself only with the help of some specialized proteins (enzymes). However, the synthesis of these enzymes can be realized only by the information coded in DNA. As they both depend on each other, they have to exist at the same time for replication. This brings the scenario that life originated by itself to a deadlock. Prof. Leslie Orgel, an evolutionist of repute from the University of San Diego, California, confesses this fact in the September 1994 issue of the *Scientific American* magazine:

It is extremely improbable that proteins and nucleic acids, both of which are structurally complex, arose spontaneously in the same place at the same time. Yet *it also seems impossible to have one without the other. And so, at first glance, one might have to conclude that life could never, in fact, have originated by chemical means. (Leslie E. Orgel, "The Origin of Life on Earth," Scientific American, vol. 271, October 1994, p. 78.)*

No doubt, if it is impossible for life to have originated spontaneously as a result of blind coincidences, then it has to be accepted that life was **created**. This fact explicitly invalidates the theory of evolution, whose main purpose is to deny Creation.

Imaginary Mechanism of Evolution

The second important point that negates Darwin's theory is that both concepts put forward by the theory as "evolutionary mechanisms" were understood to have, in reality, no evolutionary power.

Darwin based his evolution allegation entirely on the mechanism of "natural selection." The importance he placed on this mechanism was evident in the name of his book: *The Origin of Species, By Means of Natural Selection...*

Natural selection holds that those living things that are stronger and more suited to the natural conditions of their habitats will survive in the struggle for life. For example, in a deer herd under the threat of attack by wild animals, those that can run faster will survive. Therefore, the deer herd will be comprised of faster and stronger individuals. However, unquestionably, this mechanism will not cause deer to evolve and transform themselves into another living species, for instance, horses.

Therefore, the mechanism of natural selection has no evolutionary power. Darwin was also aware of this fact and had to state this in his book *The Origin of Species*:

Natural selection can do nothing until favourable individual differences or variations occur. (Charles Darwin, The Origin of Species by Means of Natural Selection, The Modern Library, New York, p. 127)

Lamarck's Impact

So, how could these "favourable variations" occur? Darwin tried to answer this question from the standpoint of the primitive understanding of science at that time. According to the French biologist Chevalier de Lamarck (1744-1829), who lived before Darwin, living creatures passed on the traits they acquired during their lifetime to the next generation. He asserted that these traits, which accumulated from one generation to another, caused new species to be formed. For instance, he claimed that giraffes evolved from antelopes; as they struggled to eat the leaves of high trees, their necks were extended from generation to generation.

Darwin also gave similar examples. In his book *The Origin of Species*, for instance, he said that some bears going into water to find food transformed themselves into whales over time. (Charles Darwin,

The Origin of Species: A Facsimile of the First Edition, Harvard University Press, 1964, p. 184.)

However, the laws of inheritance discovered by Gregor Mendel (1822-84) and verified by the science of genetics, which flourished in the twentieth century, utterly demolished the legend that acquired traits were passed on to subsequent generations. Thus, natural selection fell out of favor as an evolutionary mechanism.

Neo-Darwinism and Mutations

In order to find a solution, Darwinists advanced the "Modern Synthetic Theory," or as it is more commonly known, Neo-Darwinism, at the end of the 1930s. Neo-Darwinism added mutations, which are distortions formed in the genes of living beings due to such external factors as radiation or replication errors, as the "cause of favourable variations" in addition to natural mutation.

Today, the model that Darwinists espouse, despite their own awareness of its scientific invalidity, is neo-Darwinism. The theory maintains that millions of living beings formed as a result of a process whereby numerous complex organs of these organisms (e.g., ears, eyes, lungs, and wings) underwent "mutations," that is, genetic disorders. Yet, there is an outright scientific fact that totally undermines this theory: **Mutations do not cause living beings to develop; on the contrary, they are always harmful.**

The reason for this is very simple: **DNA has a very complex structure, and random effects can only harm it.** The American geneticist B. G. Ranganathan explains this as follows:

> *First, genuine mutations are very rare in nature. Secondly, most mutations are harmful since they are random, rather than orderly changes in the structure of genes; any random change in a highly ordered system will be for the worse, not for the better. For example, **if an earthquake were to shake a highly***

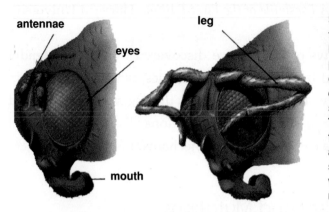

antennae

eyes

leg

mouth

Since the beginning of the twentieth century, evolutionary biologists have sought examples of beneficial mutations by creating mutant flies. But these efforts have always resulted in sick and deformed creatures. The picture on the left shows the head of a normal fruit fly, and the picture on the right shows the head of a fruit fly with legs coming out of it, the result of mutation.

ordered structure such as a building, there would be a random change in the framework of the building which, in all probability, would not be an improvement. (B. G. Ranganathan, Origins?, Pennsylvania: The Banner of Truth Trust, 1988, p. 7.)

Not surprisingly, no mutation example, which is useful, that is, which is observed to develop the genetic code, has been observed so far. All mutations have proved to be harmful. It was understood that mutation, which is presented as an "evolutionary mechanism," is actually a genetic occurrence that harms living things, and leaves them disabled. (The most common effect of mutation on human beings is cancer.) Of course, a destructive mechanism cannot be an "evolutionary mechanism." Natural selection, on the other hand, "can do nothing by itself," as Darwin also accepted. This fact shows us that **there is no "evolutionary mechanism" in nature.** Since no evolutionary mechanism exists, no such imaginary process called "evolution" could have taken place.

The Fossil Record: No Sign of Intermediate Forms

The clearest evidence that the scenario suggested by the theory of evolution did not take place is the fossil record.

According to the unscientific supposition of this theory, every living species has sprung from a predecessor. A previously existing species turned into something else over time and all species have come into being in this way. In other words, this transformation proceeds gradually over millions of years.

Had this been the case, numerous intermediary species should have existed and lived within this long transformation period.

For instance, some half-fish/half-reptiles should have lived in the past which had acquired some reptilian traits in addition to the fish traits they already had. Or there should have existed some reptile-birds, which acquired some bird traits in addition to the reptilian traits they already had. Since these would be in a transitional phase, they should be disabled, defective, crippled living beings. Evolutionists refer to these imaginary creatures, which they believe to have lived in the past, as "transitional forms."

If such animals ever really existed, there should be millions and even billions of them in number and variety. More importantly, the remains of these strange creatures should be present in the fossil record. In *The Origin of Species*, Darwin explained:

> *If my theory be true, numberless intermediate varieties, linking most closely all of the species of the same group together must assuredly have existed... Consequently, evidence of their former existence could be found only amongst fossil remains. (Charles Darwin, The Origin of Species: A Facsimile of the First Edition, p. 179)*

However, **Darwin was well aware that no fossils of these intermediate forms had yet been found.** He regarded this as a major difficulty for his theory. In one chapter of his book titled "Difficulties on Theory," he wrote:

> *Why, if species have descended from other species by insensibly fine gradations, do we not everywhere see innumerable transitional forms? Why is not all nature in confusion instead of the species being, as we see them, well*

This fossil crocodile from the Cretaceous period is 65 million years old. It is identical to crocodiles living today.

This mene unearthed in Italy is 54 to 37 million years old.

This 50-million-year-old fossil plane-tree leaf was unearthed in the USA. Plane-tree leaves have remained unchanged for 50 million years, and have never evolved.

defined?... But, as by this theory innumerable transitional forms must have existed, why do we not find them embedded in countless numbers in the crust of the earth?... Why then is not every geological formation and every stratum full of such intermediate links? (Charles Darwin, The Origin of Species, p. 172)

Darwin's Hopes Shattered

However, although evolutionists have been making strenuous efforts to find fossils since the middle of the nineteenth century all over the world, **no transitional forms have yet been uncovered.** All of the fossils, contrary to the evolutionists' expectations, show that **life appeared on Earth all of a sudden and fully-formed.**

One famous British paleontologist, Derek V. Ager, admits this fact, even though he is an evolutionist:

The point emerges that if we examine the fossil record in detail, whether at the level of orders or of species, we find – over and over again – not gradual evolution, but the sudden explosion of one group at the expense of another. (Derek A. Ager, "The Nature of the Fossil Record," Proceedings of the British Geological Association, vol 87, 1976, p. 133.)

This means that in **the fossil record, all living species suddenly emerge as fully formed, without any intermediate forms in between.** This is just the opposite of Darwin's assumptions. Also, this is very strong evidence that **all living things are created**. The only explanation of a living species emerging suddenly and complete in every detail without any evolutionary ancestor is that it was created. This fact is admitted also by the widely known evolutionist biologist Douglas Futuyma:

Creation and evolution, between them, exhaust the possible explanations for the origin of living things. Organisms either appeared on the earth fully developed or they did not. If they did not, they must have developed from pre-existing species by some process of modification. If they did appear in a fully developed state, they must indeed have been created by some omnipotent intelligence. (Douglas J. Futuyma, Science on Trial, Pantheon Books, New York, 1983, p. 197)

Fossils show that living beings emerged fully developed and in a perfect state on the Earth. That means that "the origin of species," contrary to Darwin's supposition, is not evolution, but Creation.

The Tale of Human Evolution

The subject most often brought up by advocates of the theory of evolution is the subject of the origin of man. The Darwinist claim holds that man evolved from so-called ape-like creatures. During this alleged evolutionary process, which is supposed to have started four to five million years ago, some "transitional forms" between man and his imaginary ancestors are supposed to have existed. According to this completely imaginary scenario, four basic "categories" are listed:

1. *Australopithecus*
2. *Homo habilis*
3. *Homo erectus*
4. *Homo sapiens*

Evolutionists call man's so-called first ape-like ancestors *Australopithecus*, which means "South African ape." These living beings are actually nothing but an old ape species that has become extinct. Extensive research done on various *Australopithecus* specimens by two world famous anatomists from England and the USA, namely, Lord Solly Zuckerman and Prof. Charles Oxnard, shows that these apes belonged to an ordinary ape species that became extinct and bore no resemblance to humans. (Solly Zuckerman, *Beyond The Ivory Tower*, Toplinger

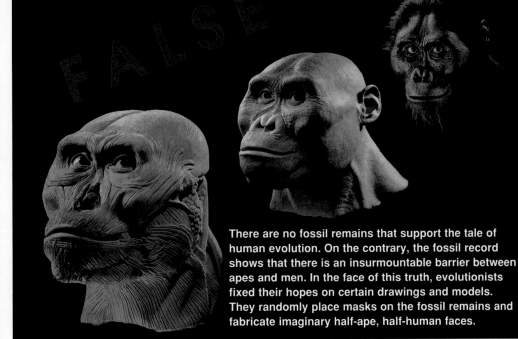

Publications, New York, 1970, 75-14; Charles E. Oxnard, "The Place of Australopithecines in Human Evolution: Grounds for Doubt", Nature, vol 258, 389)

Evolutionists classify the next stage of human evolution as "homo," that is "man." According to their claim, the living beings in the Homo series are more developed than *Australopithecus*. Evolutionists devise a fanciful evolution scheme by arranging different fossils of these creatures in a particular order. This scheme is imaginary because it has never been proved that there is an evolutionary relation between these different classes. Ernst Mayr, one of the twentieth century's most important evolutionists, contends in his book *One Long Argument* that "particularly historical [puzzles] such as the origin of life or of Homo sapiens, are extremely difficult and may even resist a final, satisfying

There are no fossil remains that support the tale of human evolution. On the contrary, the fossil record shows that there is an insurmountable barrier between apes and men. In the face of this truth, evolutionists fixed their hopes on certain drawings and models. They randomly place masks on the fossil remains and fabricate imaginary half-ape, half-human faces.

explanation." ("Could science be brought to an end by scientists' belief that they have final answers or by society's reluctance to pay the bills?" *Scientific American*, December 1992, p. 20)

By outlining the link chain as *Australopithecus* > *Homo habilis* > *Homo erectus* > *Homo sapiens*, evolutionists imply that each of these species is one another's ancestor. However, recent findings of paleoanthropologists have revealed that *Australopithecus*, *Homo habilis*, and *Homo erectus* lived at different parts of the world at the same time. (Alan Walker, *Science*, vol. 207, 7 March 1980, p. 1103; A. J. Kelso, *Physical Antropology*, 1st ed., J. B. Lipincott Co., New York, 1970, p. 221; M. D. Leakey, *Olduvai Gorge*, vol. 3, Cambridge University Press, Cambridge, 1971, p. 272.)

Moreover, a certain segment of humans classified as *Homo erectus* have lived up until very modern times. **Homo sapiens neandarthalensis and Homo sapiens sapiens (man) co-existed in the same region.** (Jeffrey Kluger, "Not So Extinct After All: The Primitive Homo Erectus May Have Survived Long Enough To Coexist With Modern Humans," *Time*, 23 December 1996)

This situation apparently indicates the invalidity of the claim that they are ancestors of one another. The late Stephen Jay Gould explained this deadlock of the theory of evolution although he was himself one of the leading advocates of evolution in the twentieth century:

> *What has become of our ladder if there are three coexisting lineages of hominids (A. africanus, the robust australopithecines, and H. habilis), none clearly derived from another? Moreover, none of the three display any evolutionary trends during their tenure on earth. (S. J. Gould, Natural History, vol. 85, 1976, p. 30)*

Put briefly, the scenario of human evolution, which is "upheld" with the help of various drawings of some "half ape, half human" creatures appearing in the media and course books, that is, frankly, by means of propaganda, is nothing but **a tale with no scientific foundation.**

Lord Solly Zuckerman, one of the most famous and respected scientists in the U.K., who carried out research on this subject for years and studied Australopithecus fossils for 15 years, finally concluded, despite being an evolutionist himself, **that there is, in fact, no such family tree branching out from ape-like creatures to man.**

Zuckerman also made an interesting "spectrum of science" ranging from those he considered scientific to those he considered unscientific. According to Zuckerman's spectrum, the most "scientific"—that is, depending on concrete data—fields of science are chemistry and physics. After them come the biological sciences and then the social sciences. At the far end of the spectrum, which is the part considered to be most "unscientific," are "extra-sensory perception"—concepts such as telepathy and sixth sense—and finally "human evolution." Zuckerman explains his reasoning:

> *We then move right off the register of objective truth into those fields of presumed biological science, like extrasensory perception or the interpretation of man's fossil history, where to the faithful [evolutionist] anything is possible – and where the ardent believer [in evolution] is sometimes able to believe several contradictory things at the same time. (Solly Zuckerman, Beyond the Ivory Tower, p. 19)*

The tale of human evolution boils down to nothing but the prejudiced interpretations of some fossils unearthed by certain people, who blindly adhere to their theory.

Darwinian Formula!

Besides all the technical evidence we have dealt with so far, let us now for once, examine what kind of a superstition the evolutionists have with an example so simple as to be understood even by children:

The theory of evolution asserts that life is formed by chance. According to this irrational claim, lifeless and unconscious atoms came together to form the cell and then they somehow formed other living things, including man. Let us think about that. When we bring together the elements that are the building-blocks of life such as carbon, phosphorus, nitrogen and potassium, only a heap is formed. No matter what treatments it undergoes, this atomic heap cannot form even a single living being. If you like, let us formulate an "experiment" on this subject and let us examine on the behalf of evolutionists what they really claim without pronouncing loudly under the name **"Darwinian formula"**:

Let evolutionists put plenty of materials present in the composition of living things such as phosphorus, nitrogen, carbon, oxygen, iron, and magnesium into big barrels. Moreover, let them add in these barrels any material that does not exist under normal conditions, but they think as necessary. Let them add in this mixture as many amino acids and as many proteins - a single one of which can by no means form by chance - as they like. Let them expose these mixtures to as much heat and moisture as they like. Let them stir these with whatever technologically developed device they like. Let them put the foremost scientists beside these barrels. Let these experts wait in turn beside these barrels for billions, and even trillions of years. Let them be free to use all kinds of conditions they believe to be necessary for a human's formation. **No matter what they do, they cannot produce from these barrels a human, say a professor that examines his cell structure under the electron microscope.** They cannot produce giraffes, lions, bees, canaries, horses, dolphins, roses, orchids, lilies, carnations, bananas, oranges, apples, dates, tomatoes, melons, watermelons, figs, olives, grapes, peaches, peafowls, pheasants, multicoloured butterflies, or millions of other living beings such as these. Indeed, they could not obtain even a single cell of any one of them.

Briefly, **unconscious atoms cannot form the cell** by coming

Can life emerge if all the conditions stipulated by evolutionists are met? Of course not! In order to show why not, let us carry out the following experiment: Place all the enzymes, hormones and proteins—everything that evolutionists regard as essential for life to form—into a barrel such as that pictured above. Then mix all these substances, using all possible physical and chemical techniques. But whatever you do, no matter how long you wait, not a single living cell will emerge from that barrel.

together. They cannot take a new decision and divide this cell into two, then take other decisions and create the professors who first invent the electron microscope and then examine their own cell structure under that microscope. **Matter is an unconscious, lifeless heap, and it comes to life with God's superior creation.**

The theory of evolution, which claims the opposite, is a total fallacy completely contrary to reason. Thinking even a little bit on the claims of evolutionists discloses this reality, just as in the above example.

Technology in the Eye and the Ear

Another subject that remains unanswered by evolutionary theory is the excellent quality of perception in the eye and the ear.

Before passing on to the subject of the eye, let us briefly answer the question of how we see. Light rays coming from an object fall oppositely on the eye's retina. Here, these light rays are transmitted into electric signals by cells and reach a tiny spot at the back of the brain, the "center of vision." These electric signals are perceived in this center as an image after a series of processes. With this technical background, let us do some thinking.

The brain is insulated from light. That means that its inside is completely dark, and that no light reaches the place where it is located. Thus, the "center of vision" is never touched by light and may even be the darkest place you have ever known. However, you observe a luminous, bright world in this pitch darkness.

The image formed in the eye is so sharp and distinct that even the technology of the twentieth century has not been able to attain it. For instance, look at the book you are reading, your hands with which you are holding it, and then lift your head and look around you. Have you ever seen such a sharp and distinct image as this one at any other place? Even the most developed television screen produced by the greatest television producer in the world cannot provide such a sharp image for you. This is a three-dimensional, colored, and extremely sharp image. For more than 100 years, thousands of engineers have been trying to achieve this sharpness. Factories, huge premises were established, much research has been done, plans and designs have been made for this purpose. Again, look at a TV screen and the book you hold in your hands. You will see that there is a big difference in sharpness and distinction. Moreover, the TV screen shows you a two-dimensional image, whereas with your eyes, you watch a three-dimensional perspective with depth.

For many years, tens of thousands of engineers have tried to make a three-dimensional TV and achieve the vision quality of the eye. Yes, they have made a three-dimensional television system, but it is not possible to watch it without putting on special 3-D glasses; moreover, it is only an artificial three-dimension. The background is more blurred, the foreground appears like a paper setting. Never has it been possible to produce a sharp and distinct vision like that of the eye. In both the camera and the television, there is a loss of image quality.

Evolutionists claim that the mechanism producing this sharp and distinct image has been formed by chance. Now, if somebody told you that the television in your room was formed as a result of chance, that all of its atoms just happened to come together and make up this device that produces an image, what would you think? How can atoms do what thousands of people cannot?

If a device producing a more primitive image than **the eye could not have been formed by chance**, then it is very evident that the eye and the image seen by the eye could not have been formed by chance. The same situation applies to the ear. The outer ear picks up the available sounds by the auricle and directs them to the middle ear, the middle ear transmits the sound vibrations by intensifying them, and the inner ear sends these vibrations to the brain by translating them into electric signals. Just as with the eye, the act of hearing finalizes in the center of hearing in the brain.

The situation in the eye is also true for the ear. That is, **the brain is insulated from sound** just as it is from light. It does not let any sound in. Therefore, no matter how noisy is the outside, the inside of the brain is completely silent. Nevertheless, the sharpest sounds are perceived in the brain. In **your completely silent brain, you listen to symphonies, and hear all of the noises in a crowded place.** However, were the sound level in your brain measured by a precise device at that moment, complete silence would be found to be prevailing there.

As is the case with imagery, decades of effort have been spent in trying to generate and reproduce sound that is faithful to the original.

Compared to cameras and sound recording devices, the eye and ear are much more complex, much more successful and possess far superior features to these products of high technology.

The results of these efforts are sound recorders, high-fidelity systems, and systems for sensing sound. Despite all of this technology and the thousands of engineers and experts who have been working on this endeavor, no sound has yet been obtained that has the same sharpness and clarity as the sound perceived by the ear. Think of the highest-quality hi-fi systems produced by the largest company in the music industry. Even in these devices, when sound is recorded some of it is lost; or when you turn on a hi-fi you always hear a hissing sound before the music starts. However, the sounds that are the products of the human body's technology are extremely sharp and clear. A human ear never perceives a sound accompanied by a hissing sound or with atmospherics as does a hi-fi; rather, it perceives sound exactly as it is, sharp and clear. This is the way it has been since **the creation of man.**

So far, no man-made visual or recording apparatus has been as sensitive and successful in perceiving sensory data as are the eye and the ear. However, as far as seeing and hearing are concerned, a far greater truth lies beyond all this.

To Whom Does the Consciousness that Sees and Hears within the Brain Belong?

Who watches an alluring world in the brain, listens to symphonies and the twittering of birds, and smells the rose?

The stimulations coming from a person's eyes, ears, and nose travel to the brain as electro-chemical nerve impulses. In biology, physiology, and biochemistry books, you can find many details about how this image forms in the brain. However, you will never come across the most important fact: Who perceives these electro-chemical nerve impulses as images, sounds, odors, and sensory events in the brain? **There is a consciousness in the brain that perceives all this without feeling any need for an eye, an ear, and a nose.** To whom does this consciousness belong? Of course it does not belong to the nerves, the fat layer, and neurons comprising the brain. This is why Darwinist-materialists, who believe that everything is comprised of matter, cannot answer these questions.

For **this consciousness is the spirit created by God**, which needs neither the eye to watch the images nor the ear to hear the sounds. Furthermore, it does not need the brain to think.

Everyone who reads this explicit and scientific fact should ponder on Almighty God, and fear and seek refuge in Him, for He squeezes the entire universe in a pitch-dark place of a few cubic centimeters in a three-dimensional, colored, shadowy, and luminous form.

A Materialist Faith

The information we have presented so far shows us that **the theory of evolution is incompatible with scientific findings.** The theory's claim regarding the origin of life is inconsistent with science, the evolutionary mechanisms it proposes have no evolutionary power, and fossils demonstrate that **the required intermediate forms have never existed.** So, it certainly follows that the theory of evolution should be pushed aside as an unscientific idea. This is how many ideas, such as the Earth-centered universe model, have been taken out of the agenda of science throughout history.

However, the theory of evolution is kept on the agenda of science. Some people even try to represent criticisms directed against it as an "attack on science." Why?

The reason is that this theory is an indispensable dogmatic belief for some circles. These circles are **blindly devoted** to materialist philosophy and adopt Darwinism because it is the only materialist explanation that can be put forward to explain the workings of nature.

Interestingly enough, they also confess this fact from time to time. A well-known geneticist and an outspoken evolutionist, Richard C. Lewontin from Harvard University, confesses that he is "first and foremost a materialist and then a scientist":

> *It is not that the methods and institutions of science somehow compel us accept a material explanation of the phenomenal world, but, on the contrary, that we are forced by our a priori adherence to material causes to create an apparatus of investigation and a set of concepts that produce material explanations, no matter how counter-intuitive, no matter how mystifying to the uninitiated. Moreover, that materialism is absolute, so we cannot allow a Divine [intervention]...(Richard Lewontin, "The Demon-Haunted World," The New York Review of Books, January 9, 1997, p. 28)*

These are explicit statements that **Darwinism is a dogma** kept alive just for the sake of adherence to materialism. This dogma maintains that there is no being save matter. Therefore, it argues that inanimate, unconscious matter brought life into being. It insists that millions of different living species (e.g., birds, fish, giraffes, tigers, insects, trees, flowers, whales, and human beings) originated as a result of the interactions

Signals from an object affect the brain by turning into electrical signals. When we say we see something, we are actually experiencing the effect of electrical signals in our brain. The brain is closed off to light. The interior of the brain is pitch black, and no light can enter where the brain is. The area known as the visual cortex is pitch black, somewhere that light can never reach, darker perhaps than anywhere you have ever seen. But you watch a brightly colored world in that pitch dark.

between matter such as pouring rain, lightning flashes, and so on, out of inanimate matter. This is a precept contrary both to reason and science. Yet Darwinists continue to ignorantly defend it just so as not to acknowledge, in their own eyes, the evident existence of God.

Anyone who does not look at the origin of living beings with a materialist prejudice sees this evident truth: **All living beings are works of a Creator,** Who is All-Powerful, All-Wise, and All-Knowing. **This Creator is God**, Who created the whole universe from non-existence, in the most perfect form, and fashioned all living beings.

The Theory of Evolution: The Most Potent Spell in the World

Anyone free of prejudice and the influence of any particular ideology, who uses only his or her reason and logic, will clearly understand that belief in the theory of evolution, which brings to mind the superstitions of societies with no knowledge of science or civilization, is quite impossible.

As explained above, those who believe in the theory of evolution think that a few atoms and molecules thrown into a huge vat could produce thinking, reasoning professors and university students; such scientists as Einstein and Galileo; such artists as Humphrey Bogart, Frank Sinatra and Luciano Pavarotti; as well as antelopes, lemon trees, and carnations. Moreover, as the scientists and professors who believe in this nonsense are educated people, it is quite justifiable to speak of this theory as "the most potent spell in history." Never before has any other belief or idea so taken away peoples' powers of reason, refused to allow them to think intelligently and logically, and hidden the truth from them as if they had been blindfolded. This is an even worse and unbelievable blindness than the totem worship in some parts of Africa, the people of Saba worshipping the Sun, the tribe of the Prophet Abraham (pbuh) worshipping idols they had made with their own hands, or some among the people of the Prophet Moses (pbuh) worshipping the Golden Calf.

In fact, God has pointed to this lack of reason in the Qur'an. In many verses, He reveals that some peoples' minds will be closed and that they will be powerless to see the truth. Some of these verses are as follows:

> As for those who do not believe, it makes no difference to them whether you warn them or do not warn them, they will not believe. God has sealed up their hearts and hearing and over their eyes is a blindfold. They will have a terrible punishment. (Qur'an, 2:6-7)

> … They have hearts with which they do not understand. They have eyes with which they do not see. They have ears with which they do not hear. Such people are like cattle. No, they are even further astray! They are the unaware. (Qur'an, 7:179)

In the same way that the beliefs of people who worshipped crocodiles now seem odd and unbelievable, so the beliefs of Darwinists are just as incredible. Darwinists regard chance and lifeless, unconscious atoms as a creative force, and are as devoted to that belief as if to a religion.

Even if We opened up to them a door into heaven, and they spent the day ascending through it, they would only say: "Our eyesight is befuddled! Or rather we have been put under a spell!" (Qur'an, 15:14-15)

Words cannot express just how astonishing it is that this spell should hold such a wide community in thrall, keep people from the truth, and not be broken for 150 years. It is understandable that one or a few people might believe in impossible scenarios and claims full of stupidity and illogicality. However, "magic" is the only possible explanation for people from all over the world believing that unconscious and lifeless atoms suddenly decided to come together and form a universe that functions with a flawless system of organization, discipline, reason, and consciousness; a planet named Earth with all of its features so perfectly suited to life; and living things full of countless complex systems.

In fact, in the Qur'an God relates the incident of the Prophet Moses (pbuh) and Pharaoh to show that some people who support atheistic philosophies actually influence others by magic. When Pharaoh was told about the true religion, he told the Prophet Moses (pbuh) to meet with his own magicians. When the Prophet Moses (pbuh) did so, he told them to demonstrate their abilities first. The verses continue:

He said: "You throw." And when they threw, they cast a spell on the people's eyes and caused them to feel great fear of them. They produced an extremely powerful magic. (Qur'an, 7:116)

As we have seen, Pharaoh's magicians were able to deceive everyone, apart from the Prophet Moses (pbuh) and those who believed in him. However, his evidence broke the spell, or "swallowed up what they had forged," as revealed in the verse:

We revealed to Moses: "Throw down your staff." And it immediately swallowed up what they had forged. So the Truth took place and

what they did was shown to be false. (Qur'an, 7:117-118)

As we can see, when people realized that a spell had been cast upon them and that what they saw was just an illusion, Pharaoh's magicians lost all credibility. In the present day too, unless those who, under the influence of a similar spell, believe in these ridiculous claims under their scientific disguise and spend their lives defending them, abandon their superstitious beliefs, they also will be humiliated when the full truth emerges and the spell is broken. In fact, world-renowned British writer and philosopher Malcolm Muggeridge, who was an atheist defending evolution for some sixty years, but who subsequently realized the truth, reveals the position in which the theory of evolution would find itself in the near future in these terms:

> *I myself am convinced that **the theory of evolution**, especially the extent to which it's been applied, **will be one of the great jokes in the history books in the future.** Posterity will marvel that so very flimsy and dubious an hypothesis could be accepted with the incredible credulity that it has. (Malcolm Muggeridge, The End of Christendom, Grand Rapids: Eerdmans, 1980, p. 43)*

That future is not far off: On the contrary, people will soon see that "chance" is not a deity, and will look back on **the theory of evolution as the worst deceit and the most terrible spell in the world.** That spell is already rapidly beginning to be lifted from the shoulders of people all over the world. Many people who see its true face are wondering with amazement how they could ever have been taken in by it.

*They said, 'Glory be to You! We have no
knowledge except what You have taught us.
You are the All-Knowing, the All-Wise.'*
(Koran, 2:32)

ISLAM DENOUNCES
TERRORISM FOOTNOTES:

1. Prof. Thomas Arnold, The Spread of Islam in the World, A History of Peaceful Preaching, Goodword Books, 2001, p. 79-80
2. http://www.ibtimes.com/why-do-people-join-isis-psychology-terrorist-1680444
3. Ahmad Diya'al-Din al-Kamushkhanawi, Ramuz al-Ahadith, Vol 1, 76/12
4. Bukhari (5778) and Muslim (109 and 110), Reported by Muslim - Eng. Trans, Vol. 1, p.62, No. 203
5. Tabari, Ta' rikh, 1, 1850, cited in Majid Khadduri, War and Peace in the Law of Islam, Johns Hopkins Press, Baltimore, 1955, p. 102
6. W.H.C. Frend, "Christianity in the Middle East: Survey Down to A.D. 1800", Religion in the Middle East, Ed. A.J. Arberry, I-II Cambridge, 1969, Volume I, p. 289
7. Prof. Thomas Arnold, The Spread of Islam in the World, A History of Peaceful Preaching, p. 71-72
8. L. Browne, The Prospects of Islam, p. 11-15
9. John L. Esposito, Islam: The Straight Path, p. 33-34
10. Bernard Lewis, The Middle East, Weidenfeld & Nicolson, London, 1995, p. 210
11. Prof. Thomas Arnold, The Spread of Islam in the World, A History of Peaceful Preaching, p. 96
12. Prof. Thomas Arnold, The Spread of Islam in the World, A History of Peaceful Preaching, p. 88-89
13. André Miquel, L'Islam et Sa Civilisation VIIe - XXe siècle, Librairie Armand Colin, Paris 1968, p. 244
14. Gesta Francorum, or the Deeds of the Franks and the Other Pilgrims to Jerusalem, translated by Rosalind Hill, London, 1962, p. 91
15. August C. Krey, The First Crusade: The Accounts of Eye-Witnesses and Participants, Princeton & London, 1921, p. 261
16. August C. Krey, The First Crusade: The Accounts of Eye-Witnesses and Participants, p. 262
17. The Alarm Newspaper Article, "Bakunin's Ground-Work for the Social Revolution," 1885 Dec. 26, p. 8
18. The Alarm Newspaper Article, "Bakunin's Ground-Work for the Social Revolution," 1885 Dec. 26, p. 2
19. The Pact of Najran, Article 6, http:// www.islami-cresources.com/Pact_of_Najran.htm
20. Karen Armstrong, Holy War, p. 30-31
21. John L. Esposito, Islam: The Straight Path, p. 58
22. Prof. Thomas Arnold, The Spread of Islam in the World, A History of Peaceful Preaching, p. 56

23. John L. Esposito, Islam: The Straight Path, p. 59
24. Francis E. Peters, Jerusalem: Holy City in the Eyes of Chroniclers, Visitors, Pilgrims, and Prophets from the Days of Abraham to the Beginnings of Modern Times, Princeton, Princeton University Press, 1985, p. 363
25. An Interview with Edward Said by the Israeli Newspaper Haaretz, Friday, August 18, 2000
26. Charles Darwin, The Descent of Man, 2nd edition, New York, A L. Burt Co., 1874, p. 178
27. Lalita Prasad Vidyarthi, Racism, Science and Pseudo-Science, Unesco, France, Vendôme, 1983. p. 54
28. Theodore D. Hall, "The Scientific Background of the Nazi "Race Purification" Program", http://www.trufax.org/avoid/nazi.html
29. James Joll, Europe Since 1870: An International History, Penguin Books, Middlesex, 1990, p. 164
30. M.F. Ashley-Montagu, Man in Process, New York: World. Pub. Co. 1961, pp. 76, 77 cited in Bolton Davidheiser, W E Lammers (ed) Scientific Studies in Special Creationism, 1971, p. 338-339
31. L.H. Gann, "Adolf Hitler, The Complete Totalitarian", The Intercollegiate Review, Fall 1985, p. 24; cited in Henry M. Morris, The Long war Against God, Baker Book House, 1989, p. 78
32. J. Tenenbaum., Race and Reich, Twayne Pub., New York, p. 211, 1956; cited by Jerry Bergman, "Darwinism and the Nazi Race Holocaust", http://www.trueorigin. org/ holocaust.htm
33. Peter Chrisp, The Rise Of Fascism, Witness History Series, p. 6
34. Hickman, R., Biocreation, Science Press, Worthington, OH, pp. 51–52, 1983; Jerry Bergman, "Darwinism and the Nazi Race Holocaust", Creation Ex Nihilo Technical Journal 13 (2): 101–111, 1999
35. Robert M. Young, Darwinian Evolution and Human History, Historical Studies on Science and Belief, 1980
36. Alan Woods and Ted Grant, Reason in Revolt: Marxism and Modern Science, London: 1993
37. K. Mehnert, Kampf um Mao's Erbe, Deutsche Verlags-Anstalt, 1977
38. Karl Marx, Das Capital, Vol. I, 1955, p. 603
39. Vladimir Ilich Lenin, Collected Works, 4th English Edition, Progress Publishers, Moscow, 1965, Volume 11, p. 216

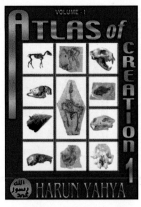

English, Turkish, French,
German, Italian, Spanish,
Russian, Chinese, Japanese,
Arabic, Indonesian, Czech,
Hindi, Urdu, Bosnian,
Swedish

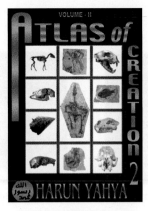

English, Turkish, French,
German, Spanish, Arabic,
Hindi

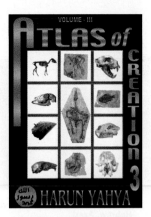

English, Turkish, French,
German, Spanish, Arabic,
Hindi

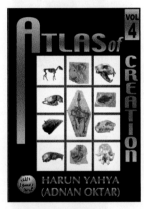

Turkish, English

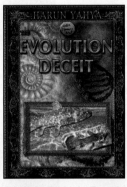

English, Turkish, French,
German, Italian, Spanish,
Russian, Chinese, Arabic,
Dutch, Indonesian, Czech,
Hindi, Urdu, Bosnian, Polish,
Farsi, Hausa, Portuguese,
Hebrew, Malay, Serbian,
Swedish

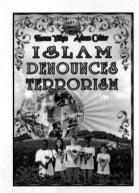

English, Turkish, French,
German, Italian, Albanian,
Dutch, Azeri, Bengali, Spanish,
Russian, Bosnian, Chinese,
Arabic, Farsi

Turkish - English

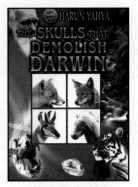

English, Turkish

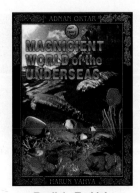

English, Turkish

English, Turkish,
Hebrew, Azeri

English, Turkish

Turkish - English

English, Turkish

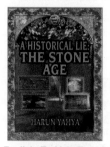

English, Turkish, French,
German, Italian, Czech,
Malay, Bulgarian,
Burmese, Hindi

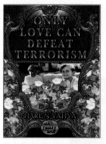

English, Turkish, French,
Albanian, Spanish,
German, Dutch

English, Turkish, French,
Italian, German, Bosnian,
Urdu, Arabic, Azeri

English, Turkish

English, Turkish, French,
Bulgarian, German

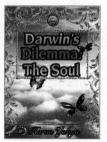

English, Turkish

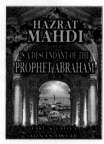

English, Turkish, Azeri

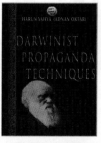

English, Turkish

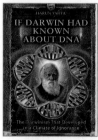

English, Turkish

English, Turkish

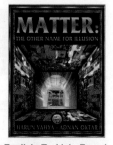

English, Turkish, French,
German, Bulgarian, Kyrgyz,
Italian, Indonesian, Hindi

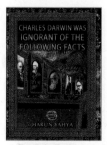

English, Turkish

English, Turkish, French, German, Arabic, Indonesian

English, Turkish, French, German, Albanian, Azeri, Spanish, Russian, Indonesian, Urdu

English, Turkish, French, Albanian, Urdu, German

English, Turkish, French, German, Kyrgyz

English, Turkish

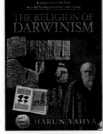

English, Turkish, French, German, Indonesian

English, Turkish, Italian

English, Turkish, French, German, Italian, Spanish, Arabic

English, Turkish, German, Italian, French, Indonesian

English, Turkish

English, Turkish

English, Turkish

English, Turkish, German, Italian, Indonesian

English, Turkish, French, Albanian, Azeri, Spanish, Russian, Urdu, Malay, Arabic, Kyrgyz

English, Turkish

English, Turkish

English, Turkish, French, German, Polish, Albanian, Dutch, Azeri, Bengali, Spanish, Russian, Bosnian, Arabic, Farsi, Indonesian, Urdu, Polish, Uzbek, Tamil, Pashto, Thai, Greek, Malay

English, Turkish, French, German, Hebrew

English, Turkish, Czech

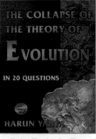

English, Turkish, French, German, Azeri, Spanish, Arabic, Indonesian

English, Turkish, French, German, Italian, Japanese, Indonesian

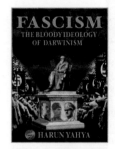

English, Turkish, German, Indonesian

English, Turkish

English, Turkish

English, Turkish

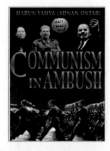

English, Turkish, Bosnian, Burmese

English, Turkish, French, German, Azeri, Spanish, Italian

English, Turkish

English, Turkish, German

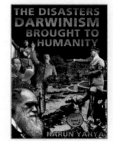

English, Turkish, French, German, Albanian, Bengali, Spanish, Arabic, Burmese, Indonesian, Serbian, M

English, Turkish, German

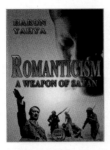

English, Turkish, French,
Azeri, Arabic, Indonesian

English, Turkish, German,
Indonesian

English, Turkish,
Malay

English, Turkish, German,
Bengali, Indonesian,
Azeri, Bulgarian, Kiswahili

English, Turkish

English, Turkish,
French, Malayalam

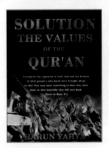

English, Turkish,
French, Italian, Arabic,
Bengali, Albanian

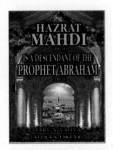

English, Turkish,
Azeri

English, Turkish

English, Turkish

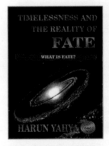

English, Turkish, Azeri, Urdu,
Malay, Farsi

English, Bosnian

English, Turkish, German,
Indonesian, Czech

English, Turkish, Arabic,
Indonesian, Bosnian

English, Turkish,
Russian

English, Turkish, Albanian

Turkish

English, Turkish, Bulgarian

English, Turkish, French

English, Turkish, French, German, Albanian, Urdu, Arabic, Kyrgyz, Azeri

English, Turkish, French, German, Albanian, Bengali, Spanish, Arabic, Indonesian, Tatar

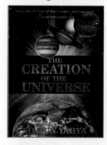

English, Turkish, French, German, Italian, Albanian, Chinese, Spanish, Russian, Arabic, Indonesian, Urdu

English, Turkish, French, German, Italian, Albanian, Chinese, Czech, Spanish, Russian, Arabic, Indonesian, Urdu, Azeri,

English, Turkish, French, Dutch, Arabic,

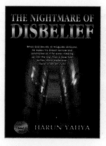

English, Turkish, French, Czech, Arabic,

English, Turkish, French, Albanian, Azeri, Georgian, Russian, Urdu, Romanian

English, Turkish, French, Albanian, Azeri, German, Bosnian

English, Turkish, Azerice

English, Turkish, Italian, Arabic, Bosnian, Azeri

English, Turkish, Azeri, German, Bulgarian, Bengali

English, Turkish, French, Bulgarian

English, Turkish, Azeri,
Indonesian

English, Turkish,
Hungarian

English, Turkish,
Pashto

English,Turkish, Albanian,
German, Farsi

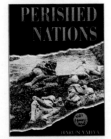

English, Turkish, French, German,
Italian, Albanian, Dutch, Azeri,
Pashto, Spanish, Russian, Bengali,
Chinese, Arabic, Farsi, Indonesian,
Urdu, Portuguese, Bulgarian

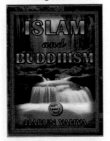

English, Turkish, Chinese,
Arabic, Indonesian, Azeri

English, Turkish

English, Turkish,
French, German, Urdu

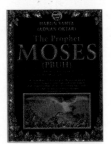

English, Turkish, French,
Albanian, Azeri, German,
Bosnian, Arabic

English, Turkish

English, Turkish,
Arabic

English, Turkish, Farsi

English, Turkish, Azeri,
German, Bosnian

English, Turkish,
German

English, Turkish,
German

English, Turkish,
Indonesian, Malayalam

English, Turkish,
German

English, Turkish,
Farsi

English, Turkish,
German

English, Turkish,
Kyrgyz

English, Turkish, French,
German, Kyrgyz, Arabic,
Spanish

English, Turkish, French,
German, Albanian, Arabic,
Burmese, Indonesian, Farsi,
Urdu

English, Turkish, French,
German, Albanian, Arabic,
Bengali

English, Turkish, French,
German, Azeri, Urdu, Russian,
Indonesian, Arabic

English, Turkish,
Azeri

English, Turkish,
French

English, Turkish,
German

English, Turkish

English, Turkish

English, Turkish

English, Turkish,
Arabic

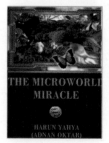

English, Turkish

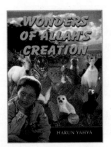

WONDERS OF ALLAH'S CREATION

HARUN YAHYA

English, Turkish, French, German, Spanish, Arabic, Indonesian, Serbian, Bosnian, Portuguese, Malay, Urdu

DEAR KIDS, HAVE YOU EVER THOUGHT? -2

the glory in the heavens

HARUN YAHYA

English, Turkish, French, Farsi, Arabic, Indonesian, Kiswahili, Bosnian, Russian, Malay

HARUN YAHYA

24 Hours In The Life Of A Muslim

English, Turkish, French, German, Uzbek, Albanian, Dutch, Azeri, Amharic, Spanish, Bosnian, Arabic, Farsi, Indonesian

NOT BY CHANCE

HARUN YAHYA

English, Turkish, German

STORIES FOR THINKING CHILDREN .I.

HARUN YAHYA

HARUN YAHYA (ADNAN OKTAR)

STORIES FOR THINKING CHILDREN 2

English, Turkish, French, Norwegian, Albanian, Dutch, Azeri, Czech, Spanish, Arabic, Farsi, Indonesian, Russian

CHILDREN! HAVE YOU EVER THOUGHT? -3-

Wonderful Creatures

HARUN YAHYA

English, Turkish, French, Albanian, Arabic, Indonesian, Urdu, Azeri

THOSE WHO EXHAUST ALL THEIR PLEASURES IN THIS LIFE

HARUN YAHYA

English, Spanish, Albanian, Turkish

HARUN YAHYA

CHARLES DARWIN AND HIS MAGIC BARREL

English, Turkish, German

THE FACT OF CREATION SERIES FOR KIDS-2-

HONEYBEES THAT BUILD PERFECT COMBS

HARUN YAHYA

English, Turkish, French, German, Dutch, Danish, Farsi, Russian, Arabic, Indonesian, Thai, Bosnian, Portuguese, Malay

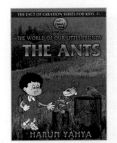

THE FACT OF CREATION SERIES FOR KIDS -1-

THE WORLD OF OUR LITTLE FRIENDS THE ANTS

HARUN YAHYA

English, Turkish, French, German, Thai, Dutch, Albanian, Bengali, Spanish, Russian, Bosnian, Malay, Danish, Arabic, Farsi, Indonesian, Portuguese, Urdu, Chinese

THE ALLIANCE OF THE GOOD

AGAINST THE MORAL DEGRADATION CAUSED BY LACK OF FAITH

HARUN YAHYA

English, Turkish, German, French

BEAVERS SKILFUL DAM CONSTRUCTORS

HARUN YAHYA

English, Turkish, German, Russian, Malayalam, Bosnian, Malay, Arabic, Indonesian, Farsi

BEFORE YOU REGRET

English, Albanian, Turkish, Spanish, German, French, Hungarian, Azeri, Dutch

HARUN YAHYA - ADNAN OKTAR

BASIC TENETS OF ISLAM

English, Albanian, Spanish, Turkish, Russian

DEVOTED TO ALLAH

HARUN YAHYA

English, Farsi, Turkish, Spanish, Albanian, Italian, French, German, Dutch, Arabic

English, Turkish, French,
Russian

English, Turkish,
Arabic, Indonesian

English, German,
Turkish, Italian, Urdu

English, Russian,
Turkish, Arabic

English, Turkish,
Albanian, Maranao,
Frrench, German,
Russian

English, Turkish,
Bengali, Czech,
Indonesian, French

English, Turkish, French,
Polish, Spanish, Urdu,
Hungarian, Bulgarian

English, German, Portuguese,
Bosnian, Arabic, Bulgarian,
Indonesian, Turkish, French,
Bengali, Russian, Italian,
Albanian

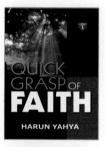

English,Turkish, Arabic,
German, Indonesian,
Russian, French,

English, Turkish,
German

English, Turkish,
German

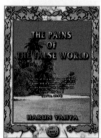

English, Hungarian, Turkish

English, Turkish,
Almanca

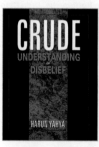

English, German,
Indonesian, Albanian,
Turkish

English, French, Indonesian,
Arabic, Italian, Turkish,
German, Albanian

English, Albanian, Kyrgyz,
French, Turkish, Burmese,
Hungarian, German

English, Turkish,
German

English, Turkish,
Indonesian

English, Turkish,
French, Arabic

English, Turkish,
German

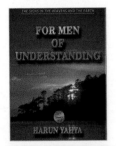

English, Turkish, French,
German, Italian, Danish, Urdu,
Spanish, Russian, Serbian,
Farsi, Indonesian

English, Turkish, French,
German, Italian, Spanish,
Russian, Indonesian, Arabic

English, Turkish, French,
German, Azeri, Urdu,
Albanian, Indonesian, Arabic

English, Turkish, French, Azeri,
Kiswahili, Spanish, Arabic,
Farsi, Indonesian, Serbian,
Macedonian

English, Turkish,
Arabic, Indonesian

English, Turkish,
French, German, Kyrgyz

English, Turkish,
Arabic

English, Turkish

English, Turkish

English, German,
Almanca

English, Turkish,
German

English, Turkish,
German

THE MIRACLE OF CREATION IN PLANTS

English, Turkish, French, Arabic, German, Serbian

SIGNS FROM THE QUR'AN

English, Turkish, Urdu

THE CAMBRIAN

English, Turkish

THE MIRACLES OF SMELL AND TASTE

English, Turkish, German, Arabic

THE MIRACLE IN THE SPIDER

English, Turkish, French, Urdu, Indonesian, Arabic

A CHAIN of MIRACLES

English, Turkish, Farsi, German, Hungarian, Indonesian, Arabic

ALLAH'S ARTISTRY IN COLOUR

English, Turkish, German, Urdu, Albanian, Bosnian, Indonesian, Arabic

THE MIRACLE OF THE IMMUNE SYSTEM

English, Turkish, French, Serbian, Albanian, Indonesian, Arabic

THE MIRACLE IN THE SEED

English, Turkish, German

CONSCIOUSNESS IN THE CELL

English, Turkish, Arabic

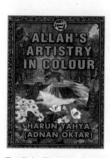

GLOBAL FREEMASONRY

English, Turkish, French, German, Albanian, Azeri, Swedish, Burmese, Kiswahili, Indonesian

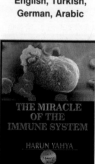

WHAT DARWINISTS FAIL TO CONSIDER

English, Turkish

MIRACLE IN THE EYE

English, Turkish, German

let's learn our islam

English, Turkish, French, German, Albanian, Spanish, Polish, Malay, Arabic, Indonesian, Urdu, Arabic

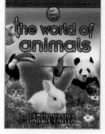

the world of animals

English, Turkish, French, German, Spanish, Polish, Farsi, Arabic, Indonesian, Bosnian, Arabic

miracles in our bodies

English, Turkish, French, German, Azeri, Albanian, Arabic, Indonesian, Bosnian, Arabic

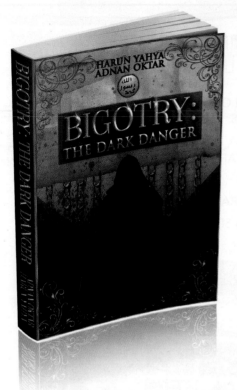

HARUN YAHYA DOCUMENTARIES ON DVD & VCD

40 Pcs. DVDs Documentary Film Set

40 DVD set with WorldWide **FREE SHIPPING**

[DVDs]:

1- The Creation of the Universe
2- The Secret Beyond Matter
3- Miracles of the Qur'an
4-The Miracle of Man's Creation
5- Perished Nations -I
6-Allah's Artistry in Color
7-Islam Denounces Terrorism
8-The Qur'an Leads the Way to Science
9-The Signs of the Last Day
10-The Truth of the Life of This World
11-The Secret of the Test
12-The Bloody History of Communism I
13-The Bloody History of Communism II
14-The Fact of Creation
15-The Miracle in the Ant
16-The End Times and the Mahdi
17-Love and Cooperation in Living Things
18-The Miracle Planet - I
19-Splendour in the Seas
20-Perished Nations -II

21-Allah is Known Through Reason
22-Deep Thinking
23-For Men of Understanding –I
24-For Men of Understanding -II
25-For Men of Understanding -III
26-Miracles of the Brain : Smell and Taste
27-The Miracle in the Cell
28-Behind the Scenes of the World Wars
29-Answers from the Qur'an
30-The Collapse of the Theory of Evolution
31-The Collapse of Atheism
32-The Disasters Darwinism Brought to Humanity
33-Altruism in Nature
34-The Miracle of Seed
35-Biomimetics: Technology Imitates Nature
36-The Names of Allah
37-Satanism: Satan's Bloody Teaching
38-The Miracle of Respiration
39-Solution: The Values of the Qur'an
40-The Miracle Planet II

10 Pcs. DVDs
Multi Language DVD Set

1-The Signs of The Last Day
2-The Truth of the Life of This World
3-Allah Is Known Through Reason
4-Deep Thinking
5-Allah's Artistry In Color
6-The Fact of Creation
7-For Men of Understanding-I
8-For Men of Understanding-II
9-For Men of Understanding-III
10-Love and Cooperation in Living Things

20 Pcs. VCDs

For Men of Understanding Documentary Series VCDs

VCD1: The End Times and Mahdi
Technology in Nature
VCD2: The Miracle of Seed
Miracles of the Brain:Smell and Taste
VCD3: Perished Nations-I
Perished Nations-II
VCD4: The Truth of the Life of This World
Solution: The Values of the Qur'an
VCD5: Architects in Nature
Allah Is Known Through Reason
VCD6: Allah's Artistry in Color
Love and Cooperation in Living Things
VCD7: The Creation of the Universe
The Miracle Planet
VCD8: Behind the Scenes of the World Wars
The Miracle of Respiration
VCD9: Signs of the Last Day
The Miracle in the Ant
VCD10: The Miracle in the Cell
Deep Thinking

SOME WEB SITES WHERE YOU CAN ACCESS THE WORKS OF HARUN YAHYA

www.king-messiah.com
www.primepeace.com
www.adnanoktarsays.com
www.harunyahyasays.com
www.redemptionofjews.com
www.evolutioninternational.net
www.religionofdarwinism.com
www.darwinismthegreatestlieinhistory.com
www.creationofman.net
www.dnarefutesevolution.com
www.theprophetjesus.com
www.mahdinevershedsblood.com
www.muslimspersecuted.com
www.islamandkarma.com
www.eastturkestan.com
www.signsofthelastday.com
www.sheikhnazimalhaqqani.com
www.darwinistsneverrealize.com
www.adnanoktarinterviews.com
www.dailycomments.net
www.primepeace.com
www.skullsdemolishdarwinism.com
www.returningtofaith.com
www.thestoneage.org
www.dayofjudgment.com
www.truthsforkids.com
www.womaninthequran.com
www.islamandbuddhism.com
www.servingislam.com
www.palestiniantragedy.com
www.theislamicunion.com
www.darwinism-watch.com
www.scienceresearchfoundation.com
www.evolutiontale.com
www.evolutionisnotscientific.com
www.mythofhomology.com
www.darwinistsdilemma.com
www.realityofdeath.com
www.harunyahyaconferences.com
www.whydarwinwaswrong.com
www.darksideofdarwinism.com
www.romanticismaweaponofsatan.com
www.darwinistcorruptioninthearabworld.com
www.bird-fossils.com
www.commentsonatlasofcreation.com
www.realityofdeath.com
www.mahdiaccordingtofoursunnischools.com
www.wisdomfromtorah.com
www.miracleoflightandcolour.com
www.reptile-fossils.com
www.mahdiaccordingtoholyscriptures.com

www.hereafterexists.com
www.formanunderstanding.com
www.quranindex.net
www.humanisamiracle.com
www.miracleintheeye.com
www.miracleinthespider.com
www.miracleofthebloodandheart.com
www.miracleintheatom.com
www.darwinismssocialweapon.com
www.mahdiaccordingtofoursunnischools.com
www.fascismandcommunism.com
www.byvirtueofharunyahya.com
www.whydarwinwaswrong.com
www.for-children.com
www.Allahexists.com
www.freeislamicbooks.net
www.worldwarsunveiled.com
www.cambriananddarwin.com
www.bbcrefuted.com
www.harunyahyasays.com
www.riseofislam.com
www.falseworld.net
www.darwinisminruins.com
www.naturalselectionanddarwinism.com
www.mythofhomology.com
www.oldestmushroom.com
www.harunyahyaimpact.com
www.nationalacademyofsciencesrefuted.com
www.divxvar.com
www.darwinistsinmourning.com
www.darwinismisso19thcentury.com
www.grievingdarwinists.com
www.darwinistsdefeated.com
www.darwinistsinpain.com
www.ambersdenydarwin.com
www.whatdarwindidnotknow.com
www.darwinslostcause.com
www.insight-magazine.com
www.brothercountry-iran.com
www.adnanoktar.us
www.miracleofhormones.com
www.natureandbiomimetics.com
www.englishkuran.com
www.psychologicalwarfaremethods.com
www.nocompulsioninislam.com